The ACFTU and Chinese Industrial Relations

Trade Unions Past, Present and Future

EDITED BY CRAIG PHELAN

Volume 12

PETER LANG
Oxford • Bern • Berlin • Bruxelles • Frankfurt am Main • New York • Wien

The ACFTU and Chinese Industrial Relations

Zhining Ma

PETER LANG
Oxford • Bern • Berlin • Bruxelles • Frankfurt am Main • New York • Wien

Bibliographic information published by Die Deutsche Nationalbibliothek.
Die Deutsche Nationalbibliothek lists this publication in the Deutsche Nationalbibliografie; detailed bibliographic data is available on the Internet at http://dnb.d-nb.de.

A catalogue record for this book is available from the British Library.

Library of Congress Cataloging-in-Publication Data:

Ma, Zhining, 1972-
The ACFTU and Chinese industrial relations / Zhining Ma.
p. cm. -- (Trade unions past, present, and future ; 12)
Includes bibliographical references and index.
ISBN 978-3-0343-0205-0 (alk. paper)
1. Industrial relations--China. 2. Zhonghua quan guo zong gong hui.
3. Labor unions--China. 4. Industrial policy--China. I. Title.
HD8736.5.M3 2011
331.880951--dc22
2010053226

ISSN 1662-7784
ISBN 978-3-0343-0205-0

Hochfeldstrasse 32, CH-3012 Bern, Switzerland
info@peterlang.com, www.peterlang.com, www.peterlang.net

Contents

Figures and Tables vii

Preface ix

Acknowledgements xi

CHAPTER ONE
A New Taxonomic Approach for Analysing Chinese Industrial Relations 1

CHAPTER TWO
The Party-state, ACFTU and Employers' Associations: Chinese Industrial Relations Actors above the Workplace Level 29

CHAPTER THREE
Grass Roots Unions and Employers: Chinese Institutional Industrial Relations Actors at the Workplace Level 75

CHAPTER FOUR
The Chinese Employee Class 105

CHAPTER FIVE
Interactions among the Party-state, ACFTU and Employers' Associations 129

CHAPTER SIX
Interactions among Grass Roots Unions, Employers and Employees 167

CHAPTER SEVEN
Conclusions and Future Studies 205

Bibliography 219

Figures and Tables

Figure 1.1 Contemporary Chinese Industrial Relations System 20
Figure 2.1 Party-state Structure in China's Industrial Relations 34
Table 6.1 Summary of Industrial Relations in Different Enterprises 200

Preface

In the context of China's growing influence over the global economy, its newly developed labour market and the subsequent series of industrial relations issues have captured much attention. However, research on industrial relations and labour problems in China is relatively underdeveloped. The classic three-party industrial relations model, which was developed for western economies, has often been difficult to apply to China's circumstances. The biggest difference between China and western countries in the matter of labour issues lies in the different institutional settings of the industrial relations systems. As a sub-system of the broader social system, the industrial relations system of a country is significantly affected by the fundamental socio-political system in that particular country.

In view of this, Chapter One of this book will first review the relevant existing industrial relations theories and explore their applicability to China. The book then continues with the proposal of a new six-party taxonomy for the analysis of Chinese industrial relations. The new taxonomy takes into account distinctive industrial relations actors with "Chinese characteristics" as well as their inter-relationships which form at different social levels. This taxonomy provides a useful tool for drawing a broad picture of the evolving industrial relations in China, which constitute the main content of the later parts of this book: in Chapters Two to Four, we analyse the historical and current situation of the six Chinese industrial relations actors, namely the party-state, employers' associations, the All China Federation of Trade Unions, grass roots unions, employers and employees; while in Chapters Five and Six, we describe the interactions between each of these actors from a historical perspective.

With the new taxonomy and the analyses that follow, this book aims to provide a new insight into Chinese industrial relations and labour studies. It attempts to present a broad picture of the Chinese industrial relations system. The discussion will be valuable for those interested in China's social development (in particular, the development of modern industrial relations in the context of the Chinese political economy).

Limitations of length, however, preclude a detailed discussion in this book of all Chinese industrial relations issues. Various future research topics have been identified in the concluding chapter, and they are undoubtedly important questions in need of enormous research efforts. Therefore, we see this book as the beginning of a series of related works, which aim to contribute to a better understanding of industrial relations in the context of Chinese political economy.

Acknowledgements

The author gratefully acknowledges the efforts of the series editor, Professor Craig Phelan of Kingston University, London, and of Mr Nick Reynolds of Peter Lang Publishing, Oxford, for their useful comments on the earlier versions of this book. The main contents of this book are largely based on the materials collected by the author during his PhD research, which was supervised by Professor Keith Hancock and Dr Michael Sullivan of Flinders University, Australia, and was supported by a Flinders University Research Scholarship.

CHAPTER ONE

A New Taxonomic Approach for Analysing Chinese Industrial Relations

Introduction

The purposes of this chapter are to explain the general background of Chinese industrial relations and then to review existing industrial relations theories to identify gaps in our knowledge. This enables us to pose a number of research questions which this book will answer.

We first discuss the research background by presenting a bird's-eye view of China's labour market and discussing the significance of this research. We also briefly review the achievements of scholars in the existing literature regarding Chinese industrial relations. We then take into account the knowledge gaps as identified in the literature review and point out, on the one hand, that there is a need to introduce western industrial relations theories for analysis of the Chinese system while, on the other hand, western industrial relations theories need to be modified when applied to China. We continue by proposing the research questions, and argue that the answers to these research questions lie in the development of a new taxonomic approach for the analysis of Chinese industrial relations.

1.1 China's Labour Market

Since the release of Deng Xiaoping's series of speeches during his 1992 "southern tour (南巡)", in which he reaffirmed his determination to clear the ideological obstacles to market-oriented economic reform,[1] China's reforms have been substantial. To name but a few, State-owned Enterprises (SOEs, 国有企业) began to be privatized in the mid to late 1990s; China finally entered the World Trade Organization (WTO) in 2001 after years of hesitation and serious negotiation; the Chinese Communist Party (CCP, 中国共产党) revised the Party Constitution to accommodate private business owners in 2002; and the state revised its Constitution to provide legal protection for private properties in 2004.[2]

This series of reforms profoundly affected not only China but also the rest of the world, as China's influence in the global economy increased significantly. Among various changes during China's reform era, the newly developed labour market and a subsequent series of labour issues captured much attention. However, research on Chinese industrial relations and labour problems remained stagnant for a long time until late 1990s. There are probably three key reasons for this:

First, over the past 100 years or so of China's history, industrial relations and labour problems have always been highly affected by the concurrent domestic political atmosphere.[3] Political influences complicated and thus hindered the development of the study of industrial relations in China.

1 Ma (2008).

2 China's reform has so far been in the economic area, with very little political content. However, if there is any merit in the Marxian theory that the economic base will determine the superstructure, it seems inevitable that the economic reform will eventually lead to political reform. The debate now is not about whether political reform will happen, but about its speed and specific direction (Heberer 2005).

3 In the 1920s, when labour consciousness first emerged, the Chinese Communist Party (CCP) immediately led it in the direction of labour-capital conflict and class struggle by applying classic Marxist-Leninist theories. After the CCP established power in 1949, and particularly after the "socialistic transformation" of domestic private companies into state or collectively owned enterprises in 1956, the CCP's leadership considered that there was no longer any fundamental conflict between labour and management in the context of socialism, so that industrial relations was considered to be only a simple version of personnel management. Finally, after the reform in 1979, and especially after 1992, when the market-oriented reforms became more in-depth, in the context of "concentrating on economic development (以经济建设为中心)", corporate level (employer-dominated) human resource manage-

Second, certain topics in the study of industrial relations are still considered to be politically sensitive,[4] thus discouraging Chinese scholars from approaching such topics. To be safe, many of them either use officially standardized, old fashioned Marxist theories or simply avoid these topics altogether.

Third, in western academic circles, the study of industrial relations has long been acknowledged as a multi-disciplinary research area at the crossroad of political science, economics, sociology, management, psychology and legal studies.[5] For many mainland Chinese social science scholars, who are more accustomed to adopting directly existing sets of theories,[6] inconsistencies in the theoretical structure of the study of industrial relations made it a less attractive field of inquiry.

In this section, we first present a bird's-eye view of China's labour market and discuss the economic and political significance of Chinese labour issues; we then identify what this research can do for enhancing better understanding of Chinese industrial relations.

---

ment theories were widely introduced from overseas. We will discuss all these major events in later chapters.

4 Such sensitive issues include (but are not limited to) union organization and collective bargaining, the role of the state in industrial relations, the construction of a fair tripartite mechanism, and joint regulation by labour, capital and the state.

5 Deery (2001), p. 6. We discuss this matter further later in this chapter.

6 This practice, which is termed in Chinese "learning by simply swallowing the whole thing (囫囵吞枣)", is particularly common among present day mainland Chinese social scientists. One reason is that the majority of Chinese scholars, mostly working in universities, are semi-public servants: they tend to use the safest, simplest and quickest way to create "academic results (学术成果)" so as to climb the bureaucratic ladder, rather than build theories of their own ("Academic Practice and Culture Re-build", *People's Daily*, 24 October 2001; "学术规范与文化重建"，人民日报，2001–10–24日). That is why, for example, Ding Xueliang, an overseas Chinese scholar condemned the system, asserting that there were no more than five qualified economists in mainland China; this viewpoint, though seemingly controversial and sweeping, was widely accepted according to a web survey ("Objective Comment: Qualified Economists Less than Five", *Chinese Youth*, "合格的经济学家 '不超过5个'比较客观", 中国青年报, 9 November 2005).

1.1.1 A Bird's-eye View of China's Labour Market

We outline a brief picture of China's immense labour market by using data from the Chinese National Bureau of Statistics. However, it is worth repeating that official Chinese data are not very reliable and need to be used with extreme caution, which will be proved immediately below. Generally, such data provide only a rough understanding of the situation and alone cannot sustain a comprehensive analysis.

According to the official data, by the end of 2006 China had a total population of 1.31 billion, of which 59.5% (782.44 million) was economically active. The employment rate (97.6%)[7] seems to be high,[8] but the figure itself is problematic, because 480.9 million of the total of 764 million in employment came from "rural employment" which includes 194.59 million in various businesses based in rural areas, while the remaining 286.31 million are in rural primary industry.[9] It is the 286.31 million employed in primary industry that pose the question: does China really need so many peasants to produce food? According to the estimation of the Ministry of Labour and Social Security (MOLSS, 劳动与社会保障部), (2007), China's farming land needs only about 170 million workers for efficient production; that is to say, there are almost 120 million labourers in rural areas who are counted as employed in statistics but are believed to be redundant and always ready for any opportunity to enter the non-primary industry labour market (mostly as blue-collar workers). For this reason, the supply of low-end blue-collar workers seems to be almost unlimited in China. The "buffer stock" of cheap labour, which is reserved in rural areas at very

7 This figure is derived by dividing 764 million (employment) by 782.44 million (economically active population).

8 Cooke points out that part-time employment is uncommon in China, in part as a result of the low-wage full-employment policy adopted by the government during the state planned economy period. In addition, driven by the Marxist emancipation book, the state encouraged women to participate in employment to gain financial independence and enhance their political and social status (Cooke (2008b), p. 1). According to the data, female employees make up 46.5% of total employment (NBS and MOLSS 2007, disc edition, Table 1.44).

9 NBS (2007), on-line edition, Table 5.2.

low cost, is the major reason for China's slow improvement in employment conditions when compared to its overall economic growth.

Owing to the Chinese government's long-held "dual management" concept which treated the rural and urban populations with dramatically different policies,[10] public services and facilities are much more available in urban areas. Therefore, theoretically, statistics regarding urban population and employment should be more reliable. But are they? According to the National Bureau of Statistics (NBS, 国家统计局), (2007), by the end of 2006, China had an urban population of 577.06 million.[11] Though there is no specific published figure for the economically active urban population, if we apply the national percentage of 59.5%,[12] the number should then be at least 343.35 million. In this case, there is a gap of 51.78 million between the estimated economically active population (343.35 million) and the published urban employment (283.1 million) plus urban registered unemployment (8.47 million). There is no official explanation for such a significant gap. There are several possible reasons: first, many employees in small enterprises do not have formal contracts, so that they were omitted from the official statistical survey; second, as unemployment subsidies provided by the Chinese government are minimal, yet required complex application and approval procedures,[13] many people simply do not bother to register as unemployed; third, the government might have directly manipulated the number of unemployed. Actual urban unemployment must be much higher than the official data. Though smaller in size when compared with those in rural areas, the "buffer stock" of unemployed labour in urban areas, which can be estimated to be at least two to three times the official number (i.e. at least around 15–20 million), is not insignificant. This, too, contributes to stagnant employment conditions in China.

10 We discuss this in more detail later in Chapter 4.

11 NBS (2007), on-line edition, Table 4.1.

12 This is a relatively conservative assumption, as we know that urban people are generally more connected with economical activities; hence the percentage of the economically active urban population should be higher than the national average.

13 Interested readers may refer to the "Regulation on Unemployment Insurance" issued by the State Council in 1999, available at <http://www.gov.cn/banshi/2005-08/04/content_20258.htm> (last accessed on 22 January 2009).

Another major indicator of a labour market is income. The declared annual average wage in 2006 was RMB 21,001 (around AUD 4,200 or USD 2,940), but this is far from the experience of the ordinary Chinese. The figure is probably due to the "averaging effect", where a high-rank manager with an annual compensation package of RMB 500,000, not to mention a CEO with an even greater package, makes the "average wages" of workers appear much higher than they are. This is a significant defect in the data, taking into account China's huge income gap between the rich and the poor.[14] Problematic though they are, the data do confirm that China falls into the World Bank's broader definition of a lower middle income economy (average income of USD 936–3,705 per capita).[15]

Aside from the above mentioned main indicators, the following information may also help to draw a broad picture of the Chinese labour market in 2006:

Educational Level of the Employed

8.63% of the employed population had tertiary degrees/certificates, 11.9% had senior high school (year 12) certificates, 44.9% had junior high school (year 9) certificates, while the remaining 36.6% were either illiterate or had only primary school (year 6) certificates.[16]

Employment by Industry Group

42.6% of the employed population were in primary industry, 25.5% in secondary industry and 32.2% in tertiary industry.[17]

14 We discuss China's growing gap between the rich and the poor later in this section.

15 World Bank's Official website information: <http://web.worldbank.org/WBSITE/EXTERNAL/DATASTATISTICS/0,,contentMDK:20421402~pagePK:64133150~piPK:64133175~theSitePK:239419,00.html> (accessed on 12 January 2009).

16 NBS and MOLSS (2007), disc edition, Table 1.46. Note that China has a nine year compulsory education system.

17 NBS and MOLSS (2007), disc edition, Table 1.5.

The Minimum Wage

Chinese city governments have the power to decide locally their own minimum wages, which range from RMB 320 (AUD 64) per month in Longnan, a second-tier city in the north-western Gansu province, to RMB 780 (AUD 156) per month in Guangzhou, the capital city of the south-eastern Guangdong province.[18]

Working Hours

Theoretically, the standard is 8 working hours per day or 40 hours per week.[19] In addition, employees are entitled to 10 days of public holidays per year and personal annual leave ranging from 5–15 days, depending on years of service in an enterprise.[20] However, the implementation of these regulations varied dramatically, largely in accordance with the employers' types of ownership.[21]

Summarizing the findings above, the first impression we may have is that China's abundant labour resources of mostly blue-collar workers with a lower education level kept China's working conditions at a relatively underdeveloped level, which helped establish China's competitive edge in the global economy. At the same time, China's vast population, which is moving from low to middle income levels, with an unprecedented economic growth rate over the decade, posed a series of issues which may well lead to socio-political instability.[22] It is within this broader context of the sheer size of the labour market that Chinese industrial relations developed during the era of economic reform. It is against this background that we conduct our research.

18 "Summary of Minimum Wages Nation-wide – 2006 version" (in Chinese), available at <http://www.labournet.com.cn/2005zdgz/2006.asp> (last accessed on 15 January 2009).
19 Article 3 in State Council (1995).
20 Article 3 in State Council (2007).
21 We discuss this in more detail in Chapter 6.
22 Interested readers may refer to Alesina et al. (1996) and Helliwell (1992) for what kind of risks the economic growth could pose to a society.

1.1.2 The Economic Significance of Chinese Labour Issues

Internationally, the competitive advantage of Chinese products, which was established mostly on the basis of cheap labour, swept world markets before the onset of the global economic crisis in 2008. For example, according to one estimate, in 2004 China produced two-thirds of the world's photocopiers, shoes, toys, and microwave ovens, half of its DVD players, digital cameras, cement and textiles, 40% of its socks, one third of its DVD-ROM drives and desktop computers, a quarter of its mobile telephones, TV sets, steel, car stereos, and so on.[23] In face of the challenges arising from cheap Chinese imports, various parties paid close attention to China's labour problems. Some interest groups in the west used the issue of low labour standards to occupy the moral high ground and fight the perceived "Chinese Threat".[24] The labour standards issue is admittedly one of the major problems in China's industrial relations (as we will see in later chapters), but the question is whether it is possible to identify a universal labour standard, taking into account the huge variation in productivity and living standards around the world.[25] Even if such a labour standard were

23 Skidelsky (2005).

24 For example, the American Federation of Labor and Congress of Industrial Organizations (AFL-CIO) has several times presented "301 Petition Regarding Violation of Workers Rights in China" to the US government. The petition alleges that the Chinese government persistently and systematically denies workers' rights, harming US workers and communities, leading to the loss of a million US jobs to China as a result of China's repression of worker rights (AFL-CIO 2006). Although the US government has formally turned down these applications, it has used such issues as a tool to put political pressure on the Chinese government (Bamber (2005), p. 7). As pointed out by Chan and Ross, in the context of globalization and free trade, there appear two strange alliances in labour relations: on the one side, western bankers and multinational companies (employers) align themselves with the governments of developing countries; on the other, western labour and human rights NGOs and trade unions stand together with their own governments (which they usually oppose) (Chan and Ross (2003), p. 1014).

25 The following experience illustrates the difficulty of setting a labour standard for a country like China, not to mention a more diversified world. In April 2008, the police and labour authority in Dong-guan, a major manufacturing centre next to

established, it might take decades, according to Bamber, before Chinese labour costs are increased to levels which compare with those prevailing in developed market economies.[26]

Domestically, concerned parties began to realize that violation of labour rights contributes to widening income gaps and deepening social tension. The gap between rich and poor continued to grow during the decade after 1995. According to data from the NBS, China's Gini Coefficient exceeded the generally accepted line of 0.4, reaching 0.46 in 2002 and 0.47 in 2004.[27] Chen argued that only by adjusting the labour protection system and establishing social security networks can the Chinese government stop the worrying trend toward widening income differences.[28] At the

---

Shenzhen and Hongkong, rescued dozens of lost children who were from Liangshan, a poorer part in Southwest China, and worked in some sweatshops in Dong-guan. But the children refused to go home because they could eat more at the factory than at home, even though they had to work 13–14 hours per day. When the journalist told the mother of a lost child that her child ate rice only every two or three days, the mother's reaction, to the journalist' surprise, was joy rather than sadness. Experts believed that poverty rather than the widely condemned "sweatshops" was the real enemy in such cases ("Research on Liangshan Child Labourers" (in Chinese), *Southern Metropolitan Newspaper*, 29 April 2008).

26 Bamber (2005), pp. 7–8.

27 As quoted by Fan (2006). Fan points out that China took only 20 years to change from one of the most egalitarian countries in the world to one with the biggest gap between the poor and the rich: China's Gini Coefficient has grown from 0.24 in 1984 to 0.32 in 1990, then to 0.47 in 2004, doubling in merely two decades. The ideas of advocates of reliance on the market, F. A. Hayek being a leading figure, dominated mainstream Chinese economic thought in the reform era, These thinkers contended that, if the distribution of earnings was the outcome of a free pricing process in the market, what the "invisible hand" produced should be deemed the most reasonable arrangement: when the market is short of labour, the employees enjoy more generous compensation; and when the market is in surplus of labour, the capitalist enjoys a lower labour cost and there should be no moral value judgement in either case (Hayek 2003). But in a modern civilized society, the question inevitably arises: should there be a morally defined bottom line for labour standards, regardless of the market situation? Should we allow the rich to get ever richer and the poor poorer?

28 Chen (2005). However, Qiao argues that, as China's comparative advantage in the international division of labour is its cheap labour, the state will continue tightening

CCP's Seventeenth National Congress held in October 2007, the central leadership for the first time raised concerns about labour protection and fair income allocation among different social groups.[29] In accordance with the Party's concerns, the state promulgated a new "Labour Contract Law" in late 2007, which came into effect on 1 January 2008.[30]

1.1.3 The Political Significance of Chinese Labour Issues

In China, almost any socio-economic activity has some kind of connection with politics. Labour problems, due to their special characteristics, have even more political content. Not only have labour issues been a significant topic in the People's Republic of China's (PRC) long complicated political history, as we see in later chapters, but power imbalances between capital and labour have resulted directly in serious labour disputes, which pose severe challenges to China's social stability and development.[31]

Unless solved properly, economic issues such as labour disputes can easily evolve into political issues, affecting the stability and harmony of the society. According to statistics from the MOLSS,[32] labour disputes have

---

its control over labour costs to maintain China's attraction of foreign investment for further economic development. Therefore, labour relations will inevitably enter a turbulent period, and the working class may suffer even more, bearing the costs of the reforms with exposure to risks such as severe unemployment, wage and benefit cuts and lower living standards (Qiao 2003).

29 CC-CCP (2007). This document virtually rejected the predominant concept upheld by Deng Xiaoping in the early 1980s of "let some people get rich first (让一部分人先富起来)". Actually, years before the CCP paid attention to the issue, scholars such as Qiao had argued that social unfairness in China, in form of an unjust income distribution, had reached such a point that there would be social turbulence if the government remained inactive in affairs such as labour protection (Qiao 2003).

30 We discuss this new law in more detail in Chapter 4, when we deal with the issue of adjustment of labour relations confronted by non-SOE employees.

31 Research Institute of MOLSS (2004a).

32 Starting from early 2008, the Ministry of Human Resource and Social Security (MOHRSS, 人力资源与社会保障部) was established to replace the MOLSS and the Ministry of Personnel (人事部). In this book, we continue to use MOLSS when it comes to issues earlier than 2008.

risen 30% annually since the 1990s. Workers involved in formally recorded labour disputes are estimated to be more than a million each year, while many more disputes were not recorded at all.[33]

Yu argues that during the decade after 1995 struggles for protection of labour rights had a "Protection by Justification (以理维权)" character, meaning that workers (especially SOE workers) took action not on the basis of "survival ethics (生存伦理)" but on the basis of orthodox Marxist "political ethics (政治伦理)",[34] wherein the working class is described as the main force of revolution, the master of the party and state, and the leader of the whole society. These ideological notions misled the Chinese working class into considering itself an inherent part of the party-state, thus (quite unintentionally) providing a useful weapon for the workers to struggle against unfair treatment. Therefore, the party-state faced embarrassment when workers struggled on the basis of such political ethics.

Incidents in the struggle for labour rights, which will be discussed in more detail in later chapters, shake the very foundation of the legitimacy of party-state rule. Taking into account the fact that China, at least nominally, is still "a socialist state under the people's democratic dictatorship led by the working class and based on the alliance of workers and peasants",[35] the political aspect of labour struggle is no trifling matter in China.

For both economic and political reasons, as discussed above, Chinese labour problems have attracted considerable attention in the international media and academic literature. However, as we will soon see, little of the literature regarding Chinese industrial relations has applied a systematic

33 Research Institute of MOLSS (2004b). Note that official data usually underestimate the seriousness of negative issues. The number of workers involved in labour disputes must be far higher than one million in reality. One million workers involved in disputes is a low percentage of the 700-odd million working population in China. If the data were true, no one would have to bother about China's labour issues. A possible reason for the underestimation is that, as will be discussed in Chapter 2, complex dispute settlement procedures have virtually prevented the majority of dissatisfied employees from taking formal action, with the result that the disputes are not recorded in official documents.

34 Yu (2006b).

35 National People's Congress (2004), p. 80.

analytical framework to draw a broader picture of Chinese industrial relations, focusing instead on specific issues such as freedom of association issues and labour disputes.

1.1.4 Existing Studies of Chinese Industrial Relations

Academics tend to identify three approaches to the study of industrial relations: the Unitarist, the Radical and the Pluralist.[36] Of the three approaches, the Pluralist approach is the industrial relations theory most widely accepted by western scholars.[37] The most popular industrial relations analytical model was founded on Dunlop's influential work of 1958, which maintained that the industrial relations system was a sub-system of the total society.

Deery summarized two important underlying assumptions of this model: first, that power is diffused among the main bargaining groups in such a way that no party dominates the other;[38] and second, that the state is an impartial guardian of the public interest, whose role is largely to protect the weak and restrain the power of the strong. Within these assumptions, industrial relations may be considered to be a process of concession and

36 See relevant discussions in Bray et al.(2005) Chapter 1 and Deery (2001), pp. 7–19.

37 To some extent, the study of industrial relations in the past 100 years or so has been a battlefield for different ideologies. On the one side, the Unitarists uphold the conservative position based on the beliefs of free market and Social Darwinism; on the other, the Radicals propose subversive revolution to overthrow capitalism and build socialism. Somewhere in between, Pluralists wish to reconcile conflict by joint job regulation. The Pluralists' position entails maintaining, reforming and developing the capitalistic free market system, and joint regulation by labour, capital and the state to safeguard the stability of the society and achieve balance between efficiency and justice (Kaufman et al. 2003). The growth of Human Resource Management (HRM) in recent years, however, has shifted attention to a more individual (micro) level of employer-employee relations, focusing on the recruitment, retention, development and motivation of employees (Dowling et al.1999). This, however, should not and cannot replace the study of interactions among different parties at a broader level, as industrial relations is not simply a branch of management science but a multi-disciplinary study that draws upon political science, economics, sociology, management science, psychology and legal studies.

38 In other words, competing forces constrain and check absolute power.

compromise in which a body of rules restrains the abuse of power and enables all parties to achieve gains.[39]

Deery's assumptions can also be rephrased by using concepts from political science so that the ideal tripartite system of labour, capital and state has to meet the following three prerequisites to function properly.

First, the law must allow independent labour unions, so that employees are *free* to join (or even establish) unions and authorize them to be collective representatives of their interests in the tripartite mechanism. Only then can labour and unions be treated as on the same side or even as one.

Second, employees should be able to exercise their *democratic* rights as individual citizens, regardless of their union membership, to influence the state's policies and regulations by their votes and through the representatives whom they have chosen. In this case, the state can be deemed to be an impartial guardian of the public interest.

Third, in a society respecting the rule of law, though there may be power gaps between labour, capital and state, the three are treated as *equal* parties in the legal framework.

These prerequisites embody the three major civil rights of *freedom* (liberty), *democracy* and *equality* in the arena of industrial relations. With the same reasoning as argued by Deery, the three-party model can stand only when freely associated labour (and unions) can deal with employers on equal ground, with the democratically elected state acting as an impartial guardian of the public interest. We will soon see in the next section that these prerequisites are not met in China, which means that the classic three-party model cannot be applied directly.

As mentioned earlier, research on Chinese industrial relations and labour problems has been stagnant for a long time. More often than not, authors utilize their original academic backgrounds in economics, management, sociology, legal and political science etc. to tackle industrial relations issues.[40] Therefore, most studies cannot be easily categorized into any of the three previously mentioned research approaches because they simply

39 Deery (2001), p. 13.

40 This problem, though to a lesser extent, also exists in western industrial relations circles even nowadays; it used to be a bigger issue when industrial relations started to be recognized as a separate stream of study in the first part of twentieth century.

did not apply them to the Chinese situation.[41] Nevertheless, we may still "borrow" some of the concepts and categorize the relevant literature into the following three broader groups:

"Unitarist" – HRM Approach

Literature in this category looks mostly at Chinese industrial relations issues from a management science (or more specifically, Human Resources Management) perspective in the context of the transition from a traditional command to market economy. Though HRM is often taken as an American or Anglo-American idea,[42] and it is arguable whether the HRM analytical framework[43] can be directly applied to enterprises in non-western contexts,[44] it nevertheless provides an interesting perspective for looking at Chinese enterprise management practices and industrial relations. Typical of the literature in this category are Chow and Fu (2000), Cooke (2004, 2005a and 2005b, 2006, 2008a and 2008b), Ding and Akhtar (2001) and

41 As it has been only a short time since the opening up of this research topic by Chinese scholars, Chinese literature on industrial relations is still unsystematic. For example, most research about the working class's situation in the transitional period focuses on only two social groups, i.e. the "peasant workers" and the "old" SOE workers, paying little attention to the workers in private and foreign enterprises. Moreover, Chinese scholars are cautious in expressing their opinions about fundamental (usually political) issues. Points are more often than not vague and obscure, and this is unfavourable to normal academic discussions. The Chinese academics' concern and caution are, of course, completely understandable. Readers with sufficient background knowledge of China can usually interpret the tactful and hidden expressions of opinion.

42 Sometimes, it is even more restrictively defined as being taken from those "best practices" among large firms, and more restrictively again, often among blue chip, private and successful firms.

43 Usually, scholars conduct analyses from the perspectives of several important HRM practices such as attracting and choosing employees (hiring), teaching employees how to perform their jobs and preparing them for the future (training), rewarding employees (compensation) and evaluating employees' performance (performance appraisal).

44 Cunningham and Rowley (2008), p. 341.

Zhu et al. (2005) etc.[45] These authors mostly have business or management science backgrounds.

"Radical" – Sociological-Political Approach

Literature in this category takes into account the unprecedented social change in China and tends to consider the worsening industrial relations and labour issues as one of the major challenges to the stability of society and the party-state political system. It therefore concentrates on the most eye-catching, confrontational issues such as the right of association, collective bargaining and strikes. It utilizes theories in sociology and political science to provide explanations and possible solutions for Chinese labour issues. Typical literature in this category includes Chan (1993, 1997, 2002, 2006), Chen (2003a and 2003b, 2006, 2007), Chang (2002), Feng (2003, 2004) and Yu (2006) etc.[46] These authors mostly have sociology or political science backgrounds.

"Pluralist" – Institutional Approach

The literature in this category is relatively scanty when compared with the other two categories, because not many Chinese scholars are familiar with pluralist industrial relations theories, while even fewer overseas industrial relations academics are familiar with China. Though limited in number of advocates, this approach tries to analyse the whole Chinese industrial relations system from a macro perspective and explain institutional

45 Other literature that falls into this broad category includes Clarke (2002, 2004); Frankel and Peetz (1998); Gallagher (2004).

46 Other literature that falls into this broad category includes Blecher (2002); Chan and Ross (2003); Chan (2005); Chen and Zhang (2005); Clarke (2005); Feng (2006); Gilbert (2005); Giles et al. (2006); Han (2005); Harper (1969); Huang and Guo (2006); Lee (1998, 2002); Leung (2002); Liu (2004); Ngai (2005); O'Leary (1998); Pringle (2001); Qi (2004); Qiao (2003); Research Institute of MOLSS (2004a and 2004b); Shen (2006); Tong (2003); Walder (1993); Wang (2003); Xu (2003); Zhang (2003) etc.

relationships between various industrial relations actors. Typical literature in this category includes Cooke (2008b), Taylor et al. (2003) and Zhu and Warner (2000) etc.[47] These authors have more diversified backgrounds than those of the other two categories.

Most of the existing literature focuses on the transition of Chinese industrial relations from the traditional form typified by practices in SOEs under a command economy towards the more modern system of a market economy. The literature indicates that, in the context of unprecedented economic transition, the process of change is mixed and complex. We will refer to these and to other relevant literature in more detail later when we come to discuss specific industrial relations issues later.

However, it is necessary to point out that most of the existing literature focuses mainly on specific aspects of Chinese industrial relations, providing little account of the overall broader picture.[48] The absence of general, comprehensive descriptive accounts of Chinese industrial relations are a major barrier for readers who are interested in the topic yet lack detailed preliminary knowledge; reading mostly "specific"-oriented papers leads only to a fragmented understanding of Chinese industrial relations. Therefore, with this book, we intend to make a modest contribution towards filling this gap of knowledge.

47 Other literature that falls into this broad category includes Clarke (2002, 2004); Frankel and Peetz (1998); Gallagher (2004).

48 Zhu and Warner (2000), Cooke (2008b) and Taylor et al. (2003) can be considered as the few exceptions. The first two are book chapters in edited collections of descriptive accounts of various countries' industrial relations and provide only brief accounts of the topic. The latter did put forward some new thoughts and insights, but, as we will see later, further revision is still required to adapt to the fast changing circumstances of Chinese industrial relations.

1.2 A New Taxonomic Approach to Analysing Chinese Industrial Relations

As noted previously, the Pluralist approach – the most widely accepted theory used by western scholars to analyse industrial relations – focuses on the interests and goals of three different parties; namely, the state, employers and employees, some via their representative organizations. It further focuses on the degree of conflict among these actors and the power resources available to them.

China's industrial relations system, however, does not fit easily within two important assumptions held by Pluralists. First, power is *not* diffused among the main bargaining groups in China but is, instead, highly concentrated in the hands of the party-state at the macro level and employers at the micro level. The party-state is generally in the dominant position. Secondly, the Chinese party-state is not an impartial guardian of the public interest but an organization with its own interests.[49]

Moreover, none of the three prerequisites[50] for a modern tripartite system are met in China, for three reasons: firstly, China's only labour union, the All China Federation of Trade Unions, or ACFTU, is not a freely associated union, but rather an extension of the party-state system.[51] Secondly, the party-state does not allow its citizens the democratic right to participate in political life and influence public policy.[52] Thirdly, China is

49 We discuss these issues in more detail in the following chapters of the book.

50 Refer back to the discussion earlier in this section.

51 Though the ACFTU monopolized the name of "labour union" for over half a century, for most of that time it neither represented the real interests of the workers nor fulfilled the responsibilities of a real union. That is why most of the free unions in the world so far have refused to recognize the ACFTU as a "labour union" (Chan (2006), p. 300). We discuss this in more detail in Chapters 3 and 6.

52 The employers, as members of the "elite class", can have some influence over relevant state policies and regulations, while labour, being in a lower class of the society, is virtually deprived of any "right of speech and involvement (话语权和参与权)", and can only passively accept whatever the state policies and their consequences may be. We discuss this in more detail in Chapters 5 and 8.

far from being a country that respects the rule of law,[53] and employers and employees are in unequal positions of power when in dispute.[54]

Therefore, China's industrial relations are very different from those of western capitalist economies and western theories cannot be applied to China without appropriate revision.[55] Regrettably, as far as the literature we reviewed is concerned, few scholars of Chinese industrial relations take the above-mentioned problems into account. Taylor et al. (2003) is an exception. Having considered the special characteristics of the Chinese trade union, Taylor et al. proposed to revise the classic tripartite model into a four-party model. This model takes the study of Chinese industrial relations one step closer to local circumstances by recognizing the distance between union and workers, thus treating the union and workers as separate actors. However, it is not sophisticated enough to build a practical, analytical model for the following reasons:

53 In recent years, the Chinese leadership has repeatedly declared its determination to build a Rule-of-Law Society (法治社会), while commentators are still debating whether the genuine idea in the mind of those officials is Rule-of-Law or Rule-by-Law ("From Rule-by-Law to Rule-of-Law" (in Chinese), *Prosecutor Daily*, "从"法制"走向"法治", 检察日报", 18 April 2008).

54 In the best case scenario, even when employees can theoretically "fight" against employers with "legal weapons (法律武器)", in reality, employees can hardly afford the time and money to turn to the legal system, because the legal procedure is so complicated and prolonged that the returns, if any, are usually far less than the cost of the lawsuit. Many employers made good use of this to exhaust employees attempting litigation (Of course, this applies also to western legal systems, but the situation in China is much worse.) We discuss this in more detail in Chapter 3.

55 This is, in fact, a problem encountered generally in China studies. As MacFarquhar and Fairbank point out, though one cannot deny the increasing influence of western ideas and examples, it would be superficial to apply western terms and methodology to China where ethical values, the family system, social norms and agrarian-commercial economy and polity have taken shape through countless vicissitudes over 3,000 years. The Chinese state and society in their contemporary guise are end products of a largely separate evolution, comparable with, but far from identical to, that of the west (MacFarquhar and Fairbank (1987), pp. 13–15).

First, the model does not recognize the unique party-state political system in China, which differs dramatically from the state system in western countries;

Second, it does not provide "space" for discussion of employer associations, which are not necessarily the same as individual employers, as we shall see in later chapters;

Third, it does not identify the differences between the ACFTU and grass-roots unions, treating them as a unified whole;

Fourth, it does not pay enough attention to the various segments of employers and employees, treating their role as actors in industrial relations as undifferentiated wholes; and,

Fifth, it does not look into specific, one-to-one relationships among all these industrial relations actors.

For these reasons, Taylor et al's approach can be considered as a starting point for the revision of classic western industrial relations theories in the development of an appropriate analytical framework for China. The knowledge gaps thus lead us to the broad research questions of this book, as listed below:

1. What revisions are needed to make the classic (western) industrial relations theories applicable to China's situation?
2. What overall picture of China's industrial relations can we develop by applying the analytical framework of a revised model?

With regard to the problems discussed above, we propose a "six-party" taxonomic approach for the analysis of contemporary China's industrial relations (see Figure 1.1). The six parties in this taxonomy refer to the major actors in contemporary China's industrial relations, namely the party-state, the employers' association, the ACFTU, grass-roots unions, employers, and employees.

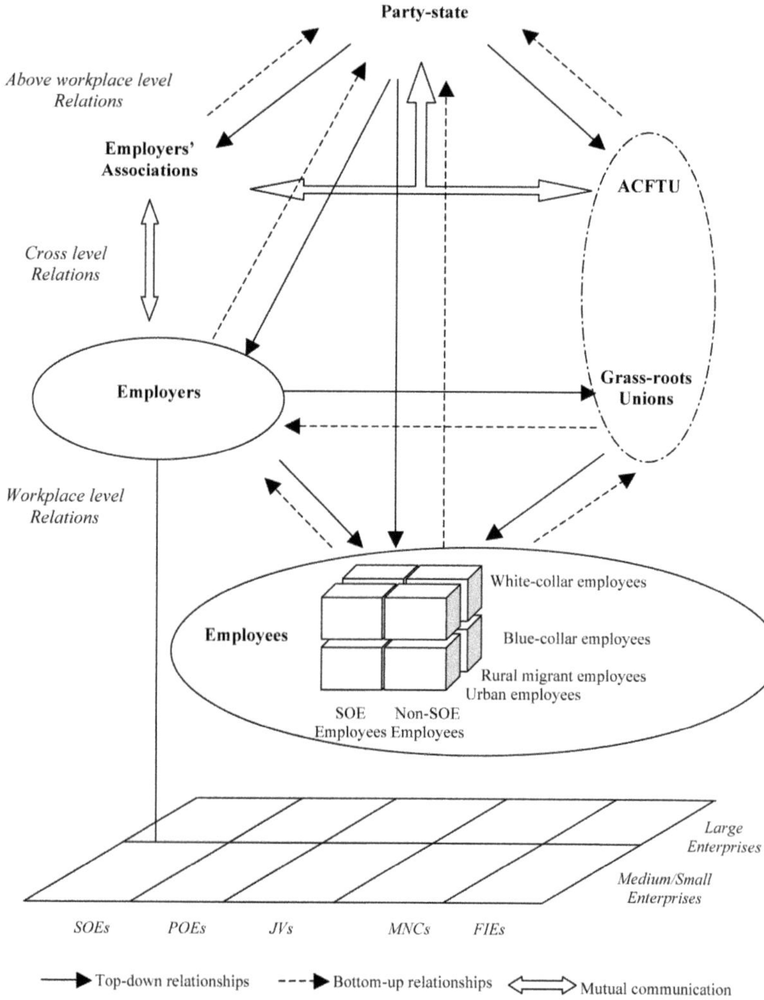

Figure 1.1 Contemporary Chinese Industrial Relations System

1.2.1 Why Identify Six Parties?

The revision of the original three-party into a six-party model is based on the following observations of China's industrial relations system:

First, since 1949, the nation's socio-economic-political activities have revolved around the so-called "party-state", the structure and functions of which differ from the state in the western liberal democracies. As we see in later analyses, the Party, i.e. the Chinese Communist Party, or CCP, plays the dominant role in the party-state system, being more important than the state in most decision-making processes. The party-state's political practices have deep roots going back to the early days when the CCP struggled to seize power. Therefore, China's industrial relations model must replace the concept of "state" with that of "party-state" in order to recognize how political power is exercised. A model focusing only on the "state" will omit erroneously the most important "invisible hand" in China, the Party.[56]

Second, the ACFTU is an extension of the party-state rather than a freely associated employees' representational organization. It embodies an inherent contradiction between furthering the interests of the party-state and promoting the interests of labour.[57] This contradiction has its root in conflicts between the ACFTU's macro- and micro-functions.[58] Even though the ACFTU and its grass-roots unions are unified organizationally, their daily practices are quite different. For this reason, it is necessary not only to treat Chinese unions separately from employees, as in Taylor et al.'s (2003) model, but also to distinguish the macro level ACFTU from micro level grass-roots unions when analysing China's union issues.

56 We discuss the structure and function of the party-state in Chapter 2.

57 See the detailed analysis in Chapters 5 and 6 of the relationships between the ACFTU and the party-state and between grass-roots unions and employees.

58 At the macro (above workplace) level, the ACFTU, as an extensional organization of the party-state, must fulfil the responsibilities allocated by the party-state, i.e. "to maintain social stability (维护社会安定)" and "to promote economic development (促进经济发展)"; while at the micro (workplace) level, the ACFTU's grass-root branches must also fulfil the obligation of "protecting the employees' rightful interests (维护职工合法权益)". (*General Provisions in ACFTU 2003*).

Third, in contrast to the party-state's strict control over labour organizations, the employers' associations developed rapidly after 1992 and are widely supported by government at various levels. Some of these organizations are official or semi-official, while others are autonomous.[59] As more in-depth economic as well as political reforms are implemented, these new-born interest groups are bound to play more important roles in China's social, economic and political life.[60] At the same time, because they are official or semi-official organizations, some of the employers' associations are not necessarily on the same side as all employers, just as the ACFTU is not necessarily on the same side as the employees. Therefore, Employers' Associations should be treated as independent actors in Chinese industrial relations.

Fourth, China's rapidly emerging market economy after the 1990s was not matched by the development of legal supervision. The operations of Chinese enterprises are multifarious, ranging from appalling "sweatshops" to modern enterprises with sophisticated human resource management capacities. The relationship between employers and employees, unlike those in systems respecting the rule of law, which tend to be relatively unified under the guidance of relevant labour laws and regulations, is much affected by employer will, which turns out to be determined usually by the scale of the employer's business and the type of the employer's ownership.[61] In the same enterprise an employee's social position also affects the employer's attitude towards him or her.[62] Therefore, it is essential that a comprehensive industrial relations model of China take into account the effects of specific

59 In China, the employers' associations are usually called "industry associations (行业协会)" or "civil chambers of commerce (民间商会)". Generally speaking, the difference between the two is that the former name is usually adopted by official or semi-official organizations, while the latter is usually used by spontaneously established ones. See the detailed discussion in next chapter.

60 The possibility cannot be ruled out that some of these employers' organizations may merge with the degenerated party-state to form eventually a rightist authoritarian regime. We discuss this in more detail in Chapters 2 and 7.

61 We discuss this in more detail in Chapter 6.

62 We discuss this in more detail in Chapter 4.

employer and employee circumstances. We segment China's employers by their ownership and employees by three social background categories.

This "six-party" taxonomy allows us to look into the specific details of each party when analysing industrial relations. Chapters 2 to 4 of the book discuss the history and current status of these six industrial relations actors.

1.2.2 Why Investigate the Specific Relationships?

Relationships among each of the six Chinese industrial relations actors are subtle. For example, the relationship between the party-state and the ACFTU is distinctly different from that between the party-state and employees. Furthermore, industrial relations at different levels are dramatically different from each other. Macro-level industrial relations are concerned with various aspects such as politics, the economy and culture,[63] while micro-level industrial relations are concerned mostly with more individual economic issues. Relationship lines also exist which link industrial relations actors at different levels, for example, those between the party-state and employers or employees.

For the reasons above, we propose to investigate separately the relationships between specific actors and to categorize these relationships into three broad groupings:

Relationships above the Workplace Level

These are relations among the three macro-level industrial relations actors; i.e., the Party-State, the ACFTU and employers' associations.

63 However, as we shall see in the analysis of the later chapters, in China, the most important consideration of macro level industrial relations is political.

Relationships at the Workplace Level

These relations are among the three micro-level industrial relations actors; i.e., the grass-roots unions, employers and employees.

Relationships across Different Levels

These are relations between the party-state and employees, between the party-state and employers, and between the employers' associations and employers. As this group of relationships has a closer connection with political science than with industrial relations study, the limited length of this book precludes us from detailed discussion of this sub-topic. We look forward to research on this matter in future works.

This taxonomy enables us to look into the specific details of each set of relationships between the six Chinese industrial relations actors. Chapters 5 and 6 of the book discuss respectively the first two groups of relationships while the last set of relationships will be touched upon in future works. We also notice that the Pluralist approach emphasizes analysis of a specific system in its historical contexts (especially when the society has gone through revolution or war), for there are always changes in the locus of actors (labour, capital and state) that impact upon the industrial relations system through time. This perspective particularly suits China's case, as we shall see in later discussions that historical elements significantly affect Chinese industrial relations. Therefore, throughout the book, we will present a picture of Chinese industrial relations in a historical context.

We attempt to propose a new analytical framework appropriate to the specifics of China's industrial relations. By establishing a taxonomy of actors and relationships, we are going to conduct research into Chinese industrial relations in a more systematic and comprehensive manner. We seek to provide answers to the following fundamental questions on China's contemporary industrial relations:

> What is the historical and current status of China's six industrial relations actors? What are the relationships among them and how might these relationships develop?

What we have proposed in this book is a new way of looking at Chinese industrial relations. Instead of following the old approach of analysing industrial relations by focusing on the three major parties, we will, firstly, add three parties "with Chinese characteristics", and secondly, pay attention to the specific relationships between each one of the six industrial relations actors.

However, the all-encompassing characteristic of this taxonomy, which is designed to be a tool for a broader descriptive account of Chinese industrial relations, makes it impossible to conduct sufficiently sophisticated field work to provide adequate empirical data for the analysis of all the sub-topics covered in the book. Therefore, instead, only already available data, official, academic, primary and secondary, will be used to provide examples of how Chinese industrial relations can be described by using this taxonomy.

For this reason, this book only acts as a starting point for the application of the new taxonomy. It is expected that a series of empirical studies focusing on more specific sub-topics of Chinese industrial relations will be forthcoming in the near future. That is to say, this book focuses on the more general and broader issues regarding the analysis of Chinese industrial relations, so that future empirical studies can progress from "general" to "specific". For example, the development of a series of labour-related laws since 1994, including the more recently promulgated Labour Contract Law (2007), has been a hotly debated specific sub-topic of Chinese industrial relations. A full account of the laws and commentary on the likely effects of specific provisions will itself be an appropriate topic for another potential PhD for post-doctoral research. Throughout this book a lot of specific issues requiring further detailed analysis will be encountered. However, although we will do our best to deal with them appropriately for our purposes, we must constantly resist the temptation to slip into details which may lead to a loss of the focus of this book.

It is also necessary to state here that, because of word limits, the book focuses only on industrial relations institutions/actors and their inter-relationships. It does not analyse specific matters regarding the processes of industrial relations; e.g., labour participation in daily operation/management, labour dispute and settlement mechanisms, or collective bargaining/

consultation procedures which lead to collective contracts. These issues will be touched upon only when we come to discuss relevant actors and their relationships.

We believe that the discussion and conclusions of the book will be valuable for those interested in China's social development (in particular, the development of modern industrial relations). In the course of this book, we offer considered views to elicit those of fellow researchers.

However, China's huge territory, vast population, long history and complex social environment all contribute to the difficulty of China Studies. As Gallagher asks, "... given the many varieties ... and ... diversity of China, is it possible to generalize about the emerging picture of labour relations there?"[64] Clearly, this book cannot cover every detail of China's industrial relations, nor did the author have the resources to conduct significant field research in China.[65] Therefore, even though the book attempts to analyse China's industrial relations from a new perspective and with a new framework, the "base materials" are not new. The book relies on primary materials such as open official documents and statistics issued by the government or relevant organizations, as well as secondary materials such as the research results of other scholars.

For the reasons above, we make only modest and pragmatic claims regarding this research. This book does not claim to be an authoritative study of Chinese industrial relations; rather, it takes the opportunity to fill some of the gaps in the literature and to present readers with contemporary material regarding the topic in such a fast changing country. Bearing this in mind, I set the following position for the book and attempt to achieve the corresponding goals:

First, to bring western industrial relations theories to the attention of relevant Chinese scholars, and, conversely, bring Chinese industrial relations issues as they are to the attention of relevant western scholars.

64 Gallagher (2004), p. 15.

65 The political sensitivities of labour studies in China are obvious and are an impediment to field research. Quite apart from this, the huge territory, enormous population and diversity of China would make it almost impossible to construct a reliable sample, as we have seen in some cases mentioned earlier in this chapter.

Second, to embark on the first attempt of revising the western industrial relations analytical model to adapt it to the realities of China.

Third, to apply the revised model and develop an overall picture of China's industrial relations which is as objective and accurate as possible.

We do not, however, attempt to propose any solution to China's immense industrial relations problems. Such proposals would need to take into account the complexities of Chinese politics, economy and society, which can hardly be accomplished in a single piece of research. We shall be content if this book contributes to a clearer analysis and description of China's industrial relations, which may help the development of a better understanding of the issue and a better strategy for tackling it.

Conclusions

China's newly developed labour market and the subsequent series of labour issues have captured much attention due to both economic and political considerations. However, little of the existing literature applies a systematic analytical framework to draw a broader picture of Chinese industrial relations. We raised research questions as to whether western industrial relations theories can be applied to China's situation, what revision(s) need to be made, and what overall picture of China's industrial relations can be developed by applying the analytical framework of a revised model. In this context we propose a taxonomy that allows for the complexities not encompassed in the frameworks of Dunlop (1958) and Taylor et al. (2003). This taxonomy of industrial relations equips us, we believe, to conduct research into Chinese industrial relations in a more sophisticated and systematic manner and provide answers in the following chapters to some fundamental questions about contemporary China's industrial relations.

CHAPTER TWO

The Party-state, ACFTU and Employers' Associations: Chinese Industrial Relations Actors above the Workplace Level

Introduction

In the previous chapter we discussed the substantial differences between China's industrial relations and those of western industrialized capitalist economies. Having regard to China's unique historical circumstances, we proposed a new analytical model for China's industrial relations system. Beginning with this chapter, we analyse Chinese industrial relations in detail by applying this model.

This chapter focuses on three major actors in macro-level industrial relations, the party-state, the ACFTU, and employer associations. We draw a broad picture of the party-state system in industrial relations and discuss its major functions. The chapter reviews the history and contemporary status of the ACFTU, discussing how it gradually shifted from a political organization to a more service-oriented one. The chapter concludes with a description of the development of Chinese employer associations, explaining briefly three distinct types of employers' associations legally operating in China.

2.1 Party-state

The biggest difference between China and western countries in the matter of state structure is the "party-state" system in China.[1]

In principle, in modern liberal democratic systems, people express their political preferences by voting, thereby legitimizing the state's power.[2] State power is then further separated into three major areas, the executive, legislature and judiciary, to prevent the possible abuse of power.[3] The concept and structure of the state in China are completely different.[4] Nominally, China has elections, but these are far from free or democratic in a western sense. China also has divisions among the executive system (the "People's" Government), the legislative system (the "People's" Congress), and the judiciary system (the "People's" Court and the "People's" Procuratorate), but

1 In this book, the party-state refers to the power combination of the Chinese Communist Party, founded in 1921, and the People's Republic of China, established in 1949. Limited by the length of the book, we do not include in this chapter an introduction to the history of the Party and the state but will touch upon certain relevant historical events when discussing specific industrial relations issues. Interested readers may refer to Fairbank (1983); Fairbank and Feuerwerker (1986); MacFarquhar and Fairbank (1987, 1991) and Zheng et al. (1997) for more detailed discussions regarding the history of the party-state.

2 Hobbes argued that people transfer their "natural right" of holding arms for self-defence to the sovereign so as to escape from "the war of every man against every man", and that this explained the origin of states (Hobbes (1651), pp. 99–114). Locke believed that people, by their own wills, conditionally transferred part of their natural rights to states so as to better protect their lives, liberty and property (Locke (1681), p. 57). Though Locke's viewpoints were traditionally considered to be a criticism of those of Hobbes, by avoiding the argument as to whether rights were transferred by fear or by liberal will, we can identify the common point that the state is founded on the rights transferred from people to cater for their need of protection.

3 McClelland (1996).

4 If we trace back the theoretical origin of the concept of the state in a "socialist country", we find the shadows of Hegel and Marx. Hegel considered the state as nothing more than an apparatus for the convenience of ruling. Marx, who was deeply influenced by Hegel, developed the thought, and incorporated it into the classic "Marxist theory of state" – the state is a tool for class struggle and oppression and is the superstructure that serves the economic infrastructure (Fukuyama 1992; McClelland 1996).

there is barely any balance of power, or "separation of powers" in a western sense, among them. The key difference lies in the matter of "legitimacy", whether the state's legitimacy derives from the people's will, and if so, how this will influences the actual operation of the state.

In China it has been observed by many critics that the people's will is dispensable. The party-state system implies that ordinary citizens need to be guided by an elite vanguard group. Therefore, beneath the state apparatus is a "hand" which manipulates the operation of the country. That hand is the Chinese Communist Party, which is beyond the control and reach of the general public.[5] This "hand" is both "visible" and "invisible". On the one hand, it is visible because party organs operate openly in all state institutions, semi-governmental organizations (事业单位) and even enterprises (mostly in SOEs and JVs). On the other hand, it is invisible because there is no document which specifically states that organizations must follow the orders of the Party. However, one of the so-called "Four Basic Principles"[6] is "Adhere to the CCP's Leadership (坚持共产党的领导)", which implicitly indicates that the Party has the final decision-making power over all major issues. This is the essence of the "party-state" system.

In the following two subsections, we look in to the structure and roles of the party-state, particularly in regards to industrial relations.

2.1.1 *Structure of the Party-state*

In China, the "party-state" system penetrates every aspect of political, social and economic life. As a sub-system of the broader social system, the industrial relations system is no exception.

5 Refer to Figure 2.1 in the later part of this section.

6 In the CCP's "Conference on Theoretical Issues" held on 30 March, 1979, Deng Xiaoping excluded four topics from debate in P. R. China, which were to be revered as the "Four Basic Principles", i.e. Adhere to Socialism (坚持社会主义道路), Adhere to Proletarian Dictatorship (坚持无产阶级专政), Adhere to CCP's Leadership (坚持共产党的领导) and Adhere to Marxism/ Leninism/ Mao Ze-dong Thoughts (坚持马列主义、毛泽东思想). The "Four Basic Principles" were also formally written into China's constitution in 1982 (National People's Congress (2004), p. 26).

The "party-state" system, however, is not unchanging. After the establishment of the People's Republic of China in 1949, it went through numerous major restructurings.[7] Especially after the "Reform and Open-door" policy commenced in 1979, the roles and functions of the party-state changed significantly. The party-state's control over and interference in purely economic or personal areas declined greatly and its roles in industrial relations changed accordingly.

Though some scholars discuss the roles of the party-state in China's industrial relations,[8] most do not analyse the matter in depth. For example, Zhang discussed the role of the party-state in union development in China, but did not look into how, as a whole, it fits into the industrial relations system and functions.[9] The writings of Taylor et al. are more detailed, and include a discussion to explain the government's position in industrial relations. The analyses, however, have a number of problems.

First, they do not clarify the difference between nominal and actual leadership. This problem is reflected in the links, both at state and local level, between the People's Congresses and government. Whereas they seem to indicate that the People's Congresses have direct power over the government, the Congresses are usually referred to as "rubber stamps (橡皮图章)" in China, meaning that they have little influence over the operation of government.[10]

Second, after years of reforms, some ministries mentioned in their discussion were restructured. For example, the original State Economic and Trade Committee (SETC, 国家经贸委) was merged with other relevant ministries in 2003 to form the new Ministry of Commerce (MOC, 商务部); and the China Enterprise Confederation-China Enterprise Directors Association (CEC-CEDA, 中企联-中企协), which was previously directly under the SETC, subsequently appeared to be acting semi-independently. In early 2008, the Ministry of Human Resources and Social Security (MOHRSS, 人力资源和社会保障部) was founded to replace

7 Xinhua News Agency (2009).

8 For examples, Feng, G. (2006); Feng, T. Q. (2003); Han (2005) and Zhang, (2003).

9 Zhang (2003).

10 Zhang et al. (2005).

the original Ministry of Labour and Social Security (MOLSS, 劳动和社会保障部) and Ministry of Personnel (MOP, 人事部).

Third, they do not pay regard to the party-state's role as legislator, regulator and judicator.

Fourth, when referring to the central level of the party system, they simply mention the Central Committee of the CCP (CC-CCP, 中共中央委员会), without further identifying two more important bodies in the hierarchy, i.e. the Politburo (政治局) and the Standing Committee of Politburo (SCP, 政治局常务委员会), which is superior to and hence more significant than the CC-CCP. As we will see in later analysis, a person's position in the party hierarchy directly affects the power of the specific organization that he/she leads.

An alternative description, which takes the above comments into account, is provided in Figure 2.1. It must be emphasised that this figure is about the party-state structure in industrial relations at the national level. Therefore:

First, it does not include the party-state structure at the local (provincial or city) level. These structures, however, are usually more or less copies of that at the national level.[11]

Second, it is not an overall description of the whole party-state system. Only organizations relevant to industrial relations are included.

Third, the occupants of positions are identified by name because China is still a society upholding "Rule of Man (人治)" rather than "Rule of Law (法治)",[12] meaning that a ministry or organization's position actually depends on its leader's personal authority and position in the party system.[13] Fourth, the party-state structure, as it affects industrial relations, undergoes frequent changes. The structure described in Figure 2.1 is based

11 The relationship between the central and the local has been hotly debated. I do not go into detail about this matter, but point out that in the party system, relationships between central and local organs entail direct leadership, while in the state system the relationships are more loose and complicated. Interested readers may refer to Guo (2000) for a more detailed discussion.

12 Tao et al. (2003).

13 For example, the position of the ACFTU fluctuated over the years in accordance with the ups and downs of its president's position in the party system. We discuss this in more detail in the next section.

on public announcements since the 16th National Congress of the CCP, last verified in January 2009.

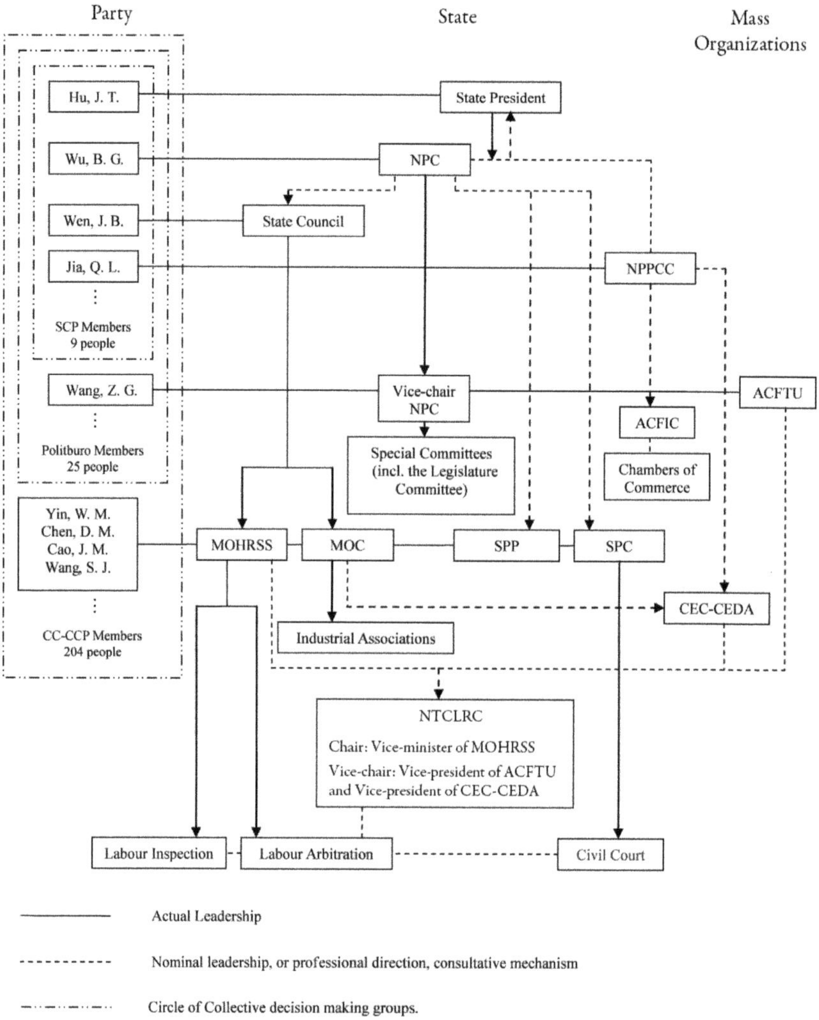

Figure 2.1 Party-state Structure in China's Industrial Relations

Keeping to the structure shown in Figure 2.1, we can now summarize the major characteristics of China's party-state system in industrial relations:

First, leaders in the party system occupy leading positions in the state system as well as in so-called "mass organizations" such as the ACFTU. As the Party has the final say in all major decisions, the power and position of a specific organization actually rely on its head's power and position in the party system.

Second, the parallel arrangements of the executive, legislature and judiciary in liberal democratic systems differ in China's state system. The Prime Minister of the State Council (head of the executive) is no. 3 in the party system, while ministers are mostly CC-CCP members. The National People's Congress (NPC) is nominally the highest authority and is headed by the no. 2 person in the party system, but the cChair of its Legislature Committee is usually occupied by an ex-minister from the government system (a non CC-CCP member), while the Supreme People's Court (SPC) and Supreme People's Procuratorate (SPP) are headed by CC-CCP members and are treated as half a rank higher than government ministries. Therefore, the executive (the State Council and the local governments) is the most powerful, while the legislature and the judiciary do not have enough representation in the power structure, or, to say it in another way, the two serve as tools of the party and government.[14]

Third, the party-state's extensions "with Chinese characteristics (具有中国特色)" are the so-called "mass organizations (群众组织)",[15] which purport to be spontaneous organizations formed by the people for specific purposes. Actually, they are all formed and headed by party-state leaders and are in essence "mass control organizations". For example, ACFTU Chair Wang Zhao Guo is a Politburo member among the top 25 leaders in the party system and concurrently vice-chair of the NPC. CEC-CEDA

14 That is why, in Chinese political vocabulary, apparatus of state is usually referred to as "Party-Government Organs (党政机关)" and the legislature and the judiciary are rarely mentioned.

15 Mass organizations relevant to industrial relations include the ACFTU and the CEC-CEDA. The ACFIC is usually considered to be a "united front organization" rather than a "mass organization" in Chinese political vocabulary.

President Wang Zhong Yu is the retired vice-president of the NPPCC and a former CC-CCP member and government minister. For this reason, some people categorize these "mass organizations" as branches of the party-state, though this is debatable as they have another face which is mass-related. We look at them in more detail in sections 2.2 (the ACFTU) and 2.3 (the employers' associations).

2.1.2 *Roles of the Party-state*

The essential function of a modern state is to protect and provide services to its citizens. These services involve diversified areas ranging from providing public goods to establishing social security systems. Western scholars, such as Dickens and Hall, Bean and Keller, summarise the state's role in the industrial relations of liberal democracies as that of legislator and labour market regulator, conciliator, arbitrator, mediator, provider of public services and employer of labour.[16] How, if at all, are these roles performed in China by the party-state?

Legislator and Labour Market Regulator

In western countries, the state develops a framework of collective and individual labour law that establishes obligations and rights for employers, employers' associations, employees and unions; the state also establishes legal minimum standards for wages, working hours, and health and safety conditions that serve to regulate competition over the remuneration and employment conditions of employees.[17] What is the position in China?

During the period 1949–79, in the context of the planned economy, there was barely any labour regulation in China. Because the whole population was virtually "employed" and managed by the party-state, there seemed to be little need for such regulation. After 1979, and especially after 1992,

16 Dickens and Hall (2003); Bean (1994); Keller (1991).
17 Ibid.

in light of the diversification of ownership, the rapid growth of the private sector, the emergent labour market and the rising number of unemployed and laid-off workers, the state issued a series of employment-related laws in order to regulate the labour market and to offer a level of employment protection for workers. The majority of the employment regulations in force were issued during the two decades after 1989.[18]

The Labour Law promulgated in 1994 symbolized a new era for China's labour legislation and regulation development. This set of legislation and regulations included not only national laws passed and proclaimed by the NPC, but also administrative regulations and departmental rules determined by the government, as well as local laws and regulations drafted by local people's congresses and governments, judicial explanations and approved international conventions. The relevant legislation and regulations since 1979, and especially after 1994, are listed below in six groupings.

National labour-related laws promulgated by the NPC include "Labour Law (1994)", "Union Law (1992)", "Occupational Disease Prevention Law (2002)", "Safe Production Law (2002)", and "Labour Contract Law (2007)".

Regulations set by the State Council include "Regulation on Protecting Female Employees (1988)", "Regulation on the Settlement of Enterprise Labour Disputes (1993)", "Rules on Unemployment Insurance (1998)", "Regulation on Prohibition of Child Labour (2002)", "Rules on Work Injury Insurance (2003)", and "Regulation on Labour Security and Inspection (2004)".

Rules formulated by MOLSS include "Treatment for Labour Contract Violation (1994)", "Rules on Collective Contracts (2003)", and "Regulation on Minimum Wage (2003)".

As the Labour Law endows provincial entities with power to legislate on operational methods, the local People's Congresses and governments enacted many local laws and regulations.

18 Cooke (2008a), p. 115. Of course, it is also true in other countries, including Australia, that the last 20 years have witnessed major developments of employment regulations.

The SPC issued the "Explanation on Certain Legal Issues in the Trial of Labour Disputes" in 2001 and 2006 respectively, and these judicial explanations affect the treatment of labour disputes.

China approved and adopted twenty-four International Labour Organization (ILO) conventions. Theoretically, these international conventions have the same legal standing as domestic laws.

At first sight, China seems to have established an adequate labour law system, with the Labour Law (and relevant national laws) as its main body, assisted by administration regulations, departmental rules, local laws/regulations, judicial explanations and international conventions. In fact, it has been argued that, with "the major exception of freedom of association", the labour standards established by the series of labour laws and regulations of China "are not markedly inferior to those of comparable countries and indeed many developed nations".[19]

But in practice, there are still many problems with China's current labour law system. As pointed out by Lin, firstly, few labour laws are promulgated by the national legislature (the NPC), with the system relying too much on administrative regulations and departmental rules which have less legal weight. Secondly, the abundance of local laws and regulations creates conflicts among different provinces as well as between local and central ministries. Thirdly, the Labour Law itself has adopted a model of compendium legislation, which means that it regulates only on principles and provides no detailed instructions for operation.[20] Cooke also argues that the ambiguities in the labour regulations often open the regulations to different interpretations, which means not only that a considerable proportion of workers are not qualified to bring their cases to the arbitration committee or court but also that rulings may be to the workers' disadvantage.[21]

The discussion above identifies major issues with Chinese labour legislation. At the core of these issues, according to Chen, is a fundamental problem. Chinese labour legislation stresses individual rather than col-

19 Cooney (2007), p. 674 as quoted by Cooke (2008b), p. 4.
20 Lin (2005).
21 Cooke (2008a and 2008b).

lective rights. The public is misled into missing the point that legislative intervention of any kind, on its own, is not adequate to the task of improving labour standards and conditions for workers. China passed numerous laws and regulations to protect workers over the two decades after 1989. But the adoption of these measures, in the almost complete absence of any parallel protection for workers' freedom of association and the right to collective bargaining, led to a situation where the law fell into disrepute through a lack of implementation and enforcement.[22]

Cooke argues that it is China's lack of effective law enforcement, rather than the lack of law or regulation, which always attracts criticism.[23] Inspection and enforcement functions are performed by the labour ministry or department in the government system and are carried out in work units to ensure implementation of laws and rules about labour and social security, under the guidance of the "Regulation on Labour Security and Inspection (2004)". According to statistics issued by MOLSS, in 2003 alone there were 1.26 million inspection cases in China, of which 1.1 million were initiatives of the ministry and local departments and 160,000 were upon report by employees.[24] There were 19,000 full time inspectors deployed nation-wide.[25]

Law enforcement is far from satisfactory. On the one hand, staff, funds and facilities are insufficient. On the other hand, local protectionism is so strong in some areas that local governments exempt certain enterprises from any inspection in the name of "protecting investment", turning labour laws and regulations into "a piece of scrap".[26] To make things worse, some labour inspection officers themselves were involved in labour abuse cases. For example, in 2007, labour inspection officers in Shanxi Province were arrested for their involvement in selling child labour to slave factories.[27]

22 Chen (2007), pp. 59–65.
23 Cooke (2008b), p. 4.
24 Information from official website of MOLSS <http://www.molss.gov.cn/gb/zwxx/2005-12/02/content_95416.htm> (last accessed on 20 January 2009).
25 Information from official website of MOLSS <http://www.molss.gov.cn/gb/zwxx/2005-12/14/content_99534.htm> (last accessed on 20 January 2009).
26 Lin (2005).
27 According to series of journal reports, *Southern Weekend*, 14 and 21 June 2007.

Conciliator, Arbitrator and Mediator

Scholars argue that the state should provide services which are intended to facilitate the resolution of industrial disputes between employers and employees, by playing the role of conciliator, arbitrator and mediator.[28]

In China, a labour dispute reconciliation system was established as early as the 1950s. After a period of disruption during the Cultural Revolution (1966–76), the system was resumed in 1987 with the promulgation of the "Temporary Regulation for Labour Disputes Reconciliation in State-owned Enterprises". This temporary regulation was amended in 1993 and implemented as the "Labour Disputes Reconciliation Regulation". The Regulation was later incorporated into the Labour Law (1994) that forms the legal basis for settling labour disputes.[29]

The labour dispute settlement system is termed "One Mediation – One Arbitration – Two Litigations (一调一裁二审)", meaning that whenever there is a labour dispute, the interested parties must first go through internal mediation, which is usually conducted by the official union. If unsuccessful, they must then apply for arbitration by the Labour Dispute Arbitration Committee (劳动争议仲裁委员会) which consists of MOHRSS officials, union representatives and enterprise (employer) representatives. Only when the parties in a dispute are not satisfied with the arbitration result can they take a lawsuit to the court, with the option, in case of dissatisfaction with a primary court decision, of appealing to a higher court and seeking settlement by a second trial. Clearly, there are defects in this system.

First, the sequence of possible dispute settlement measures, from mediation to arbitration then to litigation, prolongs the process. Hence disputes cannot be settled in a timely manner.[30] It is not uncommon to find cases

28 Dickens and Hall (2003); Bean (1994); Keller (1991).

29 Cooke (2008b), p. 16.

30 There are some signs of change. For example, the new "Labour Dispute Arbitration Law", which was promulgated on 1 May 2008, has created a new "one final arbitration (一裁终局)" system for small cases. This means that the arbitration decision in small cases (under RMB 10,000 or AUD 2,000) is considered final for the employers,

which need two years to go through all the process. Quite often, the court's decision is the same as that from the arbitration, wasting the time of the interested parties.[31] This system puts employees at a disadvantage, as they cannot afford the time and money to participate in all of the proceedings, while many employers make use of the procedure to delay payment, in the hope that employees will be exhausted and give up during the process.[32]

Second, as the whole process is under the control of the party-state (or its extension), and there is no independent organization representing the interests of employees, in the context of China's "State Developmentalism" (国家发展主义),[33] already weak workers are often placed in an even more unfavourable situation when they are in dispute with SOEs or enterprises that local governments are keen to attract and protect to maintain economic growth.

Third, according to the legal explanation given by the Supreme People's Court (SPC, 最高人民法院), parties in labour disputes are treated equally in labour contracts. Labour disputes are civil cases involving equal entities and must be tried in civil courts following civil laws.[34] Arbitration is a pre-set procedure, yet the court is not supposed to be biased by the decision and opinion of the arbitration; for this reason, the case is required to start all over again in the court system, consuming enormous amounts of time and resources.

---

while the employees still hold the right to appeal to a court. The purposes of this regulation are to expedite labour dispute settlement and lower the employees' costs in time and energy. ("Explanation of the new 'one arbitration for final' system" (in Chinese), Worker's Daily, 14 April 2008; "解读劳动争议调解仲裁法的"一裁终局"制度", 工人日报, 2008-04-14).

31 Mao (2005).

32 "Arbitration Should be Separated from Litigation in Labour Dispute Settlements" (in Chinese), Outlook, "劳动争议处理宜裁审分离", 瞭望, 10 August 2007.

33 Deng Xiaoping's famous saying that "Development is the Absolute Principle (发展才是硬道理)" was the symbol of modern China's State Developmentalism. However, people are now beginning to reflect on this policy, raising the question of its responsibility for the serious problems of environmental pollution and labour abuse of recent years.

34 Supreme Court (2001 and 2006).

The factors above make the already over-sophisticated system even more complex. Despite the party-state's seemingly good intention to provide more settlement channels, recorded labour dispute case numbers kept rising. Cooke argues that the nature of labour disputes appears to be increasingly confrontational and antagonistic, marked by an increase in the proportion of cases settled by arbitration and litigation and a decrease in resolution by mediation.[35] Fu and Choy reach a similar conclusion that more labour disputes have shifted from mediation and arbitration to litigation for final settlement.[36] This means that dispute cases have become increasingly complex and resource-consuming, widening the gulf between labour and management.[37] Relevant statistics in NBS and MOLSS (2007) support the arguments above.

For these reasons, some experts have begun to urge simplification of labour dispute settlement procedures. The focus of their suggestions is on the arbitration system, either making arbitration decisions binding or treating arbitration itself as merely an optional, rather than a required step in the procedure, and setting up special labour courts which may operate at a lower cost with simpler procedures.[38]

35 Cooke. (2008a), p. 122. Shen and Benson also argue that the key to successful mediation lies in the impartiality of the mediator and balanced bargaining power between the disputants (Shen and Benson (2008), p. 234). But as we will see in later analyses, neither of these two criteria are met in China. According to official data, the successful rate of mediation is very low: in 2006, only 63,020 out of the 340,193 cases were successfully mediated (NBS and MOLSS (2007), disc edition, Table 11.6).

36 Fu and Choy (2004). However, according to Cooke's study, only about half of the total cases were won completely by the workers, despite the fact that 94–96% of cases were lodged by the workers. What remains unclear is why a relatively high proportion of cases appealed by workers have not been won by them. Is this to do with the ambiguity in the legislation that makes it impossible to pin down employers' unreasonable behaviour? Is it due to the resource constraints encountered by the workers in fighting the cases? (Cooke (2008a), p. 123).

37 Cooke (2008a), p. 122.

38 "Unsolved Dilemma of the Labour Arbitration System" (in Chinese), *Perspective*, "劳动仲裁难局待解", 瞭望, 3 September 2007.

Provider of Public Services

A generally recognised role of the state is to provide public services such as social security and education. The breadth and depth of these services, in particular the social securities, affect deeply the decisions and behaviour of both employers and employees in industrial relations.[39] As Noon and Blyton pointed out, social welfare provision in the form of unemployment benefits, housing allowances and free medical care were designed specifically to act as a safety net, preventing citizens from being left totally at the mercy of market forces.[40] The state should act to protect the weak, otherwise it fails to fulfil its obligation.[41] China's social security system, however, is still in the midst of a dramatic transition, facing severe challenges.

First, before the reform era, especially during the period 1956–79, China's social security system was an egalitarian system with "Chinese characteristics". Ironically, a country aiming at eliminating differences among classes founded its social security system on the basis of a citizen's classification. People in the cadre class, especially those at the top of the pyramid, were privileged by the party-state.[42] Also the urban working class, 99% of which were working in SOEs, enjoyed the guarantee of life-long employment and corresponding medical care, living in a socialist system though at a lower level. In addition, the rural peasant class had to rely on its own for everything, from producing basic foods to buying medical

39 Dickens and Hall (2003); Bean (1994); Keller (1991).

40 Noon and Blyton (1997).

41 A common excuse for the state's inaction in this matter is to respect the principle of the free market, but as ILO pointed out "The State has a key role to play in creating an enabling institutional framework to balance the need for flexibility for enterprises and security for workers in meeting the changing demands of a global economy …" (ILO (2006), p. 3).

42 See the description in Chen (2005). Of course, cadres faced the dangers of playing political games, which could sometimes mean life or death in China, as in countless cases in the Cultural Revolution. For the cadres, privileges and dangers could be deemed as trade-offs.

services, if there were any in the area, as though living in a self-contained natural system.[43]

Second, beginning in 1979, and especially after 1992, China began reforming its social security system, with the initial focus on the urban population, mainly SOE workers, in addition to a newly emerging urban working class employed by non-SOEs. At the same time, privileges enjoyed by the cadre class were untouched, while the establishment of a social security system for the rural population was only placed on the agenda for preliminary discussion during the third plenum of 17th CC-CCP in October 2008. According to a joint communiqué issued by the MOHRSS and NBS,[44] in 2007 China's social security system covered around 200 million people, among whom only about 10% were rural migrant workers. Therefore, China's evolving social security system caters mostly for the urban population.

The political report delivered to the CCP's 17th National Congress in October 2007 pointed out that the development of China's social security system "should focus on (building) a basic pension system, a basic medical care system, and a subsistence allowance system ..."[45] However, even for those who are lucky enough to be covered by the social security system, all three major components have significant problems. They are detailed in the next three paragraphs.

China's pension system is supported by a combination of superannuation and pension funds run by local governments. As there is a lack of supervision and a balance of power, a series of corruption cases in the pension system rocked the country. The most infamous case was in Shanghai in 2006, where the funds involved exceeded RMB 3 billion (AUD 600 million). The actual use of the funds and the real "black hole" were never made known to the public.[46]

43 Li (2004); Knight and Song (2005); Hebel and Schucher (2006). We discuss the different treatment of urban workers and rural migrant workers in Chapter 5.

44 MOHRSS and NBS (2008).

45 CC-CCP (2007).

46 "Why So Many Big Cases Concerning the Social Security Fund" (in Chinese), *Southern Weekend*, "社保基金为何大案频发", 南方周末, 10 August 2006.

The reform of the medical care system is considered by many to have been a failure. Even the Development Research Centre of the State Council admitted in 2005 that the retreat of government support from and marketization of medical services turned such services into virtual luxurious private goods which only a minority of Chinese people can afford.[47] Even for those who are covered by the medical care system, in most cases people still need to pay up to 30% of medical care fees, for which a family may well face bankruptcy in case of a serious disease. Therefore, according to a report issued by the Ministry of Health (MOH, 卫生部), 35.7% of ill people tended to treat themselves, while another 13.1% simply do nothing but wait for natural healing.[48]

The subsistence allowance system provides little help to those in need. According to the Ministry of Civil Affairs (MCA, 民政部), in 2007 about 10 million urban households (22 million people) received a subsistence allowance from the government.[49] However, the standard of allowance was very low. Data for 2006 showed that the average national monthly allowance (RMB 169.6 or AUD 34) was only about one-third of the legal minimum wage (RMB 499.5 or AUD 100).[50]

Thus, China's social security system is in its infancy and works mostly for the urban population. The lack of social security reduced the bargaining power of employees in industrial relations, and is one of the major reasons why employees, especially rural migrant workers, are generally willing to accept unreasonably low employment conditions.[51]

47 It estimated that only about 50% of the urban population and less than 10% of the rural population were covered by the medical care system.

48 MOH (2004).

49 "Build a Safety Net for the People in Difficulties", *People's Daily*, "城乡低保为困难群众构筑安全网", 人民日报, 12 October 2007.

50 "Urban Subsistence Allowance in Comparison with Preceding Year and Monthly Minimum Wage 2005–2006", MOLSS, Public Paper; "2005–2006 年各地区城市最低生活保障平均标准与上年比较及月最低工资标准", 劳动和社会保障部，公告.

51 Lan and Ren (2004).

Employer of Labour and Labour Market Developer

In any modern society, the state is often the direct employer of a significant number of citizens. Employment conditions in the public sector play an exemplary role in society.[52]

The Chinese government used to be the biggest employer in the world. By 1978 it employed 95 million workers or 99% of the population then working in non-primary industries. Arguably, all of the rural working population were also employees of the party-state, under the state-owned land system (土地国有制度) and the people's commune system (人民公社制度). But after reforms were adopted, the Chinese government began to retreat from the labour market as a direct employer. In 1992, when reforms began to shift to transitional economic policies which attempted to transform China from a planned into a market economy, there were still about 145 million employees in state and collectively owned enterprises, accounting for nearly 92.5% of all employees in non-primary industries. By 2002, the 70 million employees left in SOEs made up less than 20% of all employees in non-primary industries.[53] According to a report issued by the former MOLSS, in the second quarter of 2006, SOEs provided only 8.2% of new job opportunities.[54] As Cooke pointed out, from the mid-1990s China experienced a sharp swing from a once rigid internal labour market dominated by the state sector to an increasingly informal and unprotected labour market.[55]

Deng Xiaoping's saying that "Development is the Absolute Principle (发展才是硬道理)", which was uttered during his land-mark "Southern Inspection (南巡)" tour in 1992, instigated the strategy of solving emerging social problems by continuous development of the economy.[56] To render this macro policy concrete in industrial relations practice, the party-state

52 Dickens and Hall (2003); Bean (1994); Keller (1991).

53 Calculations are based on NBS and MOLSS (2007), disc edition, Tables 1.5, 16 and 17.

54 MOLSS (2006).

55 Cooke (2008b), p. 18.

56 Ma and Ling (1998).

had to develop the labour market and relieve social tension by providing ever-growing employment opportunities. This is reflected in the document adopted by the 6th Plenum of the 16th CC-CCP (中共十六大六中全会) in October 2006, entitled "Resolution on Major Issues Regarding the Building of a Harmonious Socialist Society". It devoted an unprecedented clause to "The Development of Harmonious Labour Relations",[57] which mentioned the word "employment" (or "job") almost twenty times in a single paragraph.[58] For decision makers, employment is much more important than other labour related issues. This strategy of emphasizing economic development is understandable, as China was confronted by pressures on employment which no other country in the world experienced.

In a country with a poor social security system, insufficient employment means that the sheer survival of people cannot be guaranteed, and this is a severe challenge to social stability.[59] "Stability overrides anything else (稳定压倒一切)" is another of Deng Xiaoping's famous sayings. This political context makes it easier to understand why in recent years, in order to please capital, the party-state suppressed labour interests, often with violence – the very interests which a "communist and working class" regime was supposed to "represent". The underlying logic for suppressing labour interests and promoting those of capital is to trade labour rights for investment and employment.[60]

57 CC-CCP (2006).

58 The emphasis on employment does not imply that the state is necessarily planning to be the direct employer. In fact, most development policies stress increasing employment in the private sector.

59 It is also a challenge to the CCP's reformists, who have long built the regime's ruling legitimacy on the promise of continuous economic development. As Fukuyama points out, it is typical of rightist authoritarian regimes to promise continuous economic growth in their attempts to maintain ruling legitimacy without proper elections (Fukuyama 2004).

60 In this respect, Tong proposes the concept of "Resembling Labour-Capital Relations", which means that developed countries can be thought of as "capital'" while developing countries are "labour", making the relations between the two types of countries somewhat the same as strong capital vs. weak labour. The developing countries, eager to change their backward situation and to participate in the process of globalization,

Even if the sacrifice of labour rights is rewarded by higher employment, new social conflicts are simultaneously created. These conflicts may be a little less severe than the survival crisis in the case of unemployment, but their political importance should not be under-estimated, because they pose questions about the very foundation of the ruling party-state's legitimacy. Therefore, the party-state now has to look into these labour-related issues and attempt to balance employment with labour rights. This is the background to the policy of "building a harmonious society".

In summary, the party-state remains dominant in Chinese industrial relations, though it has been withdrawing from the economic areas since reform began. The structure of the party-state constitutes an almost "self-containing" industrial relations system which includes the executive, legislature and judicial branches of the state, as well as "representative organizations" of employers and employees. These measures, however, do not guarantee that its role as a modern state is fulfilled satisfactorily. The party-state, itself being a constant target of reforms in an unprecedented transitional period, did not generally perform well its roles as legislator and labour market regulator, conciliator, arbitrator and mediator, provider of public services and employer of labour and labour market developer. Though, to be fair, the party-state tried hard to transform itself to function more like a modern state, progress until 2008 was not satisfying. It had to compete with the need to keep the economy booming and with ever-growing job creation, to prevent labour-related social problems turning from economic to political turbulence.

have to integrate with capital (developed countries), sometimes having no choice but to "welcome" the exploitation (of labour). Thus some Chinese local governments suppress labour standards so as to attract foreign investment (Tong 2005).

2.2 ACFTU

As pointed out by Bray, forms of labour representation can be divided into two aspects: 1. union representation vs. non-unionism; and 2. voluntary representation vs. state-sanctioned representation.

On the surface, the ACFTU seems to belong to the state-sanctioned union type. However, Figure 2.1 implies the existence of subtle links between the ACFTU and the party-state. The ACFTU is not really a "mass organization", as it claims to be, but is rather an extension of the party-state.[61] This section will first outline the historical background and current status of the ACFTU, and then discuss further its organization and roles in contemporary China's industrial relations.

2.2.1 *Brief History of the ACFTU*

The Webbs gave a classic definition of the union as "a continuous association of wage-earners for the purpose of maintaining or improving the conditions of their working lives".[62] The origin of unions can be traced back to combinations of craftspeople in the early stage of the British industrial revolution. The scope of unionism then emerged "from the moment that ... skill alone is valueless, and is soon compelled to hire itself out to capital

61 One issue in studies of trade unions is a union's ideological and strategic relationship with the state. At one end of the spectrum is a system where the trade union has a weak relationship with the government. At the other, a union can be under absolute state domination. This latter was the case in Leninist one-party states, where the trade union was an integral organ of the party-state. Even within Communist systems, there were variations, and China occupied the extreme end of the spectrum in terms of the trade union's incorporation into, and subjugation to, the party-state and management during the Maoist period (1949–76). According to a comparative study conducted by a Soviet specialist, even in the Soviet Union in the 1950s and 1960s enterprise level trade unions played a bigger role than did Chinese trade unions in the 1980s (Chan (2006), p. 276).

62 Webb and Webb (1920a), p. 1.

… begins the opposition of interest between employers and employees, now the latter begin to group themselves together, now rises the trade society".[63] The story of unions in China, however, is completely different from such a view.

The history of the ACFTU dates back to July 1921, when the CCP was established. At the CCP's first National Congress, the "Resolution on Current Practical Works (关于当前实际工作的决议)" contended that "… the fundamental task of the Party is to establish industrial trade unions … (The Party) needs to sponsor workers' schools and enhance the class consciousness of the workers so as to make them realize the necessity of having unions …"[64] In August of the same year, the CCP established the "Chinese Labour Combination Secretariat (中国劳动组合书记部)" in Shanghai, claiming that "… (We) will combine or restructure the existing labour organizations, enhance the class consciousness of the workers, and establish closer connections between Chinese workers and foreign workers …"[65] In May, 1925, the Chinese Labour Combination Secretariat held the second national labour conference in Guangzhou. By passing the "General Statute of ACFTU (中华全国总工会总章)", the ACFTU was formally promulgated and immediately affiliated with the "Red International of Labour Unions (赤色职工国际)", which was subordinate to the Communist International (the Comintern, 共产国际).[66] At its inception, the ACFTU claimed to represent 166 unions nation-wide, with a total membership of 540,000 workers, while during the same period the CCP had only 940 members.[67]

The CCP and ACFTU were seriously damaged after the 1927 breakup between the CCP and the KMT (the Chinese Nationalist Party, 中国国民党).[68] The ACFTU was forced to go underground and its membership

63 Ludlow (1861) as quoted by Webb and Webb (1920a), p. 26.
64 As listed in Zheng et al. (1997), p. 2398.
65 Chinese Labour Combination Secretariat (1921), "Declaration of Chinese Labour Combination Secretariat", as listed in Zheng et al. (1997), p. 2398.
66 ACFTU (2006 b); Lin (1997).
67 ACFTU (2006b).
68 We discuss this further in Chapter 6.

decreased dramatically to around 30,000 workers, while the CCP also shifted its emphasis to rural areas, beginning a 22-year-long military struggle, using Mao's famous strategy of "Using Rural Areas to Besiege Cities (农村包围城市)". During the period 1927–49, two themes of CCP activities were "Rural Areas" and "Military Struggle". The position of the labour movement declined so as to be almost negligible.

In 1948, toward the end of the second civil war between the KMT and the CCP, the National Labour Conference resumed in Northeast China, which was controlled by the CCP. The ACFTU was then back in the national political forum, but its position, roles and effects could hardly be compared with those in the 1920s.

First, the position of ACFTU leaders in the Party reflected the location of the ACFTU in the Party's hierarchy. In the 1920s, they were usually members of the Standing Committee of Politburo,[69] while in 1948, the ACFTU's nominal chair, Chen Yun, was only a Politburo member ranked number 3 in Northeast CCP Committee,[70] while the executive deputy-chair, Li Lisan (李立三), was a former "representative of the wrong route". He was exiled to the USSR for more than a decade and was widely considered to be one who needed to "achieve merits to atone for his guilt (带罪立功)".[71]

Second, in the 1920s, the labour movement was the core focus of the CCP, and the ACFTU organized strikes with national political significance. But in 1948, according to the Resolution of the National Labour Conference referred to above, the ACFTU's role in the "liberated region (解放区)" was to "... organize employees to developing production, prosper the economy, care for both public and private interests, and benefit both labour and capital ... and to enhance (the employees') class awareness for boosting production in the liberated region to support the frontline"; while its role in the "KMT dominated region (国统区)" was to "... link with the

69 At one time, the ACFTU chair, Su Zhao Zhen, almost became the CCP's top leader, but he died before the appointment (Wu and Liu (2004), pp. 123–25).

70 Zheng et al. (1997), pp. 649 and 674.

71 Li and Liu (2005), pp. 292–98.

masses, gather forces, enlarge troops, prepare for the arrival of the People's Liberation Army (PLA, 人民解放军) and ensure an orderly take-over of the city".[72] Thus, the ACFTU became simply a support mechanism for the party.

Thereafter, the ACFTU was marginalized and degraded from an indispensable political force to a tool assisting the party-state machinery. The activities of the ACFTU were flat and dull after the establishment of the People's Republic of China in 1949. In the 1950s, Li Lisan and Lai Ruoyu attempted to restore the role of the ACFTU, but both faced tragic ends.[73] By 1958, the ACFTU itself propounded the slogan "struggle for the die-out of unions (为工会消亡而斗争)".[74]

In the 1960s and the 1970s, especially during the Cultural Revolution, the ACFTU was under attack from various quarters.[75] It was displaced by "Workers' Rebellious Organizations (工人造反组织)", which had various political stances. One of those organisations, the "General Commanding Headquarter for Shanghai Workers' Revolutionary Rebellion (上海工人革命造反总司令部)", produced the famous (notorious?) figure of Wang Hongwen.[76] But ironically, the chaotic period of the Cultural Revolution was the only time after 1949 that Chinese workers had the chance to associate freely.[77]

72 ACFTU (1948), "Resolution on the Roles of the Chinese Labour Movement in the Current Stage (关于中国职工运动当前任务的决议)", as listed in Zheng et al. (1997), p. 2423.

73 Li and Lai's problems were both closely linked with the hot debates at the time, which were: "Should unions and the working class follow the lead of the Party?" and "Does private interest always accord with public interests?" For details, see Chapter 5.

74 Zheng et al. (1997), p. 2428.

75 One example is that, for more than two decades after 1957, the ACFTU was not allowed to call any meeting of its national congress (ACFTU 2006b).

76 Wang made his way to the top of the CCP by leading a Shanghai Workers' Rebellious Organization. In the 1970s, he was appointed deputy chair of the CCP (a potential successor of Mao). As a member of "Gang of Four", he was arrested in October, 1976 (one month after Mao's death) together with Jiang Qing (Mao's wife) and other peers. (Ye 1993).

77 Refer to the detailed discussion in Chapter 6.

In 1978, the ACFTU's 9th National Congress was held, signifying the ACFTU's return to a politically active role. But in the 1980s, the ACFTU did nothing of significance.[78] China's economic reforms were not yet deep and the interests of workers, especially SOEs employees who made up the majority, were not yet seriously affected, while enterprises of other ownership types were still in their infancy. Labour-capital conflicts were uncommon in the 1980s. The unions' typical tasks were simply to organize entertainment and cultivate a sense of harmony in the workplace. After the 1990s, the pace of marketization in China accelerated, leading to the reform of unions. We discuss the effects of these changes on the ACFTU's roles later.

2.2.2 *The ACFTU's Status since the 1990s*

The history of the ACFTU shows that it has close relationships with the party-state.[79] How does its organisational structure reflect these relationships? This question, though not complex, has received little scholarly attention. After analysing relevant documents, we attempt to describe the ACFTU's internal structure below.

First, according to the "Statute of Labour Unions in the People's Republic of China", "... Chinese unions, are ... under the leadership of the Chinese Communist Party ..., carry out the Party policy of 'concentrating on economic development', and stick to the 'Four Basic Principles' ..."[80] These statements demonstrate that the CCP is the highest leading body of the ACFTU.

78 In the Tian-an-men Square Incident of 1989, it seemed that there was no unanimous opinion within ACFTU. Some of the ACFTU staff joined the demonstration, and ACFTU's executive vice-president Zhu Ze-hou openly supported the students' movement, issuing a public statement "Five Points on the Present Situation", urging (among other things) that the national congress meeting be brought forward (Zhang 2003).

79 We discuss this further in Chapter 5.

80 General Provisions in ACFTU (2003).

Second, according to an ACFTU document, "... (the ACFTU) *assists* provincial Party Committees in managing the cadres of the provincial ACFTU ..."[81] This means that Provincial Party Committees, rather than the ACFTU headquarters, exercise direct leadership over provincial ACFTU branches.

Third, according to the "Statute of Labour Unions in P. R. China", "... Chinese unions follow the organizational principle of managing by industry and by region ... The industrial unions' managing mechanisms[82] are subject to the decisions of the ACFTU ..."[83] This shows that the ACFTU has a double leadership (matrix) organizational structure.[84]

According to official data, by the end of 2006, there were 1.3 million grass-roots unions in China with a total membership of 169.94 million.[85] The union density nation-wide was 21.7%;[86] while union density in enterprises with existing unions was 93.7%.[87] Membership grew continuously after 1952, with the exception of the period 1996–99, probably due to the massive lay-off of millions of SOE employees who were mostly union members.[88] This trend differs dramatically from most western countries,[89] but

81 ACFTU (2006c).

82 Currently there are ten industrial unions in China, among which the unions for the railways, airlines and finance industries have solid-line leadership by industry and dot-line leadership by region, while the other seven unions have dot-line leadership by industry and solid-line leadership by region (Official Information <www.acftu.org> last accessed on 20 January 2009).

83 Article 11 in ACFTU (2003).

84 The reason for the grass-roots unions in the railway, airlines and finance industries being under the direct leadership of industrial unions is that their operations are mostly cross-regional; while on the other hand, all other grass-roots unions are under the direct leadership of the provincial ACFTU and only indirectly under the leadership of industrial unions.

85 NBS and MOLSS (2007), disc edition, Tables 11.1, 11.2.

86 This figure is derived by dividing 169.94 million (union members in 2006) by 782.44 million (economically active population in 2006).

87 This figure is derived by dividing 169.94 million (union members in 2006) by 181.44 million (employees in enterprises with existing unions in 2006).

88 NBS (2007), On-line Data, Table 23.4.

89 For example, in the United States, the labour force represented by unions continue to decline from a peak of 35% in the early 1950s to 20% in 1983, and to 13.5% in the early twenty-first century (Katz and Wheeler (2004), p. 67); while in Australia, union

as we shall see in later chapters, the rise in the ACFTU's membership had little to do with worker awareness of associating themselves. More often than not, the increase was the result of a top-down attempt deliberately to boost union membership.

2.2.3 *The ACFTU's Roles and Responsibilities*

A freely established labour union usually considers its major role to be that of representing the interests of its members and their families, either with relatively narrow concerns to do with employment conditions such

---

density fell from 49% in 1990 to 20.3% in 2006 (Lansbury and Wailes (2004), p. 127; Year Book Australia (2008), p. 261). Many scholars have suggested reasons for the decline of unionism, for example, Budd (2004); Kaufman and Kleiner (1993); Gall (2006). Their viewpoints can be summarized as: 1. By introducing HRM practices, companies have solved many lower level disputes and reduced the occurrence of conflicts, thereby relaxing tensions between employers and employees; 2. The state in western countries has actively stepped into the labour area by enacting sophisticated labour laws (legislature), by active governmental regulation and administration (executive), by arbitration and trial (judiciary), and by other arrangements such as Works Councils. These have given labour more choices for protecting its rights; 3. Economic change has significantly reduced the number of employees in the manufacturing sector where unions were traditionally strong and the replacement jobs are in the service sector, white-collar positions and self-employment, which have less of a tendency to unionism. In this context, is research on organized labour representation and unions out-dated? In my opinion this does not affect our analysis of China's unions, for the following reasons: 1. There is no spontaneous union in China that really bears the responsibilities for collective bargaining and voice. The problem with "non-union representation" is that it is ambiguous. It could mean representation by some body or person other than a union. But in the case of China, we need to allow for another possibility – that workers are not allowed to be represented by their own organization at all; 2. Only a minority of companies operating in China have fully introduced HRM practices; 3. Labour protection provided by the state is very limited; 4. In China, which is rightly referred to as the "Factory of the World", the number of employees in the manufacturing sector is still growing strongly. Therefore, the industrial relations situation in China is still in a preliminary stage. It would distort the position to rely on western research on western labour issues, ignoring the history and reality of China.

as wages, safety and equality, or with broader concerns with fairness and justice in the community.[90]

The 2003 version of the "Statute of Labour Unions in the Peoples Republic of China" stated clearly that "(China's union) is the 'bridge and transmission belt' for the connection between the party and the employed masses".[91] The concept of "bridge and transmission belt", however, was not invented by the CCP. Lenin initiated it after winning the political battle against the so-called "Worker Opposition (工人反对派)" in the 1920s.[92] When the orthodox position of the Union of Soviet Socialist Republics (USSR) was imposed throughout Communist Parties around the world, the CCP, which was at first a branch of the USSR-dominated Comintern, imported the theory and put it into practice.

As the ACFTU was run by the Party from the top down rather than by workers themselves from the bottom up, more often than not, the ACFTU put the interests of the Party above those of workers, its own members.[93] In its statute, the ACFTU requires its cadres to "... conscientiously study Marxism, Leninism, Mao Zedong Thoughts, Deng Xiaoping Theories and the 'Three Represents' Thoughts ... (and) follow the Party's basic route and policies"; while it further requires members "to deal correctly with interest relationships among the State, collective and the individual ... (and) the

90 See for examples, Australian Council of Trade Unions <http://www.actu.asn.au/AboutACTU/default.aspx> or AFL-CIO <http://www.aflcio.org/aboutus/thisistheaflcio/mission/> (last accessed on 20 January 2009).

91 General Provisions in ACFTU (2003).

92 Qi (2004).

93 Neoclassical economists regard unions as market agents extracting a rent for their members in collective bargaining. They – Friedman in particular – argued that "unions have not only harmed the public at large and workers as a whole by distorting the use of labour; they have also made the incomes of the working class more unequal by reducing the opportunities available to the most disadvantaged workers". (Friedman 1962 as quoted by Western (1997), p. 5). Clearly, in this respect, the ACFTU is not the type of union that scares the right wing, because it simply is not an organization striving for the utmost interests of its members. We discuss this further in Chapters 5 and 6.

individuals should obey the organization".[94] The ACFTU's primary role was to control rather than unite the masses, attempting to turn them into "the Party's docile tools (党的驯服工具)".[95]

The government holds a much higher position than the ACFTU in the hierarchy of the party-state system. The ACFTU cannot communicate with the government as an equal party. According to the "Statute of Labour Unions in P. R. China", "... Chinese unions safeguard the socialistic regime with the People's Democratic Dictatorship (人民民主专政), which is led by the working class and is based on the worker-peasant alliance, assisting the people's government to carry out its work ..."[96] Even for significant issues to do with the legal rights of employees, the ACFTU can only "conduct research and investigation, report the employed masses' thinking, wishes and appeals to the Party Centre and the State Council, and put forward its opinions and suggestions".[97] Thus, the ACFTU performs a supportive and assistant role in the party-state system.

In return, the ACFTU enjoys a monopolistic position, legalized by the state, in affairs related to Chinese workers. This monopolistic position is reflected both in the "Union Law of P. R. China" and the "Statute of Labour Unions in P. R. China".[98] Do the ACFTU's monopolistic position and its primary responsibility to the Party imply that it has no need to

94 General Provisions and Article 4 in ACFTU (2003).

95 This viewpoint had its origin in a 1958 conversation, "To Be the Party's Docile Tools (做党的驯服工具)", between Liu Shao Qi (No. 2 of CCP at the time and an early labour movement leader) and the editor of *Beijing Daily*, available at <http://www1.people.com.cn/GB/14677/22114/33134/33136/2464573.html> (last accessed on 16 January 2009).

96 General Provisions in ACFTU (2003).

97 ACFTU (2006c).

98 These two documents are almost the same, with no less than 80% identical contents. Even though the specific writings of those documents do not overtly state that the ACFTU is the ONLY legal union, we can discern such a meaning in the following clauses of the two documents: "... The ACFTU and its union organizations represent the interests of the employees ... at the national level, there is a unified ACFTU ... The establishment of grass-root unions, local federations of trade unions and national or local industrial unions must be approved by the union at a superior level ...".

perform the role of labour's representative or to care about the protection of labour rights? Of course, there was much criticism of the ACFTU's bureaucratic character as an official union,[99] but we should know that, after the 1990s, the situation changed markedly as the pace of marketization in China increased:

First, the biggest and most direct impact on the ACFTU was that the number of SOEs and SOE employees dropped dramatically over the years of economic transformation.[100] In the past, the ACFTU relied greatly on SOEs to recruit members by virtual compulsion. This approach did not work in enterprises of other ownership types.[101] As membership continued to fall, even the survival of the ACFTU became problematic. That is why, in a meeting about the establishment of new union branches, the ACFTU put forward the idea of "where there are employees, there shall be unions (哪里有职工，哪里就要建立工会)". Employees in non-SOEs, however, cared more about practical results. As union recruitment in these enterprises was voluntary, the ACFTU needed to demonstrate by practice, or at least, by high profile gesture, that it really cared and worked for the interests of labour. Employees did not bother to join "signboard unions". Thus the "invincible hand" of the market facilitated the self-transformation of the ACFTU.

Second, during the period of rapid social transformation, China was confronted by various social problems. As discussed earlier, in a country with a poor social security system, labour issues were linked to survival issues. It was feared that any inappropriate treatment of the matter could

99 Refer to the detailed discussions in Chapters 6 and 7 of the relationships between the union and the party-state and the union and the workers.

100 By 2002, the non-state-owned economy accounted for more than two-thirds of the GDP in China, and employees in the non-state-owned sectors were more than 70% of total urban employees. Note that in these data, employees in governmental units are counted as employees in the state-owned sector; if we put aside the public employees, SOEs employed only 16% of the total working population (Research Institute of MOLSS 2004a).

101 Actually, many local officials would rather suppress labour rights to attract investment; some even exempt enterprises from labour inspection. There are no requirements to establish unions in these enterprises (Lin 2005).

lead to turbulence. Therefore, for the maintenance of social stability, Chinese leaders could not let industrial relations continue to deteriorate. As an extension of the party-state system, the ACFTU was responsible for relieving such pressure on the party-state. It needed to "... realize the social function of the union, i.e. at the same time as safeguarding the general interests of the whole nation, to try to speak out and to protect employees' specific interests ..."[102] That is the background to a recent ACFTU slogan, which stated "organize and protect (workers') legal rights practically (组织起来, 切实维权)".

Third, there was also an economic consideration in the ACFTU's attempt to expand its coverage. According to the union law, "... enterprises and working units with established union organizations should hand in levies which amount to 2% of the *total salary of all employees* ..."[103] In an extreme case, even if only one employee in a company joined the ACFTU and claimed the establishment of a union branch, theoretically the ACFTU held the legal right to levy 2% of the *total salary of all employees* from the company. Such a huge economic incentive would of course motivate the ACFTU to realize "where there are employees, there shall be unions (哪里有职工，哪里就要建立工会)".

All of the above elements caused the ACFTU to become more active over the decade after 1997. But the question of the ACFTU's effectiveness remains. For example, in the over-heated "Wal-mart vs. Union Incident", a "happy ending" eventually took place, appealing to the needs of both the ACFTU and Wal-Mart:

> ... On the morning of 8 November, 2006, Wal-Mart China Headquarters held a union establishment ceremony in a high-profile manner. Xu De Ming, vice-chair of the ACFTU, came all the way from Beijing to present the signboard to the union branch. Guangdong provincial government officials, provincial ACFTU cadres, and the CEO of Wal-Mart China attended the ceremony. Ms Wang Yu. Jia, Employee Relations Director of Wal-Mart China, became the first chair of the union ... Source: "Wal-mart China Headquarter Establish Union in Shenzhen", Southern Metropolitan News, 9 November 2006

102 General Provisions in ACFTU (2003).
103 Article 42 in National People's Congress (2001).

It is impossible to estimate the percentage of such "signboard unions" controlled by management among the 1.3 million grass-root unions recognised in official statistics, but clearly, such practices are not rare.

Another issue is that, according to Cooke, union officials seemed not to believe that their duties should change in spite of the new circumstances, nor did they have enough resources and power, skills and legal knowledge to fulfill their collective bargaining role or defend their members' rights.[104] Aside from ideological misperceptions inherited from the old days, in Chan's opinion, this issue was due at least partly to the fact that the international trade union movement kept isolating the ACFTU so that when the business sector had a profound influence on China, introducing neoliberal ideas and training a large crop of Chinese managers in the art of human resources management through an increasingly capitalist-style corporate structure, an external countervailing presence was sorely absent to help build an anti-neoliberal capability in China.[105]

In summary, the market economy called for a service union which pursued the interests of its members. The problem confronting the ACFTU was whether or not to change its role from an organization of political control to an economic service organization.[106] The core of the problem was whether a legally monopolistic organization possessed the intention and motivation to trigger self-reform, and if so, how effective reforms would be? If the monopoly position was broken, making room for the free association of labour, would there be a chain reaction such as that which led to the emergence of Solidarity in Poland? This is a complex political issue beyond the reach of this book.

104 Cooke (2008b), p. 11. We will discuss this issue in more detail in Chapter 7.

105 Chan (2006), p. 300.

106 Cooke argues that the role of the unions, or more specifically, the union officials' perception of their duties, has not changed in time to reflect the new reality (Cooke (2008b), p. 11).

2.3 Employers' Associations

Compared with the strict controls that employee organizations confront, the environment for employers' associations is much looser. The biggest difference lies in the fact that there is only one legal employees' organization in China (i.e. the ACFTU) while there are many legal employers' associations currently existing in China and even more are likely to emerge.

We need to clarify two terms, "Industry Associations (行业协会)" and "Chambers of Commerce (商会)" which we encounter later. Many scholars tend to equate the two. But these two terms have specific meanings in China. "Industry Associations (行业协会)" are established by government departments[107] and supervised either by the government departments or by the State-owned Assets Supervision and Administration Commission (SASAC 国资委), with links to the China Enterprise Confederation-China Enterprise Directors Association (CEC-CEDA, 中国企业联合会-中国企业家协会). The "Chambers of Commerce (商会)", on the other hand, are organizations established relatively spontaneously by civilian businessmen, most of whom are affiliated with the All China Federation of Industry and Commerce (ACFIC, 全国工商联), with a few others affiliated with the party or government departments, while some are without proper registration.

Thus, there are three major categories of employer associations in China: the official "Industry Associations" headed by the CEC-CEDA; the semi-official "Chambers of Commerce", affiliated with the ACFIC; and the completely spontaneous "Civil Chambers of Commerce".[108]

107 These government departments are typically industrial departments in the planned economy system, which became redundant later in the series of government reforms. Refer to the detailed discussions in Chapter 5.

108 Yu (2006).

2.3.1 CEC-CEDA

The China Enterprise Confederation-China Enterprise Directors Association (CEC-CEDA, 中国企业联合会-中国企业家协会) is not well known to the general public, even within China. It was formerly known as the China Enterprise Management Association (中国企业管理协会), and was founded in March 1979 as a subsidiary of the then State Economy Committee (国家经委). In April, 1999, it received approval to rename itself the CEC-CEDA.[109] Despite its short history, CEC-CEDA was granted recognition as "the only representative of employers" in the National Tripartite Conference on Labour Relations Co-ordination (NTCLRC, 国家协调劳动关系三方会议). It participated in the activities of some international organizations, such as the International Labour Organization and the International Organization of Employers by claiming to be the only representative of Chinese employers.[110]

How could such an organization acquire this status so quickly? The answer lies in its special connection with the party-state.[111] When compared with the other employers' associations in China, such as the ACFIC

109 Yuan (2004).

110 Article 8 in CEC-CEDA (2003).

111 We will explore in more detail the relationship between the CEC-CEDA and the party-state in Chapter 5. Here, a short list of the CEC-CEDA's key leaders will provide a quick idea of its relationship with the party-state: the founding chair of the CEC-CEDA was Yuan Bao Hua (former minister of State Economy Committee and member of the CC-CCP) and the honorary chairman was Bo Yi Bo (former vice-premier of State Council and member of Politburo-CCP); Bo Yi Bo died in January 2007 and his son, Bo X. L., who used to be the Minister of Commerce, became the indirect leader of CEC-CEDA. The current chairman is Chen Jin Hua (former vice-chair of the NPPCC, ex-minister of the State Planning Committee, and member of the CC-CCP). All of these were key figures in the party-state system. Furthermore, the CEC-CEDA has a group of former or current party-state leaders as its consultants: the list includes Zhu Rong Ji (former premier of State Council and member of SCP-CCP), Tian Ji Yun (current vice-chair of the National People's Congress and member of Politburo-CCP), and Wang Zhong Yu (current vice-chair of the National People's Political Consultative Conference and member of CC-CCP, former director of State Economy and Trades Committee).

(discussed in the next subsection), the CEC-CEDA, being a direct descendant of the party-state, was undoubtedly a more reliable industrial relations vehicle for the party-state. The party-state felt more comfortable with it as the "representative" of employers (on behalf of the party-state). Therefore, when the party-state needed a "representative of employers" to make complete the structure of the newly established NTCLRC, the CEC-CEDA was summoned to take up the role, even though none of the CEC-CEDA's reputation, historical background or level within the party could be compared either with that of its supposed "rival", the ACFTU or of its counterpart, the ACFIC.

From the perspective of the party-state, having a dependable "representative of employers" was essential for its absolute control over the new industrial relations co-ordination mechanism. As we have now seen, the three parties in the NTCLRC, MOHRSS, ACFTU and CEC-CEDA, are all direct or indirect subsidiaries of the party-state.[112] The "Statute of CEC-CEDA (2003 revised version)" confirms its role in the tripartite system:

> Article Two This association is the united organization for the enterprises, entrepreneurs (employers) and enterprise groups. It represents the enterprises and entrepreneurs (employers) in the NTCLRC, which comprises the MOLSS, the ACFTU and this association.
>
> Article Seven [It] protects the legal rights of the enterprises and entrepreneurs (employers), represents the enterprises and entrepreneurs (employers) in co-ordinating labour relations, guides regional and trade enterprise confederation/enterprise directors' associations to participate in a complete tripartite scheme for co-ordination of labour relations.
>
> Article Eight This association is China's only representative in the International Organization of Employers, and actively participates in the ILO and IOE's relevant activities, as well as communicating and co-operating with other countries' employers' organizations. Source: CEC-CEDA (2003)

112 We discuss these relationships in more detail in Chapter 5.

In an internal document, CEC-CEDA admits that "the CEC-CEDA's key function is to co-ordinate labour relations ... to work under the instructions of the NTCLRC regarding the establishment of tripartite system in all cities and in counties and districts with appropriate economic base and conditions ... The CEC-CEDA actively promotes the development of branches nation-wide ..." In all cities with established tripartite systems, 72% have CEC-CEDA as employers' representatives.[113]

We have no difficulty, then, in identifying CEC-CEDA's official position. Its level is about equal to that of the former Economy and Trades Committee (ETC) or of the State-owned Assets Supervision and Administration Commission (SASAC). Why then did the party-state use CEC-CEDA, rather than ETC or SASAC?[114] We submit that the likely reason is that anointing governmental bodies such as the ETC or SASAC as "representatives" of employers (capitalists) in a "socialist country" was ideologically absurd. Thus, the tripartite system copied from the western countries created a need for CEC-CEDA to be in the forefront.

There is a view that CEC-CEDA was becoming gradually independent after the dismissal of ETC[115] because 55% of CEC-CEDA's members were in non-SOEs, so that it represented the interests of both SOEs and the non-SOEs.[116] For these reasons, Yuan argued that CEC-CEDA rightly represented employers of different backgrounds.[117] But there are three problems with claims that CEC-CEDA was independent with an adequate representation base.

113 Information from CEC-CEDA's official website: <www.cec-ceda.org.cn> (last accessed on 20 January 2009).

114 Though, according to the same source, there are still about 17% tripartite organizations with the ETC or SASAC acting as the "representatives" of the employers.

115 It is true that, since the dismissal of the ETC in 2003, no government ministry claims to have direct leadership of the CEC-CEDA.

116 Information from CEC-CEDA's official website: <www.cec-ceda.org.cn> (last accessed on 20 January 2009).

117 Yuan (2004). Yuan was the founding chair of the CEC-CEDA. Hence his contention cannot be treated as objective.

First, in CEC-CEDA's organizational structure, the most important department is the party committee office. Its role is "to revolve around the association's key jobs, ensuring the party's role at the centre of political life, providing political protection and supervision ..."[118] Furthermore, as we have seen, all of the key leaders of CEC-CEDA were current or former party-state officials.

Second, according to the "Regulation on the Registration and Management of Social Organizations", issued by the State Council, all "Social Organizations", including CEC-CEDA, must have a "business supervisory unit (业务主管单位)" in place. There is no public information as to which ministry took up that responsibility after CEC-CEDA's original "business supervisory unit" (the ETC) was dismissed. But it is certain that CEC-CEDA must have a "business supervisory unit" in the current legal environment.[119]

Third, there are also doubts about the representative base of CEC-CEDA. According to CEC-CEDA's website, it "has 3,000 direct enterprise members and 436,000 'connection member enterprises (联系会员企业)'". There is no explanation of how the number of "connection member enterprises" is calculated. But even if we accept the number of 436,000, this accounts for less than 10% of all enterprises in China.[120] It is still far from a reasonable basis for any claim to "represent" China's employers.

Thus it is highly questionable whether CEC-CEDA is really organizationally "independent" and has a sufficient representative base to qualify as the sole representative for China's employers in domestic and international tripartite systems.

118 Information from CEC-CEDA's official website: <www.cec-ceda.org.cn> (last accessed on 20 January 2009).

119 Item Four of the "Statute of CEC-CEDA" states that "this association accepts the guidance and supervision from the business supervisory unit and the social organization registration and administration unit".

120 According to National Statistics Burea's data, by the end of 2004, there were 5.16 million enterprises in China's non-primary industries (NBS 2005).

Confronted by these questions and "the danger of being replaced by other organizations",[121] some officials inside CEC-CEDA hoped to resolve problems by the intervention of the party-state. In an internal meeting, some CEC-CEDA cadres urged that

> since the union (the ACFTU) has the protection of Union Law, and the employers' organization (the CEC-CEDA) has an unclear position, participants in the meeting argued for pushing the relevant state bodies to pass a law or regulation to ensure [the CEC-CEDA's] (monopolistic) position.[122]

Though the party-state eventually turned down such a request, this meeting revealed that the work methods of some of the CEC-CEDA leaders were still those of typical bureaucrats who were used to gaining monopolistic or quasi-monopolistic privileges by top down authority.

Reviewing CEC-CEDA's activities during the decade since 1997, we find little meaningful contribution to the tripartite system, other than that of "representing" employers in various meetings and applauding whatever policy the government put forward.[123] CEC-CEDA was even less representative and more impotent than the ACFTU. After the late 1990s, ACFTU at least raised concerns over worker interests and rights, making efforts to soften strained labour relations, even though the actual effects are very limited. CEC-CEDA, on the other hand, did little. Therefore, we question CEC-CEDA's legitimacy as the "representative" of China's employers.

121 An internal document of CEC-CEDA stated that "for historical reasons, CEC-CEDA's membership coverage is insufficient ... if we cannot adapt to the ever changing market environment, there exist the danger of CEC-CEDA being replaced by other organization" (Information from CEC-CEDA's official website available at <http://www.cec-ceda.org.cn/ldgx/info/content.php?id=158> (last accessed on 16 January 2009).

122 CEC-CEDA meeting minutes for "Conference on Building Up Employers' Organizational Capability", July 2006 (Information from CEC-CEDA's official website: <http://www.cec-ceda.org.cn/ldgx/info/content.php?id=969> last accessed on 20 January 2009).

123 Refer to the detailed discusiion regarding NTCLRC in Chapter 5.

2.3.2 ACFIC

Compared with CEC-CEDA, the All China Federation of Industry and Commerce (ACFIC, 全国工商联) has a much longer history and higher political reputation.

The ACFIC has its origin in 1949, when the CCP issued an "Instruction on Organizing the Federation of Industry and Commerce". It was established formally in 1953 as "a mass organization and a civil chamber of commerce with the characteristics of a 'united front (统一战线)'[124] under the leadership of the CCP, and as a participating unit of the National People's Political Consultative Conference (NPPCC, 全国政协)".[125] At its inception, ACFIC's main body of members comprised private enterprises. Acting in accordance with the "General Tasks of the Transitional Period (过渡时期总任务)", the ACFIC helped to persuade private business owners "to accept education on patriotism and socialism, and to do their part to restore and develop the national economy, enhancing the socialistic transformation of the existing capitalistic industry and commerce".[126] After completion of "the socialistic transformation (nationalization)" of the private sector in 1956, the ACFIC's tasks shifted to persuading members "to accept the socialistic transformation and serve socialistic construction". After the Reform and Open-door policy was initiated in 1979, the fourth general meeting of the ACFIC adopted the slogan "firmly follow the Party, do the best for the four modernizations". At its fifth general meeting in 1983, ACFIC defined itself as "a mass organization composed of socialistic labourers and patriots supporting socialism and unification of the country in the sector of industry and commerce ..."[127] In 1991, the CC-CCP issued an instruction to the ACFIC, redefining it as

124 The "united front (统一战线)" was considered to be one of the major tools for the success of the CCP's revolution. Mao pointed out that "... it is the united front of all revolutionary elements under the leadership of the (communist) party ... It is the major weapon with which we defeated the enemy ..." (Mao 1949).

125 Information from ACFIC's official website: <http://www.acfic.org.cn/cenweb/portal/user/anon/page/introducePage.page> (last accessed on 20 January 2009).

126 Chen (1953).

127 General Provisions in ACFIC (2007).

> a mass organization and a civil chamber of commerce with the characteristics of "united front (统一战线)", assisting the government to administer the non-state-owned economy and being the bridge between the party-state and the representatives from the non-state-owned economy.[128]

By the first half of 2006, there were altogether 3,119 ACFIC branch associations around the country with 1.97 million members.[129]

The ACFIC was more of a political than an economic organization. It can be described as a political organization aiming to unite employers (capitalists) in industry and commerce.[130] These characteristics are recognised in statutes:

> Article One The ACFIC is a mass organization and a civil chamber of commerce under the leadership of the CCP; it is the bridge and transmission belt between the party-state and the representatives of the non-state-owned economy, assisting the government to administer the non-state-owned economy.
>
> Article Three The principles for the ACFIC are: uphold the great flag of Deng Xiaoping Theories, study and practise the important thoughts of "Three Representation" ... stick to the Party's basic route and policy in the preliminary stage of socialism ...
>
> Article Four The ACFIC's key roles and functions:
> - Participate in political consultation regarding nation-wide political, economical and social issues, play the role of democratic supervision, be actively involved in political discussions;
> - ...
> - Recommend the political arrangements for representation of the sector of industry and commerce;
> - ...
> - Undertake assignments delegated by the governments and relevant apparatus.
>
> Source: ACFIC (2002)

128 CC-CCP (1991).

129 Information from ACFIC's official website: <www.acfic.org.cn> (last accessed on 20 January 2009).

130 That is, it is a "united front organization (统战组织)".

In the 1953 version of the "Statute of ACFIC", Clause Four of Item Three stated that "… (the ACFIC) represents private business owners' legal rights nationally, reflects opinions and puts forward suggestions to the people's government, co-ordinates with the ACFTU on labour relation issues regarding private enterprises …" But when new organizational arrangements for CEC-CEDA emerged in the 1990s, these functions were eliminated from ACFIC's responsibilities.

Though the ACFIC was an extension of the Party-state system, a so-called "united front tool", it had more subtle relationships with the party-state,[131] and cannot be deemed to be a "direct descendant (嫡系)" of the party-state. Therefore, even though ACFIC has a longer history and better reputation than CEC-CEDA, and is a bigger organisation, it has been barely involved in NTCLRC's mechanisms.[132] Although the ACFIC plays an active role as an employers' association, its importance and potential should not be underestimated. Possible future political and structural reforms provide an environment for it to develop its role in Chinese industrial relations.

2.3.3 Other Employers' Associations

Is there any possibility that a fully spontaneous employers' association will emerge and prosper in China's political and economic environment? While there was much debate about the organization and development of Civil Chambers of Commerce operating as employers' associations,[133] the attitude of the party-state has gradually become clear. At the NPC held in March 2005, Premier Wen Jia Bao's Government Report contained a paragraph referring to the role of government in business. Its role was to

131 We discuss these relationships in more detail in Chapter 5.

132 In all those cities with established tripartite systems, only 11% of local TCLRCs chose the local FIC as the employers' representatives.

133 For examples, Chen and Ma (2004); Gao (2000); Li and Wang (2005); Ma (2002); Yu et al. (2002), Yu and Wu (2001); Zheng and Jiang (2003).

> … enhance the transformation of the government's functions … push further ahead the separation of government and enterprises (政企分开), the separation of government and capital (政资分开) and the separation of government and public utilities (政事分开) … hand back all those matters, in which the government should not get involved, to the enterprises, the social organization or the agency apparatus …

Guangdong province, in the front line of economic reform, issued a "Regulation on Trade Associations" in December 2005, providing a much looser environment for the self-association of enterprises within specific industries. Shenzhen city, being "in the front line of the front line", went a step further by establishing the "Shenzhen Trade Association Service Department", enforcing a new system of "no official level, no official staffing, no supervisory unit (无级别、无编制、无主管)" for trade associations.

Of course, in the context of China's political circumstances, this opening was limited and conditional.

First, looser regulations were issued only by local authorities. Regulation at upper levels, such as the "Regulation on the Registration and Management of Social Organizations", issued by the State Council in 1998, did not undergo significant amendment. In practice, with conflict between local and national regulations, the more strict national regulations continued to be followed.

Second, even in the "Regulation on Trade Associations" in Guangdong province, there were items stating that

> … the civil affairs department of the people's government is the registration and administration unit for the trade associations, other relevant government departments can supervise the activities of the trade associations in their specific administrative areas and can guide the trade associations by putting forward suggestions, announcing information and issuing directive policies …

Furthermore, registration and administration units had the authority "to prohibit the preparation and formation (of trade associations)" or to "order [an association to be] dismissed according to law".[134]

134 Articles 7, 11 and 36 in Guangdong Provincial People's Congress (2005).

Third, in Guangdong, the Provincial Party Committee issued a document in February 2006 commenting on "how the party and government can lead the trade associations in the n ew era of reform", and urging the "establishment of an interactive mechanism that involves the party, the government and the trade associations".[135] Officials in Shenzhen city also openly stated that "... (we) must prevent the trade associations from becoming political pressure groups ... party committees at all levels should feel confident in building up the party branches in all trade associations ..." According to one report, among the 2,300 full time staff in 160 trade associations in Shenzhen, there were only 353 party members.[136]

A big gap remains between the theory and practice of free association. But the emergence of trade associations is a solid step towards free association. According to data provided by the Ministry of Civil Affairs, by the end of 2005 53,000 trade associations were registered nation-wide. Their growth is the fastest among all social organizations. We can foresee that there will be more spontaneous organizations which will really represent the interests of employers in Chinese industrial relations.[137]

It is a pity, however, that in a "socialistic country", nominally "led by the working class", the breakthrough of reform affecting free association came not from the association of workers and employees but from the association of employers and capitalists. This caused some puzzlement as to why the party-state feels more comfortable dealing with capitalists than with the working class.[138] While the interests of employers can be

135 Articles 1 and 22 in Guangdong Provincial Party Committee and Government (2006).

136 "Civilization Makes Trade Associations in Shenzhen Stronger" (in Chinese), *Liaowang News Weekly*, "民间化让深圳行业协会硬起来", 瞭望新闻周刊", 7 August 2006.

137 In Chapter 6, we discuss further what those employers associations have done to promote employers' interests.

138 More examples of this type can be found in Chapter 7 when we discuss the relationship between the party-state and the employers (capitalists) and the relationship between the party-state and the employees. It is interesting that the party-state seems to share some common views with the Unitarist approach of the industrial relations theory, which, being right wing, tends to consider (free) labour unions as

represented eventually by their own associations, employees still have to rely on the official union to "represent" their interests. If this situation does not change, the power gap between the employers and employees will only become wider.

Conclusions

In this chapter we discussed three industrial relations actors at the macro level, namely, the party-state, the ACFTU and the Employer Associations:

First, having regard to the problems of Taylor et al.'s (2003) summary of the party-state structure in China's industrial relations, we suggested a more sophisticated diagram (Figure 2.1) to describe the relevant party-state structure in industrial relations. We then analysed further the party-state's role in industrial relations as legislator and labour market regulator, conciliator, arbitrator and mediator, provider of public goods, and employer of labour and labour market developer. We concluded that the party-state, itself a constant target of reform during an unprecedented transitional period, did not perform well in these roles, though it tried to do so.

Second, taking into account the history and post-1997 status of the ACFTU, we concluded that it was an extension of the party-state, playing the role, as set by the party-state, of "bridge and transmission belt for the connection between the party and the employed masses". Being privileged by the party-state, however, did not mean that the ACFTU had no role to play as labour's representative, or to care about the protection of labour rights. Since the 1990s, the market economy called for a service union which would pursue the interests of its members, yet the ACFTU was constrained by being a party-state extension.

---

troublemakers who raise transaction costs for solving labour problems, and tends to entrust major responsibilities to the employers for handling industrial relations issues at the workplace.

Third, three major types of employer associations operate legally in China: official "Industry Associations" headed by the CEC-CEDA, semi-official "Chambers of Commerce", affiliated with the ACFIC, and more spontaneous "Civil Chambers of Commerce". These three types of employers' associations are distinct from each other due to their respective origins and characteristics.

CHAPTER THREE

Grass Roots Unions and Employers: Chinese Institutional Industrial Relations Actors at the Workplace Level

Introduction

In the last chapter, we identified and discussed three major industrial relations actors above the workplace level in China: the party-state, the ACFTU, and employers' associations. In this chapter, as well as the next, we shift our focus to industrial relations actors at the workplace level. In particular, this chapter focuses on two institutional actors, namely, grass roots unions and employers.

We argue that there are significant differences between the ACFTU and grass roots unions, stressing that reforms in the latter affect elections and daily performance, though the real effects of the reforms remain uncertain. Turning to employers, we explain the mixed economic model in China and contend that Chinese employer behaviour should be analysed on the basis of segmenting enterprises by operational scale and ownership type. Individual employees are the subject matter of the next chapter.

3.1 Grass Roots Unions

As noted in Chapter Two, the relevant literature[1] on Chinese industrial relations seldom singles out grass roots unions as separate actors, usually treating them with the ACFTU as a whole. If this was acceptable in the past, when the ACFTU and grass roots unions behaved almost identically in the context of a state-owned economy, it is no longer so, because the positioning, roles and functions of the ACFTU and of grass roots unions are quite different from each other in the context of a transitional society heading towards a market economy.

China's transition to a market economy, bringing SOE reform and restructuring and the rapid development of non-SOE sectors, caused significant change in the operation of all kinds of enterprises in China. Unions, especially grass roots unions at the workplace level, were confronted by new challenges which include, but are not limited to, the cessation of compulsory recruitment in non-SOEs, SOE lay-off (下岗) issues and growing labour disputes caused by a harsher working environment, particularly in Privately Owned Enterprises (POEs) and general Foreign Investment Enterprises (FIEs). All these factors drove the reform of grass roots unions.

From the analysis in the previous chapter, we learnt that the ACFTU is a highly political organization. As China's central leadership stressed economic reform without a road-map for political reform, significant reform of the ACFTU was unlikely. Grass roots unions, however, were more down-to-earth and much less politically sensitive, facing issues such as the ordinary workers' everyday livelihood and dealing with the more practical tasks such as the negotiation of payment rates and working conditions. In the context of the new CCP leadership's policy of "constructing a harmonious society (构建和谐社会)", reforms of grass roots unions began to take off after the new "fourth generation" leadership came into power in 2003. In the following subsections, we discuss these reforms.

1 For examples, Chan (1993, 2002, 2003); Leung (2002); Gilbert (2005); Zhang (2003); Qi (2004); Feng (2006) etc.

3.1.1 *Structural Changes in Grass Roots Unions' Working Environment*

In the early stage of reforms and the Open-door Policy during the period 1978–92, China developed a so-called "economic system with public ownership as the mainstay and other forms of ownerships as supplements (以公有制为主体、其他所有制为补充的经济制度)", which meant that the public sector continued to play a dominant role in the economy as well as in the labour market.[2]

In an economic system dominated by the public sector, grass roots unions dealt mostly with SOE employees, who were automatically and compulsorily recruited as union members. Grass roots unions retained the top-down mentality which characterised the ACFTU at the macro-level, playing mainly a political role in control of the working population. Though we did not locate any empirical research on the practices of grass roots unions during this period, the following document issued in 1984 gives a hint of what the ACFTU and party-state required of the grass roots unions in their everyday operations:

> Grass roots unions are the basis for the Union (ACFTU) to connect with the masses and carry out various tasks ... (We shall) strengthen the construction of grass roots unions and give full play to the union's speciality in realizing the Party's general missions and objectives ... Grass roots unions shall adhere to Socialism, adhere to Proletarian Dictatorship, adhere to the CCP's Leadership, and adhere to Marxism/ Leninism/ Mao Zedong Thoughts ... [Grass roots unions shall] fully play the roles of being the transmission belt between the Party and the working masses, being the important social pillar supporting the People's Democratic Dictatorship (人民民主专政), and being the school for spreading communism [to the working people] ...[3]

Grass roots unions at this stage were endowed with political functions typical of any Leninist trade union,[4] which were, as outlined in subsection 2.2.3, in line with those sustained by the ACFTU. During this period, there was little difference between the ACFTU and grass roots unions, except that they operated at different levels of social control.

2 For detailed descriptions of this policy, refer to the publicized political reports of the 12th and 13th CCP's national conference (CC-CCP 1982; CC-CCP 1987).

3 General Provisions in ACFTU (1984).

4 Qi (2004).

After 1992, the grass roots unions' working environment underwent significant structural change. The most significant change is that they lost much of their guaranteed membership base, which was provided traditionally by SOEs.[5] As pointed out in the last chapter, by 2002, only 70 million employees remained in state and collectively owned enterprises, merely half of the 1992 number and less than 20% of all employees in non-primary industries.[6] As over 80% of employees worked in non-SOE sectors which were out of the reach of the party-state, the diversification of enterprise ownership types made labour relations more complex than before. Labour disputes began to emerge in the public realm whereas previously most labour issues were confined to and settled within the "work unit (单位)". As a consequence, the number of recorded labour dispute rose significantly from 48,121 cases in 1996 to 317,162 in 2006.[7] Furthermore, together with the influx of foreign capital, modern western management systems and style impacted significantly on traditional ways of managing enterprises and unions.[8]

In response to these changes, the ACFTU issued a new version of the "Regulation on Enterprise Union's Work" in 2006, significantly reducing the political content in the original regulation[9] by shifting emphasis to "... lawfully fulfil the basic responsibility of protecting employees' legal rights, co-ordinate labour relations in the enterprises, push forward the construction of harmony in enterprises, and facilitate enterprises' healthy development ..."[10] Measures were also taken to reform grass roots unions so as to match the changes. Among them, two reforms were significant. The first related to election of grass roots union leadership, or the "representation" issue, while the second related to how grass roots unions should perform their roles, or the "function" issue. We discuss these two matters in the following two subsections.

5 Theoretically, the fact that a firm is privately owned does not necessarily preclude compulsory union membership. But it has been lucky (or unlucky?) for the Chinese workers that the policy-makers did not enforce union membership in non-SOEs.

6 Refer back to discussions in 2.1.2 of Chapter 2.

7 NBS and MOLSS (2007), disc edition, Table 9.1.

8 Refer to the analysis by Wang (2003) and Tong (2003).

9 I.e. ACFTU (1984).

10 Article 4 in ACFTU (2006).

3.1.2 Grass Roots Unions Elections

Despite the fact that Chinese employees were not allowed to organize their own independent unions, relatively free and democratic elections within the existing union structure were widely accepted. Wang connected elections with the development of new forms of democracy in China, arguing that they were another major reform following the release of control over peasants' self-governance in rural areas and residents' self-governance in urban areas.[11] Other scholars, though, were less optimistic but generally positive about union reform during the decade after 1997.[12]

Grass roots union elections were an attempt to solve "representation" and legitimacy issues in China's monopolistic union system. As we saw in the last chapter, the ACFTU is a top-down structured union controlled by the CCP at all levels and can be deemed an extension of the party-state system. For this reason, its legitimacy as an organization "representing the working class" was long questioned.[13] One of the ACFTU's major problems was that union leaders at all levels used to be appointed by and were therefore responsible to "the upper leadership (上级领导)"[14] rather than their worker members. A bureaucratic working style was fostered in such a top-down and semi-governmental operational environment.[15] These practices did not cater to employee needs in the emerging market economy.[16]

11 Wang (2005).
12 E.g., Wang (2003); Chen and Zhang (2005) etc.
13 For such criticism, refer to Harper (1969); Chan (2002); Leung (2002); Zhang (2003); Liu and Zhang (2005) etc.
14 According to the union statute, the "upper leadership" refers to the superior Party committee as well as the superior union governing body. (Refer back to the discussion in 2.2.2).
15 Deng Xiaoping, on different occasions, commented that "... unions shouldn't be the 'tail' of the administration ... union cadres shouldn't consider themselves as administrative officials" and "... union shouldn't be an organization for a few people to collect workers' membership fees, play 'the master' and pursue personal interests ..." (as quoted by Xu 2006). In the Chinese official language, all those "shouldn'ts ..." refer to existing practices.
16 As the employees in the non-SOE sectors now enjoy the right of job mobility and can choose whether to join the union or not, they demand that the union should

Reform of China's unions so as to lessen bureaucracy and enhance their adaptability to the market economy, without causing possible chain effects such as those caused by Poland's Solidarity, was a hard nut to crack for China's policy makers. Following a strategy of "reform in a gradual manner", authorities encouraged limited direct elections in grass roots unions in the hope of solving representation and responsibility issues with a more controllable workplace and without dramatic changes to the official union system.

Grass roots union elections were first trialled in part of Shekou District[17] as early as 1986 and were extended to the whole district in 1988. Since then, in Shekou, not only have leaders of grass roots unions been elected, but also leaders of the union federation at the district level. The experiment was then extended to Guangdong Province. It is estimated that by 2003 one third of grass roots unions in Guangdong Province, or, approximately 40,000 out of 120,000 unions, held direct democratic elections.[18]

Summarizing those experiences in official documents, the ACFTU passed several regulations to formulate the practice of elections in grass roots unions. Such documents include the "Temporary Regulation on Grass Roots Unions' Elections" and "On Grass Roots Unions' Representative Conference", which were issued in 1992, as well as the "Regulation on Enterprise Unions' Work", which was issued in 2006. In addition, some ACFTU provincial branches also issued local rules on the election of union chairs.[19]

The question remains, though, whether the ACFTU's grass roots unions were really democratized. This question requires us to look into the specific regulations as well as their implementation.

---

first demonstrate its value before they are willing to join it and to pay for their membership (Xu 2003).

17 Shekou is an industrial district under Shenzhen Economic Special Zone, Guangdong province.

18 "Direct Election Is Not A Show, One Third of Guangdong's Grass Roots Unions Are Elected Directly" (in Chinese), *Southern Metropolitan Paper*, "直选不是做秀, 广东1/3企业基层工会直选产生", 南方都市报, 9 July 2003.

19 E.g., Shanxi Provincial ACFTU (2006).

Regulations on Grass Roots Unions Elections

Most of the items in the ACFTU's 1992 document "On Grass Roots Unions' Representative Conference" can be seen as consistent with basic democratic rules such as open competitive elections, secret ballots and the majority principle. For example, the regulations stipulated that "all representatives in grass roots unions' representative conferences shall be chosen in a competitive election by secret ballots"[20] and that "candidates must obtain majority support in ballots conducted in their working units to be granted the formal title of representative".[21] At the same time, however, we must note that there were also clauses meant to protect the existing system and to prevent a bottom-up qualitative change of power which may be triggered by direct elections. For example, the regulations stipulated that "... grass roots union representatives should ... persist in following the Party's basic lines ..."[22] and that "... the representatives' responsibilities are to lead the implementation of the Party's lines, policies and tactics ..."[23]

The most limiting clause is perhaps one which states: "after the representatives are elected, the list of names of the elected representatives shall be handed to the grass roots union committee for investigation of qualifications".[24] This clause grants the power of final decision to the grass roots union committee, which is usually controlled by the corresponding CCP branch. Why does the qualification investigation take place afterwards and not before the elections? If a person is found to be unqualified after he/she wins an election, is it not a waste of time and resources to arrange for another election? Why not hold the investigation at the outset? Those who are familiar with the political processes in China know that when something is against normal logic, it usually suits the logic of political

20 Article 5 in ACFTU (1992c).
21 Article 5 Item 7 in ACFTU (1992c).
22 Article 5 Item 1 in ACFTU (1992c).
23 Article 5 Item 13 in ACFTU (1992c).
24 Article 5 Item 9 in ACFTU (1992c).

expedience.[25] Investigation beforehand, of course, can filter out obvious dissidents, but there are also "hidden" dissidents who can be identified only by their words and actions during the election campaign. Therefore, this clause provides a "safety brake" for the ACFTU and the party-state behind it. If a candidate exhibits a tendency to disagree with the existing system, the authorities can still deem him or her unqualified even if the person wins the election.

We can see, therefore, that the ACFTU and the party-state behind it held a complex attitude towards direct elections in grass roots unions. They realized that direct elections were a two-edged sword. On the one hand, elections reduced bureaucracy in the official union and enhanced the effectiveness and efficiency of the grass roots unions. On the other hand, if not controlled "properly", elections triggered a chain of events and even endangered the political system as in Eastern Europe during the 1980s and 1990s. That is why the Regulations contained both democratic and limiting clauses.

The Implementation of Direct Elections in Grass Roots Unions

Guo Wencai, the chief director of the ACFTU's Organizational Construction Department, commented in 2003 that direct elections at the grass roots level focused on unions in medium/small and non-SOE enterprises, not in SOEs at that stage.[26] Implementing direct elections first in medium/small enterprises fitted clearly with the long-held economic reform mentality of "Grasping the Large While Releasing the Small (抓大放小)",[27] while

25 Interested readers can refer to Bo (1998) and Wu (2002). These two famous books contain many vivid examples of power manipulation in Chinese history.

26 "Union Reforms in the Transitional Period" (in Chinese), *Southern Weekends*, "转型期的工会改革方向", 南方周末, 3 July 2003.

27 The policy of "Grasping the Large While Releasing the Small (抓大放小)" can be traced back to the speech made by Deng Xiaoping during his famous "Southern Tour" in 1992, and can be formally found in State Council (2003). Though this policy was initiated as a measure for the SOE reforms, it is now widely applied to various other reforms such as union reform, finance reform, and medical care reform etc.

the focus on non-SOE enterprises was a consequence of marketization. Employees in non-SOE enterprises were accustomed more to working in a market economy environment. They were more pragmatic, therefore, about the costs and benefits of their choices, needing to be convinced that joining a union would bring net benefits. As grass roots unions in non-SOE enterprises were established mostly on a voluntary basis,[28] the ACFTU, if it was to attract members, had to make gestures to show that its intention was to work for the interests of labour. Undoubtedly, one of the best gestures was to support direct elections in these enterprises. Workers were not interested in joining "signboard unions" such as those manipulated by authorities in SOEs.

In addition, the complexity of the role of unions in SOEs delayed union reform in those enterprises. After the establishment of the SOE system in the 1950s, unions in SOEs performed multiple functions, assisting enterprise administration,[29] and acting as agents for the party-state in leading the working class. For this reason, the 2006 version of the "Regulation on Enterprise Unions' Work" continued to stipulate that "the candidates for union chair in state and collectively owned enterprises shall be nominated by the party organization at the same level together with the superior union ... the union chair shall be treated as assistant to the party/administration at the same level; if he/she is a CCP member, he/she shall be a member of the party's leading organization ..."[30] Therefore, the phenomenon of "no separation between government and enterprises (政企不分)" remained in SOEs,[31] with little indication that reform of union elections was to be implemented in SOEs before they were fully marketized.

28 I.e. non-SOE employees have the right to decide whether or not to establish a grass roots union, and/or whether or not to join a grass roots union if it is established; while in the SOEs, grass roots union are all in place and all employees automatically become members.

29 Unions in SOEs usually perform part of the roles of the HR department, mostly in organizing employees' recreational activities.

30 Article 24 in ACFTU (2006).

31 Hu (2001).

In summary, policy makers tried to reduce the political aspects of grass roots unions. They were willing to grant more flexibility and freedom to those operating in medium/small and non-SOE enterprises.[32] However, it is premature to suppose that the ACFTU's grass roots unions were democratized. The democratization of grass roots unions was a long and drawn out process,[33] with no clear answer to the question whether reforms were destined to proceed to the upper level of the ACFTU itself. Yet, it can be reasonably expected that the roll-out of the direct elections in grass roots unions will eventually affect the operation of upper levels.

3.1.3 Grass Roots Unions' Roles

There are two major issues in the changing roles of grass roots unions. One concerns the ways in which the grass roots unions, in time of peace, perform their roles in collective bargaining and ensuring the realization of labour contracts. The other is about how, in times of trouble, grass roots unions are involved in the protection of employees' legal rights.

Collective Bargaining and Daily Monitoring

Theoretically, the ACFTU encourages all grass roots unions to be actively involved in collective bargaining and daily monitoring processes. The "Regulation on Enterprise Unions' Work" stipulates that "... (enterprise

32 This tendency can also be revealed by comparing items in the 2006 "Regulation on Enterprise Unions' Work" with those in the 1984 "Temporary Regulation on Grass Roots Unions' Work". We can see that most of the political wording in the old version was deleted and replaced with instructions on how to "connect closely with the masses, care for their production and livelihood, warm-heartedly serve employees, and strive to construct a 'reliable home' for the staff..." (Article 5 in ACFTU 2006). There are also clauses emphasising "the openness of union affairs, adherence to the 'masses line' and democracy" (Article 19 in ACFTU 2006).

33 As shown earlier in this section, even in the most reformed province of Guangdong, only about one third of grass roots unions have gone through the democratic election process, and SOE union reform is not on the agenda at all.

unions should) help to instruct the employees in signing labour contracts with the enterprises; co-ordinate/negotiate and sign collective contracts as equals with the enterprises on the matters of payment, working hours, labour quota, rest and holidays, safety and hygiene, and insurance and welfare etc.; and monitor the implementation of the collective contracts ..."[34] In practice, implementation of collective bargaining was treated more seriously in non-SOEs than in SOEs,[35] though nominally the proportion of employees covered by collective contracts was much higher in SOEs than in non-SOEs.[36] The reason is that collective contracts in SOEs were achieved by co-ordination, with little need for real negotiation, between official union and administration cadres, while in non-SOEs, contracts had to go through more practical negotiation processes.[37]

For grass roots unions which took on the actual role of collective bargaining, the ACFTU's guiding strategies were reflected in a series of policy guides entitled "Enterprise Union: On the Way to Co-ordination and Negotiation".[38] These articles reiterate that "... [unions] should make the employees realize that the rise of salaries and welfare must be in line with the enterprises' profitability, and that the staffs' individual interests are closely connected with those of the enterprises. The enterprise should

34 Item 3, Article 18 in ACFTU (2006).

35 Gallagher (2004); Xu (2003); Wang (2003); Tong (2003).

36 It has been argued the collective bargaining/consultation system does not provide a real independent framework for regulating employment relations and that the majority of collective contracts were model agreements made between the employer and the union without direct involvement of workers or any real negotiation process (Cooke (2008a), pp. 15).

37 Taylor et al. have a different view, arguing that in the process of achieving a collective contract, whether in SOEs or non-SOEs, there is rarely any real negotiation with little substantive content contained in the contract. I believe that this conclusion is too sweeping. Because of the complicated state of China's industrial relations, it is extremely difficult to make a proper generalized judgment on the effectiveness of collective negotiations (Taylor et al. (2003), pp. 187–206).

38 The words "co-ordination" and "negotiation" instead of "bargaining" reflect the Chinese preference for a harmonious approach rather than the more confrontational attitudes that are sometimes held by western unions.

care for its employees, while the employees should strive to reach the production target and to improve the enterprise's profitability. Only by these means can the interests of both sides be maintained through co-ordination and ultimately achieve a 'win-win' solution ..."[39] Clearly, the ACFTU's leadership, following the party-state's guiding ideology of "constructing a harmonious society", wish to foster a more "win-win" harmonious atmosphere in collective bargaining at the grass roots level.[40]

This approach was in line with most unions around the world. As pointed out by Freeman and Medoff, as unions are not simple textbook monopolies but collective organizations of workers with diverse interests, they rarely set wages, unlike the monopoly firm which sets prices to maximize profits. Rather, they bargain over wages with employers. Moreover, a union's ability to raise wages is limited by the possibility that, if all else stays the same, higher union wages will induce employers to reduce employment.[41]

Some researchers reveal through case studies[42] that reasonable demands[43] were achieved through win-win style negotiation after employees were organized and showed their collective power. Some case studies demonstrated that employees' collective support was the key for union action, and that collective action not only placed pressure on management but also strengthened union power, protecting shop stewards and making them feel freer to speak for members.[44]

39 ACFTU (2007).

40 It is worth pointing out that there is significant difference between the ACFTU's guidelines and an orthodox Marxist perspective, which locates the essence of labour issues in the unequal distribution of political power and economic wealth among different social classes and strongly questions the possibility of constructing and maintaining a win-win relationship between labour and capital (Hyman (1975), pp. 10–13, 27–31).

41 Freeman and Medoff (1984), p. 6.

42 E.g. Tong (2003); Wang (2003); Han (2005).

43 This means that unions only make demands which are within the affordability of the enterprises.

44 Wang (2003).

Effective collective bargaining and daily monitoring cannot develop without active, collective power constructed on the basis of employee support. The source of employee support comes from their recognition of the union as the representative of the employees' interests and not the interests of the upper-level leaders. Only when this happens are employees willing to give collective support to the union's actions. As we saw in the last subsection, free, direct elections, which will greatly enhance employees' recognition of unions, were not the norm in China. Though some of the grass roots unions in non-SOEs started to shift their practices in this member-oriented direction, many unions did not do so. We can be only cautiously optimistic about grass roots unions' overall performance in collective bargaining and daily monitoring during the decade after 1997.

Protection of Employees' Legal Rights

Aside from the classic market mechanism of exit-and-entry,[45] the union's voice provides another mechanism for dealing with social or economic problems. "Voice" means discussing with an employer conditions that ought to be changed, rather than resigning from the job. In modern industrial economies, and particularly in large enterprises, a trade union is the vehicle for collective voice, which provides workers as a group with a means of communicating with management.[46] Therefore, unions were a useful tool for developing so-called industrial democracy.[47] Was this the situation in China?

45 The classic market mechanism is "exit-and-entry", in which individuals respond to a divergence between desired and actual social conditions by exercising freedom of choice and mobility. In the labour market, exit is synonymous with quitting, while entry consists of new hires by the firm. By leaving less desirable for more desirable jobs, individuals penalize the bad employer and reward the good, leading to an overall improvement in the efficiency of the economic system. Much economic analysis can be viewed as a detailed study of the implications of this kind of adjustment and of the extent to which it works out in real economies. As long as the exit-entry market mechanism is viewed as the only adjustment mechanism, institutions like unions are invariably seen as impediments to the optimal operation of the economy (Freeman and Medoff (1984), pp. 7–8).

46 Freeman and Medoff (1984), pp. 7–11.

47 Many capitalists and some scholars, though, oppose industrial democracy as an infringement of the right of management to manage (Brooks 1920).

MOLSS statistics show that labour disputes increased at an annual rate of 30% from the early 1990s, when China began its transition to a market economy.[48] Labour disputes were no longer as exceptional as they were previously, when most labour issues were confined to and settled within the SOE "work unit (单位)" and were rarely treated formally as disputes. Labour disputes happened every day around the country, and union cadres learnt to live with them, though they had a serious problem in identifying the unions' role in an employee's so-called "Right Protection Activities (维权活动)".[49]

On the one hand, the union was theoretically duty-bound to provide protection for an employee's legal rights. Under the ACFTU's policy of "organize and practically protect (workers') legal rights (组织起来, 切实维权)", which was issued at its 14th National Conference in 2003, unions at various levels were encouraged to be more active in employees' "Right Protection Activities (维权活动)". Admittedly, unions at all levels were taking some action. For example, most local unions established "Legal Right Protection Centres". Some hired full-time lawyers to provide legal assistance to workers in need,[50] and at the national level, the ACFTU activated a nation-wide telephone hot-line (12351), as well as a website <www.12351.org.cn> for legal consultation on dispute matters.[51]

On the other hand, local unions were a solid reporting line leading to the local party committee. In a political system which appraised local official performance by GDP growth in their areas of responsibility, local

48 Research Institute of MOLSS (2004b).

49 "Right Protection Activities (维权活动)" is a commonly found term in recent years. It refers to those activities organized spontaneously, outside the traditional official system, by a specific group of people in an attempt to defend their own legal rights through various measures, such as legal actions, appeals, and demonstrations etc.

50 According to the data released by the ACFTU, by the end of 2005, there were 3,856 legal assistance offices in various levels of unions, with more than 10,000 staff and 669 full-time union lawyers (as quoted by "Union Legal Assistance Become Systemized" (in Chinese), *Workers' Daily*, "工会法律援助渐成体系", 工人日报, 30 January 2007).

51 Information from the official website <www.12351.org.cn> (last accessed on 20 January 2009).

party branches and government administration had more incentive to create a looser business environment so as to attract capital and enliven the local economy.[52] As a consequence, grass roots unions were sandwiched between employees and superior official organs, being in the embarrassing position of trying to please both sides, often without success. It was not uncommon to find union cadres standing on the side of capital and local authority instead of their members when "negotiating" with employees in labour disputes. In extreme cases workers sued union cadres for their inaction or inappropriate action.[53]

That is the reason why many scholars[54] do not believe that China's unions played a significant role in protecting workers' legal rights.[55] Though some union cadres tried genuinely to do so while others only tried to make workers believe that they did so, there were probably many more officials who simply sat idle and kept out of trouble.[56] According to a survey, workers in disputes tended to seek help from governmental departments and the media rather than from their unions.[57]

52 "Why There Is Competition among Local Governments" (in Chinese), *21st Century Economic Report*, "中国的地方政府间竞争何以如此突出", 21世纪经济报道, 13 July 2006.

53 "Workers Sue Union Chair for His Inaction" (in Chinese), *Guangzhou Daily*, "工会主席不作为我支持工人告他", 广州日报, 16 November 2006.

54 For example, Chan (2002); Chen (2003); Feng (2006); Han (2005); Leung (2002); Qi (2004); Zhang (2003) etc.

55 Cooke argues that, while some local union authorities claim that industrial relations tend to be less problematic in enterprises with a union than those without one, this seemingly better industrial relations climate should not necessarily be seen as the positive outcome of unionism. Rather, it may be that enterprises that recognize unions are those which have better employment relations in the first place, with or without unions, and that union recognition is "icing on the cake", i.e. a by-product of the good enterprise climate (Cooke (2008a), p. 132).

56 As pointed out by Howell, union officials, straddled uncomfortably between these two sets of often conflicting interests (of the members and of the party-state), have responded to disputes in diverse and ambiguous ways (Howell (1998), pp. 164–69).

57 Xu and Shi (2006).

Whether in times of peace or trouble, the dilemma of grass roots unions' conflicting roles leads to a further question: if there was no reform in the union system at the macro level,[58] was there any significant improvement in the union model as a consequence of reforms such as grass roots union elections at the micro level? The relevant literature[59] suggests that when problems were confined within specific enterprises, for example collective bargaining on a specific labour contract, reforms at the micro level helped improve the unions' operation. However, grass roots reforms did little to solve problems which were beyond the scope of individual enterprises. Such problems include the treatment of systematically laid-off workers in SOEs, legal procedures for labour dispute settlement, and interference from local governments.

In summary, grass roots union reforms made some progress after the 1990s, especially the improvement of union representation by means of limited direct election at the workplace level. However, the operational systems of higher level unions were not reformed in accordance with those of the grass roots unions,[60] so that many issues were not resolved. Therefore, the policy of reform at the grass roots level, while keeping the macro level union system untouched, resulted in the predicament that upper level unions, with the backing of the party-state, are a major barrier to further union reforms at the workplace level. This suggests that the union representation and responsibility issues were not solved at the workplace level, though it is always possible that grass roots union reform will trigger or force the reform of upper level unions.

58 For example, the Union Law has technically placed the union in the position of mediator and arbitrator, rather than the representative of the workers; and as pointed out previously (with more to be touched upon in Chapter 7), union cadres see it as their duty, first and foremost, to follow the interest of the party-state and distance themselves from worker members when they decide to take collective action.

59 For example, Chen (2003a and 2003b); Feng (2006); Tong (2003); Wang (2003); Han (2005).

60 I.e. the ACFTU and its branches above the workplace level remain to be run in a top-down manner in contrast to the gradually more bottom-up working style in the grass roots unions.

3.2 Employers

Management styles are connected with the cultural and economic contexts in which firms operate. Marginson and Sisson categorize companies into two types of ownership and control systems: the Anglo-American "outsider" system and the European-Japanese "insider" system. They argue that the former is characterised by higher degrees of institutional share ownership and emphasis on short-term returns, while the latter is characterised by interlinked corporate, institutional and/or family shareholdings, less-developed stock markets, and emphasis on long-run performance. Marginson and Sisson also maintain that, in these circumstances, the "insider" system is more likely to encourage its managers to treat their staff as long-term assets than the "outsider" system.[61]

However, China's case is much more complicated, with neither an "insider" nor "outsider" but rather a unique "mixed" system. After "Reform and Open-door" policies began after 1978, and especially since 1992, Chinese enterprises have become more and more diverse. Industrial relations practices ranging from infamous "sweat shops" to highly modernized enterprises applying human resource concepts exist simultaneously, though they are distributed unevenly. The complexity and variety of China's industrial relations landscape has often confused researchers, causing difficulties for the study of industrial relations.

Besides external factors such as the economic and political environment, the enterprise's internal characteristics also directly impact upon employer behaviour. These characteristics can be divided into two categories. First, on the employer's side, operational scale and ownership type determine an employer's basic behaviour. Secondly, on the employee's side, the specific social-economic stratum to which an employee belongs[62]

61 Marginson and Sisson (1994).

62 For example, whether an employee is a blue-collar or a white-collar worker, whether an employee is an urban resident or a migrant worker from the rural area etc. Refer to the discussion in the next chapter.

also directly affects an employer's attitude towards and treatment of the employee. We discuss the latter factor in the next chapter. In this section, we focus on the former.

Operational scale and ownership type profoundly affect the industrial relations practices of employers in China. Most of the industrial relations literature pays insufficient attention to this matter. In the minority of studies that do consider it, the focus is usually limited to a specific ownership type.[63] As pointed out by Cooke, "there have been relatively few studies that examined the industrial relations in China ... and even fewer that examined whether they demonstrated characteristics distinct to ownership type and size of undertaking."[64]

Therefore, I propose to use "Operation Scale" and "Ownership Type" as two dimensions for differentiating Chinese enterprises. Following the analysis in Chapters Two to Four, which focuses on the situation of industrial relations actors rather than interactions among them, in this section we introduce only the basic situation of these employers, leaving the discussion of relations between the employer and various industrial relations actors to Chapters Five and Six.

3.2.1 Operation Scale of Employers

Scholars propose different standards for determining the operational scale of an enterprise. Cunningham and Rowley summarized various international definitions in which different criteria, such as the numbers employed, volume of output or sales, value of assets, and even energy consumption, are used.[65] The standard used by the NBS, however, is the most authoritative in China and is thus followed in most Chinese research. The NBS defines a "large enterprise" as one that simultaneously meets the following three

63 For example, Liu (2004); Chen (2003); Yu (2006); Lee (1998) focus their research on SOEs, while Wang (2003) and Tong (2003) focus their research on JVs, and Xu (2003) focuses his research on POEs.

64 Cooke (2008a), p. 112.

65 Cunningham and Rowley (2008), pp. 354–56.

criteria: first, 2,000 or more employees; second, annual sales volume of RMB 300 million (AUD 60 million) or greater; and third, total asset value of RMB 400 million (AUD 80 million) or greater. All other enterprises are defined by the NBS as medium/small enterprises.[66]

According to the NBS census data in 2004, there were 46,610 large enterprises operating in China, making up only 1.4% of the total, while 3,202,732 medium/small enterprises made up the remaining 98.6%.[67] However, it is worth pointing out that these numbers do not include so-called "Individual Household Business Units (个体户)", which were usually below the scale of 8–12 people and clearly belong to the medium/small enterprise category.[68] There were no precise statistics of "Individual Household Business Units (个体户)",[69] but according to figures released by the State Administration for Industry and Commerce (SAIC, 国家工商局), the estimate was around 25 million in 2006.[70] Therefore, for the sake of accuracy the official term "all Chinese enterprises" is more precisely "all Chinese enterprises formally registered under the Corporation Law".[71] If we take the number of "Individual Household Business Units" into consideration, medium/small enterprises made up 99.8% of all Chinese enterprises.

66 "New Standard Higher the Entrance Requirement for Large Enterprises" (in Chinese), *Guangming Daily*, 12 September 2003, available at <http://news.xinhuanet.com/newscenter/2003-09/12/content_1078593.htm> (last accessed on 6 January 2009).

67 NBS (2005).

68 According to the Chinese regulation, "Individual Household Business Units" are not considered as enterprises. Theoretically, their operation should be based on self-employed individuals and their family members, and the maximum number of employees should not exceed eight; but in reality, it is not uncommon to find some "Individual Household Business Units" employing dozens of people.

69 The NBS announced that "Individual Household Business Units" would be taken into account when the second economic census was conducted in 2008 (CCTV news report, 10 November 2007).

70 Data as quoted by "Monopoly is the Accelerator for the Disappearance of Individual Household Business Units" (in Chinese), *Chinese Youth Paper*, "垄断是650万个体户消失的加速器", 中国青年报, 18 September 2007.

71 Hereafter abbreviated to "all formally registered Chinese enterprises".

Large enterprises were distributed unevenly across the country, with over 60% located in the four maritime provinces of Shandong, Guangdong, Jiangsu and Zhejiang. It is worth noting that, though the national ratio between SOE and non-SOE large enterprises was around 50–50, in the four maritime provinces the number of non-SOE large enterprises significantly exceeded that of their SOE counterparts. The percentages of non-SOE large enterprises were, respectively, 81.3% for both Guangdong and Zhejiang Provinces, 64.7% for Jiangsu Province and 53% for Shandong Province.[72]

The NBS' census data also showed that large enterprises provided 41.4% of all employment opportunities, while medium/small enterprises accounted for 58.6%.[73] For the same reason as discussed above, these numbers are problematic, because the census took into account only jobs provided by formally registered companies with formal labour contracts, so that the 166 million jobs recorded in the census excluded employment provided by the "Individual Household Business Units (个体户)" as well as those in formal medium/small enterprises but without formal labour contracts. According to official data, total employment in 2006 was 764 million.[74] If we deduct the 286.31 million employed in rural primary industry,[75] the total employment in non-primary industry should be around 478 million. If the two sets of data are combined, the total picture is very different. As management practices in large enterprises were relatively formal, we may accept the census number regarding jobs in large enterprises of 68.7 million. Dividing this number by 478 million, we find that jobs in large enterprises might have made up only around 14% of all employment.

In summary, 99.8% of Chinese enterprises were medium/small scale and provided around 86% of employment. Therefore, it is necessary to pay special attention to medium/small enterprises when researching labour issues in China.

72 NBS (2005).

73 Ibid.

74 NBS and MOLSS (2007), disc edition, Table 1.1.

75 NBS (2007), on-line edition, Table 5.2.

3.2.2 Ownership Type of Employers

In China's model of a mixed economy, there were five major enterprise ownership types: State (Collectively) Owned Enterprises, Privately Owned Enterprises, Joint-ventures, Direct Subsidiaries of Multi-national Companies and General Foreign Invested Enterprises. This categorization was based largely on the "Regulations on Dividing Enterprises' Registration Type",[76] issued jointly in 1998 by the NBS and the State Administration for Industry and Commerce (SAIC).

In the decade after the Regulation was promulgated China has undergone significant economic change. Some of the regulations no longer accurately reflect the state of socio-economic development. However, because the Regulation remains in effect, and most of the statistics and research in China continue to follow its standards, we have little choice but to accept its definition of specific sub-groups. Nevertheless, we will categorize enterprises in a different manner.[77] We explain below the specific definitions of ownership types and their respective basic situations.

State (Collectively) Owned Enterprises

State (Collectively) Owned Enterprises,[78] for the purpose of this book, include State-owned Enterprises (国有企业), Collectively-owned Enterprises (集体企业) and State-wholly-owned Companies (国有独资公司), as described in the Regulation:

1. State-owned Enterprises are enterprises whose assets all belong to the state.

76 In this section, abbreviated to "the Regulation".

77 I re-categorize the enterprise ownership types. For example, the State (Collectively) Owned Enterprises (SOEs) include State-owned Enterprises (国有企业), Collectively-owned Enterprises (集体企业), and State-wholly-owned Companies (国有独资公司), as described in the Regulation. However, for each sub-group, I follow the standards in the Regulation.

78 Hereafter abbreviated to "SOEs".

2. Collectively-owned Enterprises are enterprises whose assets belong to the collective.
3. State-wholly-owned Companies are limited companies wholly owned by state investment organizations or state authorized departments.

According to the NBS census data in 2004, 16% of all formally registered Chinese enterprises,[79] or around 519,895 in number (16% of 3,249,342), belonged to the SOE sector. These SOEs had absorbed RMB 10.1 trillion (AUD 2 trillion) of state capital, amounting to 56% of all capital in formally registered Chinese enterprises.[80] As SOEs not only had access to enormous government funding but were also protected by various regulatory measures, they often gained monopolistic or oligopolistic advantages and occupied top ranking positions in their industries. For example, the sixteen Chinese mainlander enterprises enlisted in Fortune 500 in 2007 version were all SOEs,[81] while 69.8% of the China's own Top 500 enterprises in 2007 were SOEs.[82]

However, the influence of SOEs in the labour market declined dramatically after 1978, and especially after 1992. As mentioned in the previous chapter, the weight of SOE employment (percentage of total non-primary industry employment) dropped from 99% in 1978 to 92.5% in 1992, then to 20% in 2002, while in the second quarter of 2006, SOEs provided only 8.2% of new job opportunities.[83] In Cooke's opinion, the sharp decline of employment in the state sector was achieved mainly through down-sizing, plant closure and privatization of SOEs as part of the state-driven reform. Beginning in the early 1990s with the aim of revitalizing outmoded and largely loss-making SOEs, the momentum of SOE reform reached its peak

79 As discussed earlier, this number did not include the so-called "Individual Household Businesses (个体户)".

80 NBS (2005).

81 Official website of Fortune China: <http://www.fortunechina.com/fortune500/index.htm> (last accessed on 20 January 2009).

82 Official website of CEC-CEDA: <http://www.cec-ceda.org.cn/huodong/2007china500/11.htm> (last accessed on 20 January 2009).

83 Refer back to discussions in sub-section 2.1.2 of Chapter 2.

in the late 1990s after the then Premier Zhu Rongji announced a SOE reform plan in 1997. In the ensuing five-year period between 1998 and 2002, over 27 million workers were laid off.[84] Clearly, there was a huge disparity between the SOEs' input and contribution to the labour market, at least, as far as the capital they absorbed and the employment they provided were concerned.[85]

Privately Owned Enterprises

Privately Owned Enterprises (POEs), in this book, include Stock Co-operative Enterprises (股份合作企业) and Stock-holding Limited Companies (股份有限公司),[86] as well as the general Privately Owned Enterprises described in the Regulation:

1. Stock Co-operative Enterprises are based on a co-operative mechanism and are invested in mainly by employees, with a certain percentage of investment from society;
2. Stock-holding Limited Companies issue shares on the stock market. Share-holders' liabilities are limited by their investments, and the company's liability is the extent of its assets;
3. Privately Owned Enterprises are established by and invested in by individual partnerships, employing labour in pursuit of profit.

84 Cooke (2008b), pp. 2–3.

85 This is further evidence that China needs continuous efforts in SOE reform to reduce further the number of inefficient SOEs.

86 These enterprises are mostly securitized SOEs which were transformed into essentially private enterprises; but there are also some Stock-holding Companies which are privately owned from the very beginning. According to Guo's study, about 80% of the transformed medium-small size SOEs were sold to management. In these cases, the original SOE cadres became private owners of the enterprises. The remaining 20% were purchased by other investors. Whatever their origin, the employees of these completely transformed SOEs, if not made redundant, became employed workers of real private enterprises (Guo 2006).

According to the NBS census data for 2004, there were about 2.5 million formally registered POEs operating in China.[87] As discussed earlier, this number did not include the 25 million "Individual Household Business Units (个体户)", which apparently belonged to the POE sector. If we take them into account, the POEs would have made up 97.4% of all Chinese enterprises.

The POE is by far the fastest developing enterprise type in contemporary China. Between 1956[88] and 1978, the entire private enterprise category disappeared completely. After 1978 POEs sprang up rapidly, developing vigorously though unevenly throughout the economy. After the late 1990s, the growth trend was even stronger, with double digit annual growth rates in registration, number of employees and registered capital.[89] According to 2004 data, around 117 million people were employed in formally registered private enterprises, accounting for about 29% of all employees in non-primary industries.[90] It is estimated that, in addition, there were about 100 million people working casually, most of whom were employed by medium/small size POEs or the "Individual Household Business Units (个体户)". These casual workers were not included in formal enterprise statistics, but if they are taken into account, the POE sector actually provided over 50% of jobs in non-primary industries. According to a report issued by MOLSS, in the second quarter of 2006, POEs provided about 79.8% of new job opportunities.[91]

87 As the definition of POE differs between this book and the official document, the number here is calculated on the basis of NBS (2005).

88 1956 was the year when the so-called "Socialistic Transformation of Capitalistic Enterprises" was completed.

89 Medium-small Enterprise Research Centre, Social Science Academy of China (2005).

90 NBS (2005).

91 MOLSS (2006).

Joint-ventures

Joint-ventures (JVs) in this book include Joint-Investment Enterprises (Hongkong/Macau/Taiwan Capital), Joint-Investment Enterprises (Foreign Capital), Joint-Co-operation Enterprises (Hongkong/Macau/Taiwan Capital), and Joint-Co-operation Enterprises (Foreign Capital), as described in the Regulation:

1. Joint-Investment Enterprises (Hongkong/Macau/Taiwan Capital) are established by Hongkong/Macau/Taiwan investors with mainland enterprises on the basis of the "Joint-Investment Enterprise Law of PRC";
2. Joint-Investment Enterprises (Foreign Capital) are established by foreign investors with mainland enterprises on the basis of the "Joint-Investment Enterprise Law of PRC";
3. Joint-Co-operation Enterprises (Hongkong/Macau/Taiwan Capital) are established by Hongkong/Macau/Taiwan investors with mainland enterprises on the basis of the "Joint-Co-operation Enterprise Law of PRC";
4. Joint-Co-operation Enterprises (Foreign Capital) are established by foreign investors with mainland enterprises on the basis of the "Joint-Co-operation Enterprise Law of PRC".

Many joint-ventures were products of either earlier reforms or regulations which constrained the magnitude of foreign investment in certain industries. During the early stage of the "Open-door policy", the Chinese government decided that in order to control the operations of foreign companies in China, foreign investments would be confined to joint ventures with local, state partners.[92] For example, in the automotive manufacturing industry, foreign investors could have no more than 50% of the share. Therefore, they had to establish JVs with Chinese partners, usually SOEs, if they intended

92 Cooke (2006), p. 109.

to enter the Chinese market.[93] According to the data released by the SAIC, by the end of 2007, 106,000 JVs operated in China, making up 37% of foreign investment related enterprises, 3% less than in 2006.[94]

Direct Subsidiaries of Multi-national Companies

This enterprise type is not listed separately but treated simply as FIEs in the Regulation. However, taking into consideration MNCs' unique operational model and its significant difference from the general category of Foreign-Invested Enterprises (FIEs), we single out Direct Subsidiaries of MNCs as an individual ownership type. Direct Subsidiaries of MNCs refers to the subsidiaries of large multi-national companies[95] which were established and registered in China on the basis of the "Foreign Invested Enterprise Law of PRC".

When large, multi-national companies invest in a national economy, the exemplary and downstream effects impact significantly. Therefore, central and local governments were very active in attracting more investment from large multi-national companies.

According to data released by MOC, in 2005, 94% (470 in number) of the Fortune 500 companies had established over 3,000 subsidiaries. Over 90% of these direct subsidiaries of multi-national companies were in the eastern coastal areas, in particular Shanghai, Guangdong, Beijing, Jiangsu, Tianjin, Liaoning, and Shandong.[96] More than 55% of MNC investments were in capital and/or technology-intensive industries, such as electronics, telecommunication, machine manufacturing, chemical production etc.[97]

93 For the most updated detail restrictions on foreign investment in a specific industry, refer to NDRC and MOC (2004). The Chinese government now permits 100% foreign ownership in most industries and the number of new wholly owned foreign subsidiaries surpassed that of equity joint ventures for the first time in 1998 (Cooke (2006), p. 109).

94 Information from SAIC's official website: <http://www.saic.gov.cn/zwxxq/zwdt/zyfb/t20080310_32681.htm> (last accessed on 19 January 2009).

95 There is no absolute definition of a large multi-national company. However, we may use the widely publicized Fortune 500 as a reference.

96 Among these areas, Beijing and Shanghai are the most favoured for the MNCs' regional headquarters, with more than 95% of headquarters being located in these cities.

97 MOC (2007).

General Foreign Invested Enterprises

General Foreign Invested Enterprises (FIEs) include Hongkong/Macau/Taiwan Capital Invested Enterprises and Foreign Capital Invested Enterprises[98] as described in the Regulation:

1. Hongkong/Macau/Taiwan Capital Invested Enterprises are wholly invested in and owned by Hongkong/Macau/Taiwan investors on the basis of the "Foreign Invested Enterprise Law of PRC";
2. Foreign Capital Invested Enterprises are wholly invested and owned by foreign investors on the basis of the "Foreign Invested Enterprise Law of PRC".

China was one of the two largest foreign direct investment (FDI) recipient economies in the world during the period 2000–5.[99] According to NBS census data in 2004, FIEs made up about 5.4% of all formally registered Chinese enterprises (around 152,000 in number), and about 94% of FIEs were medium/small enterprises. However, 6% of large FIEs provided 50.7% of jobs in this sector.[100]

The majority of these FIEs draw their capital from Hongkong, Macau, Taiwan or other Asian countries such as Japan, Korea, and Singapore. By the end of 2007, over 70% of FIEs came from these Asian countries and territories. Hongkong, a part of China since 1997, was still treated as "foreign-related" in the statistics and was ranked number one in the FIE sector, with 106,000 enterprises and capital investment of USD 405 billion. Manufacturing accounted for 67.4% of the FIEs. Most were labour-intensive manufacturing companies catering to outsourced "OEM (Original Equipment Manufacturer, 外包代工厂)" production for international markets.[101] According to data issued by the former MFTEC, in 2002 FIEs

98 But excluding the Direct Subsidiaries of MNCs as discussed above.

99 *International Statistics Yearbook* (2004) as quoted by Cooke (2006), p. 105. The United States remained the largest foreign direct investment (FDI) recipient over the years.

100 NBS (2005).

101 Information from SAIC's official website: <http://www.saic.gov.cn/zwxxq/zwdt/zyfb/t20080310_32681.htm> (last accessed on 19 January 2009).

accounted for 52.2% of China's exports.[102] MOC estimated that around 25 million people worked in FIEs.[103] This estimate seems questionable, however. If we divide 152,000 FIEs by 25 million workers, the average employment in a FIE was merely 165 workers, which seems unlikely because FIEs were mostly labour-intensive manufacturing companies. A possible reason for the probable under-estimation of numbers is that MOC took only workers with formal labour contracts into consideration.

Conclusions

In this chapter, we discussed two institutional industrial relations actors at micro level, namely, grass roots unions and employers.

First, the positioning, roles and functions of the ACFTU and grass roots unions became quite different in the context of China's transition towards a market economy. Measures were taken to reform grass roots unions so as to match the external changes. However, the authorities held a complex attitude towards direct election reform in grass roots unions, knowing that they are a two-edged sword. Because grass roots unions were sandwiched between employees and superior official organs, it is questionable whether they played a significant role in protecting workers' legal rights, no matter whether elected by members or appointed by authorities.

Second, after 1992, Chinese employers became more diverse, ranging from infamous "sweat shops" to highly modernized enterprises applying human resource concepts. We argued that, besides external factors such as the business and political environment, an enterprise's internal characteristics, in particular its operational scale and ownership type were even more significant in impacting directly on industrial relations behaviour. Therefore, we identified "operation scale" and "ownership type" as two

102 As quoted by Jin (2003).
103 MOC (2007).

dimensions for differentiating Chinese enterprises. Based on this model, we outlined the general situation among various types of employers. Later discussion in which the diversity of enterprise types is taken into account will show that the classification of enterprises relates significantly to industrial relations practices in China.

CHAPTER FOUR

The Chinese Employee Class

Introduction

In the last chapter we identified and discussed two major institutional actors in China's micro-level industrial relations system, the grass roots unions and employers. In this chapter, we shift the focus to individual actors at the workplace level, the employees.

As Shen pointed out, after the international community recognised that China had become the "world's factory", the sociological significance of this was clear enough. The world's biggest "employee class" had emerged in China.[1] As to the magnitude of this economic class, according to official data, by the end of 2006 the economically active population in China's non-primary industries was around 478 million.[2] Except for a few business owners and the self-employed, the majority of this population belonged to the employee class. Furthermore, it is estimated that for the past few years, the net growth of the working population was around 20 million annually.[3] Therefore, the total working population in China's non-primary industries in 2008 was approximately 500 million. Who, then, are in the employee class? How is this class stratified? What is its situation in contemporary industrial relations? This chapter attempts to answer these questions.

1 Shen (2006).
2 Calculation is based on NBS and MOLSS (2007), disc edition, Table 1.1 and on NBS (2007), on-line edition, Table 5.2.
3 MOLSS (2007).

4.1 The Concept of the Employee and Stratification of the Chinese Employee Class

The concept of "employee" needs first to be clarified. According to one definition, an employee is someone who is employed by other people and relies on the employment payment as the major income source.[4] We narrow the definition to focus only on enterprise employees, not taking into account public servants, the military and employees in other semi-governmental organs.[5] In this case, the number of enterprise employees is around 425 million.[6]

Clarification is also needed of the relationship between the terms "working class" and "employee". In previous decades, in China, as well as in other (former) "socialist" countries, the term "working class" was a political concept with special meaning. In the Marxian canon, "working class" refers mainly to production (industrial) workers, which excludes management and technical professionals.[7] The CCP, however, developed

4 Liu et al. (2005), p. 9.

5 According to the Research Institute of MOLSS (2004a), government-related employees constitute about 15% of the total working population in China. There are surely industrial relations issues in managing the many government employees, such as clerks. But as most government-related employees are CCP members and therefore are allied with the party-state as a "common body of interest (利益共同体)", their employment relations with the "employer" (the party-state) are essentially political rather than industrial in the usual sense. Limited by space, I cannot deal with this group in this book.

6 I.e., 85% of the 500 million working population in China is roughly 425 million.

7 This is a highly debated topic, as Marx himself did not clearly define who is within the working class. In his most famous and programmatic document, the Manifesto of the Communist Party, he stated: "... Society as a whole is more and more splitting up into two great hostile camps, into two great classes, directly facing each other: Bourgeoisie and Proletariat ... The bourgeoisie has stripped of its halo every occupation hitherto honoured and looked up to with reverent awe. It has converted the physician, the lawyer, the priest, the poet, the man of science, into its paid wage labourers ..." From this description, it seems that Marx meant to include technical professionals in the working class. However, elsewhere in the Manifesto as well as in

a new concept of "working class" to include not only industrial workers but also business service staff, enterprise management, military staff and state cadres. Intellectuals were also included after the Cultural Revolution.[8] To some extent, the term "working class", at least in the context of official ideological discourse, can be regarded as an artificially created political concept, intended to provide legitimacy for the CCP's rule. Therefore, the term contains more symbolic than real meaning in China.[9] All employees are, theoretically, part of the "working class",[10] while some members of the "working class", such as certain enterprise managers, state cadres, and intellectuals are not necessarily employees in the strict sense.[11] Therefore, to avoid confusion, we shall try to avoid the term "working class". Where it is used, it will be in quotation marks, meaning that it is a special political concept with "Chinese characteristics".

We can now discuss the stratification of enterprise employees in China's contemporary industrial relations. Clearly, a social group as huge as 425 million people cannot be treated simply as a single whole. How should we disaggregate it to provide more specific and meaningful descriptions of various sub-groups?

Capital, his discussion revolved around industrial workers. The question as to who other than industrial workers can be considered as a part of the "working class" has been a long-debated theoretical topic in all "socialistic" countries.

8 Xu and Shi (2007).

9 "Seminar on China's Macro Economy and Reform Development Trends (Summary Notes)" (in Chinese), Internal Papers, "中国宏观经济与改革走势座谈会纪要", 内部资料, 4 March 2006.

10 Theoretically, but not necessarily so in reality, for example, the "rural migrant employees (农民工)", whom we discuss in the coming subsection, are already employed as industrial workers, but are still considered as rural population and hence treated as "peasant class" in China because of the longstanding "residency registration (hukou, 户口)" system.

11 This issue is complex. Mid/low level enterprise managers, state cadres and intellectuals generally fit the definition of employee; but high-end enterprise managers and state cadres usually enjoy stock options or allowances which are substantially higher than their salaries, and some intellectuals have intellectual property income which is substantially higher than their salaries. Such people cannot usefully be considered as employees.

In the relevant literature, only a few authors analyse the stratification of the Chinese enterprise employee class. Three major propositions are offered by scholars. Ping, taking into consideration the enterprise ownership issue, argues that SOE employees should be distinguished from non-SOE employees.[12] Shen, taking into account the issues of "differences between urban and rural areas (城乡差别)", proposes the stratification of "new workers" migrating from rural areas in contrast to the "old workers" in SOEs.[13] Liu advocates the stratification of the employee class in terms of mental or physical labour.[14] Recognizing the meaningfulness of all of these approaches, we utilize them for our classification, but with certain revision and development.

The first revision concerns the second stratification approach. Shen's vague distinction between "new workers" and "old workers" (which refer to migrant workers originally from rural areas and SOE workers respectively) entails a logical problem because some employees (e.g. urban non-SOE workers) are neither "new" nor "old" workers according to this definition. We therefore replace Shen's distinction between "new" and "old" workers with one between "rural migrant employees" and "urban employees".

Our second, relatively minor and somewhat semantic, revision is to change Liu's old-style expressions "mental labourers" and "physical labourers" to the more common concepts of "white-collar" and "blue-collar" employees.

Thus we investigate employee situations from three perspectives: rural migrant employees vs. urban employees; SOE employees vs. non-SOE employees; and white-collar employees vs. blue-collar employees.[15] Chinese employees can thus be segmented by these three dimensions. In the following sections, we will discuss these three major dichotomies of employees and their respective situations in China's contemporary industrial relations.

12 Ping (2005).

13 Shen (2006).

14 Liu et al. (2005).

15 We should note, however, that the three stratifications overlap. For example, an employee, originally from rural areas, who is a blue-collar worker in a private company has simultaneously the characteristics of a "non-SOE employee", a "rural migrant employee", and a "blue-collar employee".

4.2 Rural Migrant Employees vs. Urban Employees

The first period of Chinese labour market development, from the mid-1950s to 1979, was a highly regulated, or more precisely, controlled, labour market through administrative policy under the state planned economy.[16] Labour mobility was highly restricted, monitored by the "residency registration (hukou, 户口)" system, which classified people as either "urban residency registration holders (城市户口居民)" or "rural residency registration holders (农村户口居民)". By this means, China established a kind of "social closure (社会屏蔽)" that prevented the majority of the Chinese population, the rural residency registration holders,[17] from sharing social resources in urban areas. Though the system was loosened after 1979, it is still legally in effect, affecting the lives of every mainlander Chinese.[18]

Before reforms started in 1979, China had a planned economy which did not allow space for a real labour market. The state was responsible for assigning labour, and work units normally did not have a say in recruitment or lay-off. The purpose of this system was not to optimize labour as a "resource" but to ensure "100% employment". This was due to the notion that under socialism there is no unemployment and government should make efforts to expand employment and create jobs for its people.[19] In particular, in urban areas, the "planning committee (计委)" produced labour quotas for Labour Departments and the Labour Department worked out detailed recruitment arrangements for each enterprise. In rural areas, the practice was a kind of "natural employment (自然就业)", which meant that rural youth automatically became members of the "people's commune (人民公社)" and participated in collective farming work, except for those having very rare opportunities such as entering university, being recruited

16 Cooke (2008b), p. 1.

17 According to official data, rural population made up 82% of total population in 1978 (before reform); this percentage has been in a continuous downward trend, descending to 56% in 2006 (NBS 2007, on-line data, Table 4.1).

18 Li (2004), pp. 28–40.

19 Zhu and Dowling (2002), p. 570.

by the army, or, even more rarely, being recruited by urban factories. Rural labourers were not allowed to seek employment in urban areas.[20]

One may even hypothesize that the state's monopoly over labour allocation and reallocation, combined with the exclusive distribution of basic resources such as food, housing and welfare, had a deeper impact on people's compliance with the socialist system than its direct political control. For this reason, Hebel and Schucher argued that changes in the organization of labour and its related institutions are of crucial importance for both economic and political systems.[21]

After 1979, rural residents, also referred to as "peasants (农民)", were allowed to work in urban areas, signifying the emergence of a labour market, though at a very preliminary stage. Before 1992, however, most urban residents worked in SOEs. Therefore, even though the labour market started to emerge, there was no significant free flow of labour in the early years of reforms. During these years, rural migrant employees strove for survival outside the SOE sector. As a result, the practice of allowing the market to decide employment and, later, wages had a profound impact on the urban labour market when the economy started its transition.[22]

The period between the mid-late 1990s and 2003–4 was a time of tumultuous change for many urban workers. Employment shocks as well as shocks to traditional benefits were large and widespread,[23] while the then fledgling social security system did not provide sufficient assistance to people in need. The situation was somewhat eased in the period 2003–4, when the most painful period of SOE restructuring seemed to have passed, and there was more government input into the social security system.[24] But employees continue to confront new challenges.

20 Li (2004); Knight and Song (2005).

21 Hebel and Schucher (2006).

22 Li (2004); Knight and Song (2005).

23 The shocks were two-sided: on the one side, urban workers' "iron rice bowls" in SOEs were broken; on the other, urban workers now faced the direct competition of cheap labour from rural areas.

24 Giles et al. (2006); Ping (2005).

After the period 2003–4, the original dualistic employment system collapsed almost completely. Theoretically, China has a free labour market, where enterprises recruit people on the basis of criteria such as age, education and experience, and rarely take "residency registration (hukou, 户口)" into account.[25] According to official estimation, in 2007, there were about 200 million rural migrant employees working freely in the urban areas,[26] versus the 293.5 million urban employees.[27] Can we say, then, that there is now no difference between rural migrant employees and urban employees? The answer is not so clear-cut.

First, as a legacy of China's long-held dualistic management system, gaps between urban and rural areas remain significant, especially in matters such as education and "personal relations (guanxi, 关系)", which are both determinants of whether or not one can successfully win a job and what kind of job one can obtain.

Second, urban residents enjoy social security, public services and medical care, which are not completely open to rural migrants. These advantages give more underlying support to urban employees' bargaining power. Rural migrant employees have to accept more severe employment arrangements when confronted with basic survival issues.

Clearly, these problems cannot be solved overnight. As a result, according to official statistics, in 2007, the average income of urban residents is about 3.33 times that of rural residents; the urban-rural income gap was in fact even bigger than the number of 2.57 in 1978 (before reform).[28] It is expected, therefore that the gap between rural migrants and urban employees will continue.[29]

25 Except that in some SOEs a few positions still require "urban residency registration (城市户口)".

26 MOLSS (2007).

27 NBS and MOLSS (2008), disc edition, Table 1–1.

28 NBS (2008), Table 9–2.

29 Cai and Yang (2000); Wu and Han (2006).

The Chinese government has not been idle, however. After the widely reported "premier claiming back salaries in arrears for migrant workers"[30] incident in 2003, the party-state leadership showed more willingness to solve the problems of rural migrant employees. In March 2006, the State Council issued a document "On Solving the Issue of Peasant Workers", requiring all regions and governmental departments to remove all discriminatory regulations and restrictions against rural migrant employees, to eliminate administrative levies on enterprises when they employ rural migrant employees, and gradually to merge the rural population into the social service system, in particular the medical care and education systems.[31]

Though things have seemingly turned for the better, rural migrant employees remain a weak social group. In comparison with urban employees, rural migrant employees work longer but are usually paid less.[32] Perhaps such gaps are an unavoidable aspect of modernization and urbanization. Only after government policies are fully implemented will gaps between rural migrant employees and urban employees become less significant, which is the case in most developed countries.

4.3 SOE Employees vs. Non-SOE Employees

During almost thirty years of reforms and development, China's labour relations have undergone profound changes, with an unprecedented complexity emerging. On the one hand, marketized labour relations in the

30 On 24th October 2003, when Premier Wen Jiabao was inspecting the San Xia area, a peasant housewife complained to him that her husband's salary was kept in arrears for a year out of malice. At Premier Wen's order, the money was paid the next night. This incident was reported by New China News Agency and it triggered a nationwide "storm" for clearing arrears of pay to rural migrant employees.

31 State Council (2006).

32 Zhang (2006); Gao (2006).

non-SOE sector have gradually become dominant,[33] while on the other hand, aspects of the old planned economy, particularly in the SOE sector, await further reform.[34]

Thus, the Chinese employee class can be split into two major groups: SOE employees and non-SOE employees. Their interests and requirements are distinct. Gilbert argued that there are two separate "new labour movements" in China: SOE workers protest and strike to defend their jobs, while non-SOE workers in the private/foreign-owned sector revolt against dismal conditions and despotic management.[35] Labour relations in China entail complex issues. For SOE employees, the problem is how to transfer their identities as state workers to those of marketized labourers, while for the non-SOE employees who are already in the marketized sectors the problem is to improve the power imbalance between labour and capital so as to minimize the serious violation of labour rights.[36]

4.3.1 SOE Employees

The status of "workers" under the planned economy was a political one as much as an economic one.[37] Under Maoist state socialism, Chinese workers, almost 100% working in state or collectively owned enterprises, acquired considerable social and economic entitlements, ranging from

33 According to the Research Institute of MOLSS (2004a), by 2002, the non-state-owned economy had already accounted for more than two-thirds of the GDP in China, and employees in the non-state-owned sectors constituted more than 80% of China's total economic population.

34 Former Premier Zhu Rongji, when discussing the issues of economic reform (particularly the SOE reforms) in the 9th NPC press conference, in March 1998, said: "... landmines or abyss, whatever is in front, I will persevere forward dutifully, sparing no efforts to die (不管前面是地雷阵还是万丈深渊，我都将一往无前，义无反顾，鞠躬尽瘁，死而后已) ..." The last part of Zhu Rongji's comment is actually a quotation from an ancient Chinese politician, signifying his determination to confront various possible political dangers when he launched the SOE reforms.

35 Gilbert (2005).

36 Research Institute of MOLSS (2004a).

37 Cooke (2008b), p. 6.

lifetime employment to substantial benefits including low-cost housing, health care, pensions, and education,[38] but they did not enjoy real and meaningful civil and political rights. The government installed a paternalist system in SOEs that provided an institutional guarantee of workers' economic status as well as a mechanism of controlling workers through "organized dependence".[39]

When reform began, state policy was to convert SOE employees' identity as state workers to that of marketized labourers by giving them economic compensation to leave SOEs. For the minority that remained, the objective was to convert their identity as permanent state employees to that of workers with term contracts.[40] This was the origin of the "lay-off tide (下岗潮)" which hit SOE workers' during the late 1990s and early 2000s, as reformed SOEs needed many fewer workers than were employed originally.[41] The once relatively harmonious management-labour relationship[42] was replaced with one that was characterized by conflicting interests, rising disputes and increasing inequality in contractual arrangements between management and labour.[43] In the context of significant job reduction in the SOEs, "preserving the rice bowl (保饭碗)" was the theme of SOE labour relations during the period 1997 to 2004.

On-going reforms in SOEs after 1987 resulted in profound changes to the employment relationships between workers and their state employers.

38 Such employment status in SOEs was termed in Chinese "the three irons (三铁)", referring to the iron rice bowl (铁饭碗), the iron chair/position (铁交椅) and the iron wage (铁工资). In addition, work units (单位) offered permanent employees a cradle to grave, enterprise-based welfare system, which was even more comprehensive than in the conventional Eastern European model. A large number of SOEs could be referred to as "mini welfare states", as their functions extended well beyond production and business to include subsidized housing, leisure activities and facilities and social security benefits (Zhu and Warner (2000), pp. 118–19).

39 Chen (2007), p. 62.

40 Research Institute of MOLSS (2004a).

41 As we have seen in the last section's discussion, the purpose of the original "socialistic" labour system was not to optimize labour as a "resource" but to ensure "100% employment", leading to the existence of many redundant state employees in the SOEs.

42 At least, it superficially seems to be so.

43 Cooke (2008b), p. 11.

Most notable were the end of employment security and reduction in workplace welfare provisions. These changes undermined, and in some cases practically ended, the paternalistic bond between state employer and its workers.[44] Researchers investigating the responses of SOE employees to SOE reforms labelled those responses "Non-Collective Action (无集体行动)",[45] "Collective Action under ideas of 'Moral Economics' or 'Protection by Ideological Justification' (道德经济学/ 以理维权下的有集体行动)",[46] or "Collective Inaction (集体无行动)".[47] Though these three

44 Cooke (2008b), p. 7.

45 By analysing material derived from interviews in five SOEs (all of which had gone through some kind of ownership transformation) in four cities, Liu (2003) concluded that most SOE workers choose the option categorized as "Non-Collective Action (无集体行动)" (this means that they more often avoid collective action by exiting the enterprise, or complying with the management, or appealing individually to upper authority). The underlying rationale in workers' minds is the "Logic of Obeying the Rule (守法逻辑)". Liu argues that this logic has two aspects: 1. some workers recognize the legitimacy of the reforms and therefore find no reason for collective action; 2. other workers are aware of possible punishment for collective action and therefore choose to obey.

46 Chen (2003b, 2006) argued that SOE workers are resistant to enterprise transformation, because they believe that many enterprise transformations completely remove workers' rights of participation, ignore their basic interests, and even intrude upon their legal rights. Workers support "Collective Action", according to Chen's research in Shang-hai and Luo-yang, and to some cases revealed by the *Worker's Daily*. Labour actions of this sort remain largely "moral economy" oriented. Protesting workers, in other words, are locked into the concept of rights inherited from the past, and attempt to redress perceived injustices by recourse to the norms of the old days, rather than by seeking to redefine and contest their rights in the new property relations. This attitude exposes the political and institutional constraints in workers' consciousness and on their ability to define and defend their interests in the economic transformation. But as long as the official rhetoric remains unchanged, it acts as workers' weapon against reality. "Protecting state assets" is indeed a powerful slogan that the state cannot openly rebuff. Yu (2006) supported Chen's viewpoint and reached a similar conclusion – "Protection by Ideological Justification (以理维权)" – in his unique investigation in Anyuan Mining Site. (Yu researched the Anyuan Mining Site because of its unique significance in the history of the Chinese working class and the CCP. Refer to the discussion in Chapters 6 and 7).

47 On the basis of a field visit to seventy SOE workers in Guangzhou during 1995–96, Lee (1998) analysed labour behaviour in the transitional period from the perspective

distinct interpretations have theoretical and empirical merit no single model can possibly summarize the size and complexity of China's industrial relations system. All three describe different aspects in different locations at different times.

During SOE reforms, the significance of the management team grew steadily, gradually forming a powerful vested interest group (既得利益集团) in its own right, while the position of employees at the rank-and-file level correspondingly deteriorated. In the original planned economy, labour relations in SOEs were relations between the state and individual employees, with the economic rights of labour protected by an egalitarian welfare system. That is to say, in the past, SOE managers and workers were, at least theoretically, equal "masters (主人翁)" of the enterprise. SOEs were maintained by this "spirit of masters (主人翁精神)" reaching a form of equilibrium in labour relations. Once the gap, whether economic or political, between SOE management and rank-and-file was enlarged significantly by reforms, the old relationship equilibrium in SOEs broke down. A new equilibrium, however, was not created to take its place.[48]

In the transition period starting from the mid to late-1990s, labour relations practice in SOEs has been one where rank-and-file SOE employees face "quasi-capitalist" employment under labour contracts. For management level SOE employees, the situation is more complex. Capitalist practices such as options and performance-based bonuses exist, as do the old practices of administrative orders and personnel control with state interference. As pointed out by Gallagher, the "dual" labour system is the product of the transformation of labour relations in the absence of large-scale privatization and political change.[49]

---

of class experience. She believed that "Collective Inaction (集体无行动)" described SOE workers' responses. "Collective Inaction" is demonstrated by workers' apathy, noncompliance, evasion of public duties, lack of enthusiasm, absenteeism and inefficiency in the workplace.

48 Liu (2006).

49 Gallagher (2004), p. 13.

4.3.2 Non-SOE Employees

In the marketized sectors of the economy, labour relations are complicated by dramatically disparate employer practices. Some enterprises are relatively well regulated and compliant with labour laws, but many others violate laws and invade basic labour rights. We discussed this issue in the previous chapter from the perspective of "employers".

According to the Research Institute of MOLSS, in the marketized non-SOE sector, regulation mechanisms and systems are, in general, not yet established, and power relations between labour and capital are unbalanced. Ever-increasing labour-capital conflict entails enormous hidden perils for the stability and further development of China.[50] As Knight and Song pointed out, though marketized labour relations are already dominant, the labour market is still in a very rudimentary phase.[51]

As mentioned earlier, non-SOE employees' interests and needs are distinct from those of SOE employees. For example, a survey of 1000 POE employees in Wenzhou[52] demonstrates that most private employees favour labour-capital co-operation and reject traditional socialist theories of "class struggle". Interestingly, though 78% of interviewees agreed with the necessity of forming a union, 32.5% did not know that a union already existed in their enterprise.[53] For those who were aware of the union's existence, 45.7% expressed dissatisfaction with its current secretary.[54]

The survey indicated that, while SOE workers relied on old concepts such as "rights of the working class", which had a profound effect on the "Planned Economy System (计划经济体制)" and socialist ideology, to jus-

50 Research Institute of MOLSS (2004a).

51 Knight and Song (2005).

52 Wenzhou, located in the southern part of Zhejiang province, is famous for its prosperous private sector economy.

53 This is a typical case where there are "bosses' unions", established jointly by the bosses and the local ACFTU to accomplish the top-down target of "new union set up". In many cases, these "unions" exist only in documents and statistics, without any practical operation.

54 Xu (2003).

tify their actions, non-SOE employees, with official unions rarely involved, began to develop their own awareness of a separate identity. They attempted to seek self-protection by forming unions, though they would rather co-operate with employers than be "represented" by an unreliable official organization.[55] Support for co-operation with employers may be considered a prudent, pragmatic choice by a shrewd "free economic man".[56]

Non-SOE employees expressed a greater desire to adjust labour relations with employers through co-operation,[57] and contracts were deemed to be one of the most important bases for equal co-operation in the enterprise. Thus, labour contracts ought to play a significant role in non-SOE industrial relations.[58] The Chinese government was also well aware of this. After 1994, when the labour contract system was put forward as part of the new Labour Laws,[59] the Chinese government promoted its implementation.

Scholars view the effects of the 1994 version of the labour contract system differently. Gallagher argued that it had the effect of setting a relatively equal "starting point" for all employees. It lowered life-long employment in SOEs to employment for limited terms, while simultaneously

55 Wang L. C. (2003) conducted a case study in a joint venture in Xiang-tan. This study demonstrated that, in a market economy, employees would almost inevitably come together and form their own organizations to represent their interests. Employees gain a collective self-consciousness which gradually evolves into spontaneous collective action and a request for organizational recognition. Existing grass roots unions have to respond to the challenge with a working mechanism which resolves competing interests, slowly weakening themselves as political organizations.

56 Perhaps, the best evidence for this statement is the response to the question "Are you willing to hand in 1% of your income as a union levy?" If the union really worked for the employees, 70.1% would agree to do so, but only 36.7% expressed willingness with respect to the current union (Xu 2003).

57 Of course, such co-operation is not unconditional: when necessary, the employees will exercise their right to "exit" by "voting with their feet".

58 In many cases, the labour contract is almost the only protection that a non-SOE employee can have when he/she attempts to turn to legal resolution of labour disputes.

59 The labour contract system constituted a chapter in the 1994 version Labour Law, with 20 clauses and roughly 1,700 characters. Clearly this was a very preliminary document and left much room for arguments and arbitrations.

creating a cloak of the "rule of law" for subsequent "lay-offs (下岗)"), and raised non-SOE employee protection[60] to that of clearer contracted employment relations.[61] Xu, however, argued that though China's formalized contract system may originally have had the purpose of protecting the weak, when an "officially standardized contract" was enforced, it deprived employees of the basic right to decide terms in their own contracts.[62]

Implementation of the labour contract system is often unsatisfactory in non-SOEs. According to an investigation conducted by the NPC's Standing Committee in September, 2005, less than 20% of medium/small non-SOEs, and an even lower proportion of the "Individual Household Business Units (个体户)", had labour contracts in place. For enterprises with contracts, around 60% were short-term or less than three years duration.[63]

Confronted by various problems in the implementation of the 1994 labour contract system, the Chinese government proposed revisions and intended to upgrade the system, which was only a by-product of the 1994 Labour Law, to a stand-alone law. In March 2006, it put forward a "Labour Contract Law (draft)" and in March 2006 took the unusual step of making it available for public consultation.

According to media reports, the government received more than 190,000 suggestions, most of which were from employees, when the one month consultation period ended. The most attention-grabbing incident, however, occurred on the very last day of the consultation, when the two biggest foreign investor organizations in China, the European Union Chamber of Commerce (EUCC) and the American Chamber of Commerce (ACC), handed in their suggestions and proposals. The EUCC proposed 11 revisions and argued that the new legislation would impose strict regulation on the flexibility of employers, increase production costs enormously and force foreign investors to re-consider future investment. The ACC's submission comprised 42 pages covering almost all items in the

60 Most of them originally worked without any contract.

61 Gallagher (2004), pp. 22–25.

62 Xu (2003).

63 "Breakthrough in the Labour Contract System" (in Chinese), *People's Daily*, "劳动合同制度有突破", 人民日报, 29 March 2006.

drafted law and ending with the claim that "we believe that this (legislation) will have a negative impact on China's investment environment". Other MNCs' reactions were also strong. For example, the Shanghai MNC HR Association, which represents 54 enterprises employing 260,000 people, collectively threatened to withdraw investment if the law was passed.[64]

To some extent, we can see the argument as a contest between two major streams of thought about industrial relations. Those upholding neo-classical economic ideas in favour of the "free market economy" insisted that the new law should be based on contract law and treat all parties, in theory, equally. Those upholding "neo-socialist" ideas in favour of public welfare contended that labour and capital are unequal from the very beginning, especially in such a labour-abundant economy. The imbalance is already there and the new law should increase the protection for labour in order to reach a new equilibrium in labour relations.

The argument continued for more than a year from March 2006 to June 2007 and the "Labour Contract Law (draft)" went through many revisions and was put aside for some time.[65] The law was eventually passed by the NPC Standing Committee in June 2007. The most revised section concerns the role of the union. A previous draft proposed that any amendments to work regulations must first go through the union. This was strongly opposed by employer associations. The revision only vaguely says that "any amendment of work regulation shall consult the union's opinions".[66] Furthermore, there are also technical revisions about probation periods, non-competition agreements, lay-offs and collective bargaining.[67]

64 "Foreign Investors Toughly Resist the Proposed 'Labour Contract Law'" (in Chinese), *21st Century Economic Report*, "外商强硬拒绝《劳动合同法》草案 威胁要撤资", 21世纪经济报道, 11 May 2006.

65 "China Toils Over New Labour Law", *Wall Street Journal* (Chinese Edition), "新劳动合同法好事多磨", 华尔街日报中文版, 7 May 2007.

66 Taking into account the ACFTU's characteristics as an "official union", it is not really a bad thing that the union power is restrained.

67 Interested readers can compare the draft (National People's Congress 2006) and the promulgated law (National People's Congress 2007).

Despite the revisions, the final version of the new law provides legal protection for weak labour. It deals specifically with the most commonly found labour abuses, particularly in non-SOEs, such as not signing a labour contract, or signing only a short-term contract, not purchasing social security insurance for workers and escaping employers' responsibilities by subcontracting.[68]

According to Cooke, this law, together with the other two less controversial and thus less known, employment/labour-related laws promulgated in 2007, namely, the Employment Promotion Law and the Labour Dispute Mediation and Arbitration Law, mark the beginning of a new era in which the Chinese government seeks to re-regulate the labour market through legislative intervention, in order to provide greater employment protection to workers, particularly those outside the state sector.[69] In face of severe working conditions, non-SOE employees have finally been given more legal tools for their self protection.[70] The previous lack of legal protection may be a major reason why the number of labour disputes increased significantly after the mid-1990s. The ambiguity of the 1994 labour contract system had led to different understandings of employment conditions from an employer and employee point of view. According to the *China Labour Statistics Yearbook*, issued jointly by NBS and MOLSS, labour disputes in non-SOEs jumped from 36,000 in 1997 to 147,000 in 2003, while the percentage of labour disputes in non-SOEs out of all cases jumped from 50% in 1997 to 65% in 2003. However, the data also reflects the weaker position of non-SOE employees relative to that of SOE employees. We mentioned in the last chapter that non-SOE employees account for about 85% of all enterprise employees in China, and their working conditions, especially those in the POEs, are usually worse than those in SOEs. The fact that they accounted for only 65% of disputes and even fewer before 2003 demonstrates that when non-SOE employees are treated unfairly,

68 National People's Congress (2007).

69 Cooke (2008b), p. 2.

70 Of course, whether or not the new law will be fully implemented and enforced remains to be tested.

fewer have the capacity formally to lodge a dispute case. Compared with SOE employees who felt justified in raising disputes,[71] more non-SOE employees chose to keep silent and to leave quietly.[72]

4.4 White-collar Employees vs. Blue-collar Employees

The literature provides little evidence of comparative research on China's white-collar and blue-collar employees. Some scholars[73] mention this matter parenthetically and tend to deal with it in the context of social class and stratification.

A report issued by the China Academy of Social Science argued that Chinese society can be stratified into seven social layers:[74]

1. senior government officials, large enterprise management, senior intellectuals and "liberal professionals (自由职业者)";
2. mid/lower level government officials, ordinary enterprise management, junior intellectuals and "liberal professionals (自由职业者)";
3. ordinary clerks and technicians in government and enterprises;
4. technical workers;
5. semi-technical/semi-physical workers and service staff;
6. pure physical labourers; and
7. "lay-offs (下岗)", the unemployed and people receiving government privation allowances.

71 Or, sometimes, they even participated in protests and demonstrations, which were theoretically illegal but usually tolerated by the government (reflecting the ideological predicament that a "working class" regime could hardly "crack down" on labour movements).

72 There may be another reason for the disparity in disputes: many of the non-SOE employers would have been very small; and as in most countries, there tend to be fewer formal disputes when the employer is small.

73 For example, Li (2005); Sun (2004); Shi (2006) etc.

74 Li et al. (2005), p. 54.

The Academy's research was focused not on the stratification of the employee class but on that of the whole society. People in the first and seventh layers are technically not employees and hence not within the scope of our research. Nevertheless the stratification used by the Academy is pertinent, because as we look into the other five social layers, we see that social stratification is based largely on education and the technical levels of a worker's job. Workers in the second and third layers are white-collar employees doing mental work, while workers in the fourth, fifth and sixth layers are blue-collar employees doing physical work.[75]

The "difference between mental and physical work (脑体差别)" is one of the long-held "three major distinctions (三大差别)"[76] in Chinese society, reflecting the belief that "the one who labours mentally controls, while the one who labours physically is controlled (劳心者治人, 劳力者治于人)".[77] Such traditional differences between the mental and physical influenced thinking, except for the short period of 1960s–70s, when the main line of thinking was "politics in command (政治挂帅)" and the focus was on "'reducing' the differences".[78]

Because of the limited availability of relevant statistics, we cannot actually confirm the proportion of blue-collar and white-collar workers among China's 425 million enterprise employees. My own working experience in a number of enterprises suggests that the workforce basically follows the

75 Shi (2006)'s research provides further evidence for this point. She found that the entrance requirement for white-collar professions is diploma or above.

76 The "three major distinctions" refers to "differences between workers and peasants (工农差别)", "differences between urban and rural areas (城乡差别)", and "differences between mental and physical work (脑体差别)".

77 This saying originally appeared in "Mencius (孟子)", one of the authoritative works of the Confucian school which had dominated the Chinese way of thinking for over 2,000 years (and beyond).

78 During that special period, blue-collar employees doing physical work were the political favourites of the generation. They not only had "iron rice bowls (铁饭碗)" that provided guaranteed income and welfare, but also enjoyed prestigious political positions. However, since the economic reform started in 1979, blue-collar employees have gradually lost their enviable welfare and political privileges, and the "differences between mental and physical work" has re-emerged as the usual social phenomenon (Sun (2004), pp. 85–92).

"80/20 rule". A report issued by MOLSS[79] also provides indirect evidence that 78% of new job opportunities required an education level of year 12 or below, which indicated that these were blue-collar jobs.[80] If we accept this estimation, then there are around 340 million blue-collar out of the 425 million enterprise employees in China.

As blue-collar jobs are mostly physical, with little technical input, they are highly insecure and workers can commonly be replaced by others at any time. Hence, competition among the 340 million blue-collar employees is already intense. To make matters worse, as mentioned in Chapter One, around 120 million redundant labourers in rural areas are ready for any opportunity to enter the non-primary industry labour market as blue-collar workers. In this context, blue-collar employees rarely have any bargaining power in the labour market, which leads directly to their weak position. Yet, for the same reason, the supply of workers from rural areas creates China's comparative advantage in labour costs, enabling it to become the "world's factory".[81]

The operations of Chinese enterprises correlate highly with the international market.[82] In the context of economic globalization, China's manufacturing enterprises confront a continuous squeeze on price by international buyers. To maintain competitiveness, Chinese employ-

79 MOLSS (2006).

80 It is worth pointing out that in western countries some jobs, which need a certain kind of vocational training instead of a tertiary degree, are performed by tradesmen such as fitters and turners, printers, electricians, plumbers and carpenters; and there are also service workers such as waiters and shop assistants, all of whom are not generally be described as blue-collar in western countries. In China, however, all these employees are usually considered as blue collar workers.

81 "Is China Losing Its Comparative Advantage in Labour Cost?" (in Chinese), *China Youth*, 25 August 2005; "中国劳动力的竞争优势正在失去？", 中国青年报, 2005–08-25.

82 According to Li Yu Shi, vice director of the Research Institute of MOC, exports account for 30% of China's GDP, and China's dependency on foreign trade can be as high as 60%. ("Comments on China's Foreign Trade Development", *Financial Times* (Chinese Edition), "我国对外贸易的发展与评价", 金融时报, 24 February 2005).

ers try to lower production costs, and, as the major production cost in labour-intensive manufacturing industries is employee wages and welfare, blue-collar employees are severely affected by international competition. It is unrealistic to expect Chinese employers to raise the level of compensation packages for blue-collar employees. Some experts argue that it will be the government's responsibility to ensure that blue-collar employees' basic labour rights are protected and that employers' exploitation is not further intensified.[83]

Sun L. P. (2004) and Qiao J. (2003) presented a pessimistic view that, because China relied on cheap labour resources as a competitive advantage in international competition, the state keeps a tight hand on labour costs so as to maintain the momentum of attracting foreign capital and developing the economy.[84] Hence, China's blue-collar employees experience low wages and conditions.[85] According to a survey in Guangdong in 2005, 80% of blue-collar employees had a monthly salary in the range of RMB 500–1500 (AUD 100–300),[86] which was in the lower income class in Guangdong. Workers have little choice but to accept these conditions.[87]

83 "Experts' Perspectives on the Economic Transition in Pearl River Delta" (in Chinese), *Security Times*, "专家谈珠三角经济转型：从汗水经济到智慧经济", 证券时报, 25 July 2006.

84 For this reason, Sun (2004) very obscurely suggested that the Chinese government is the most "right-wing" government in the world, as most of its public policies were set on the side of capital. But as indicated in our last chapter's discussion, developing countries, being eager to change their backward situations and to participate in the process of globalization, sometimes have no choice but to "welcome" the exploitation of labour. The desire to attract foreign investment is one underlying reason why some Chinese local governments tend to suppress labour standards.

85 Qiao (2003).

86 This income hardly differs from that of 10 years ago, while China's economy maintained a 7–10% annual growth rate in the same period. This reflects the fact that blue-collar employees have gained little benefit from the country's overall development.

87 The survey was conducted by Guangdong Provincial Party's School in July–September 2005, covering 1,500 interviewees. The abstracted content can be found in "Guangdong Working Class's Current Situation" (in Chinese), *Southern Metropolitan*, "广东工人阶级现状", 南方都市报, 28 April 2006.

White-collar employees typically have managerial and/or technical responsibilities; thus, the circumstances of white-collar employees are usually much better and are less exposed to the "exploitative behaviour" of employers. Hence, their issues attract relatively less attention in studies of Chinese industrial relations. Nevertheless, "hidden exploitation" is widespread, mainly in the form of "voluntary overtime". In 2006, the death of two young white-collar employees,[88] caused by continuous overtime without proper rest, aroused an enormous public response, causing many major companies to suspend the practice of office overtime at night. To be fair, such extreme exploitation is rare, especially when compared with the thousands of work-related injuries and deaths faced by the blue-collar employees.[89] That so many companies suspended the practice of office overtime at night after the incidents indicates the relatively stronger position of white-collar over blue-collar employees.

Compensation packages for white-collar employees are also normally much better than for blue-collar employees. There are no formal data[90] available on this matter, but according to a brief informal survey,[91] white-collar employees in Guangdong had a monthly salary range of RMB 2000–10,000

88 One was a R and D engineer in Huawei (a high tech. company), while the other was a project manager in Pepsi Cola.

89 Because of the sensitivity of such data, the actual numbers of work-related injuries and deaths are never officially publicized. It has been estimated that about 1 million work-related injuries, which led to the death of 130,000 people, occur annually in China. Refer to "Safe Production Is an Essential Part of China's Continuous Development" (in Chinese), *Safety in Mechanical and Electrical Industries*, "安全生产是中国可持续发展的重要组成部分", 机电安全, 6 December 2004. We may compare the Chinese number with the position in Australia: in 2003/04 there were 332 deaths in Australia as a result of work-related injuries. (Australian Social Trends 2007, available at <http://www.abs.gov.au/ausstats/abs@.nsf/latestproducts/63ED457234C2F22DCA25732C002080A7?opendocument> last accessed on 27 February 2009). This equates to a rate of 3.5 per 100,000 employed people in Australia; while the Chinese estimated rate is 17 per 100,000 employed people.

90 There are some salary surveys conducted by human resource service companies. As these are informal surveys, and there are fees for access to the data, the author decided not to use them.

91 The survey was conducted at the end of 2005 in Guangzhou, covering 50 interviewees working in enterprises of various ownership types. The interviewees were

(AUD 400–2000), and most companies adjusted their salaries annually according to the general economic situation and the performance of the company. This suggests that white-collar employees' incomes are roughly 2 to 20 times those of blue-collar employees. A significant difference is that white-collar employees have an opportunity to share in the benefits of economic growth,[92] to which blue-collar employees normally have no access.[93]

Differences between mental and physical work affect not only the immediate working conditions of employees but also their future development. Before reform and the economic transition, blue-collar employees had some chance of being promoted to clerical/managerial positions, but such chances have gradually diminished, solidifying this social group with little cross-class social flow.[94] Moreover, this affects the next generation. As education operates to reproduce distinctions in society, and an individual's family backgrounds tends to correlate with scores in school, a society, such as China, which overemphasizes the importance of educational background,[95] will keep reproducing existing social distinctions.[96] Shi produced evidence which supports such views. After 1979, the correlation

---

all white-collar employees from clerical level up to junior manager level, excluding senior managers and technical professionals.

92 Because of its rapid economic growth, China has been in great need of managerial and technical talent since mid-1990s. Actually, many white-collar employees do not depend entirely on the companies to raise their salaries; a more usual practice is to raise one's salary by changing jobs and moving to higher positions. My own case as a sales professional in a few enterprises is an example: my salary in 2005 (as a sales director in an FIE) was roughly 20 times that of 1995 (as a sales representative in an MNC).

93 The income gaps between employers, white-collar and blue-collar employees are a topic for further research to which I refer in my concluding chapter.

94 "Research on China's Contemporary Social Stratification" by the China Academy of Social Science, as quoted by Sun (2004), p. 92.

95 This is also a long-held tradition in the Chinese society, as indicated by the famous folk saying "All the other occupations are low-grade, when compared with academic book-learning (万般皆下品，唯有读书高)". It is the usual practice for Chinese recruiters to consider a degree or diploma as a very significant criterion for virtually any white-collar jobs.

96 Sun (2004), pp. 93–96.

between parents' and children's professions has become significantly more positive, meaning that more children, especial children from blue-collar families, follow their parents' work paths.[97]

In summary, Chinese white-collar employees enjoy much better employment conditions than blue-collar employees, and this situation continues because of the over-abundance of non-technical workers in China.

Conclusions

A detailed overview of how Chinese employees are stratified was necessary in order to analyse their situation in contemporary China's industrial relations system. By synthesizing, with certain revisions, three existing stratification approaches, we segmented Chinese employees using a three-dichotomy approach. We then discussed briefly the circumstances of three different groups of employees, namely, SOE employees vs. non-SOE employees, rural migrant employees vs. urban employees, and white-collar employees vs. blue-collar employees. We argued that, for historical and cultural reasons, each group of employees has distinctive employment conditions.[98]

97 Shi (2006).

98 Though people would find that employees of different groups always have different conditions in most societies, the degree of such condition gaps are much more significant in China than in developed economies.

CHAPTER FIVE

Interactions among the Party-state, ACFTU and Employers' Associations

Introduction

In the previous three chapters we considered six major actors in China's contemporary industrial relations system, namely, the party-state, the ACFTU, employers' associations, grass roots unions, employers, and employees. We focused on the specific circumstances of each actor individually rather than the interactions between them. In this and the next chapters, we shall consider the interactions, respectively, above the workplace level, at the workplace level, and across different levels.

In this chapter, we analyse interactions between the party-state, ACFTU and employers' associations above the workplace level. We first analyse the interactions between the party-state and the ACFTU during various historical periods, demonstrating that even though the ACFTU was an extension organization established by the party-state, the relationship was not always simply a "subordinate obeying the superior (下级服从上级)". Second, we show that the various employers' associations, including CEC-CEDA, ACFIC and the Civil Chambers of Commerce, have a distinctive relationship with the party-state. Finally, we analyse the National Tripartite Conference on Labour Relations Co-ordination (NTCLRC), and conclude that this is not a tripartite mechanism in the real sense but yet another quasi-bureaucratic organization.

5.1 Party-state and ACFTU

How the party-state and the ACFTU interact is the main focus of the Chinese study of industrial relations. Our study is helped by a large volume of academic literature and historical material.[1]

In subsection 2.2.1, "Brief History of the ACFTU", we explained briefly the profound historical linkage between the party-state and the ACFTU, pointing out that the ACFTU was established by the CCP before it came to power for the purposes of agitating workers for revolutionary activities and of controlling them when it gained power. The question which is always asked is whether the ACFTU is always under the absolute leadership of the party-state; that is, whether the relationship is simply one of a "subordinate obeying the superior (下级服从上级)"? This question is the topic of much academic debate.

5.1.1 Party-state and ACFTU 1921–49

In Chapter Two, we pointed out that a very early "incarnation" of the ACFTU was the "Chinese Labour Combination Secretariat (中国劳动组合书记部)", established by the CCP in Shanghai in August 1921. In May 1925, the "Secretariat" held its Second National Labour Conference in Guangzhou.[2] By passing the "General Statute of ACFTU (中华全国总工会总章)", the "Secretariat" formally promulgated the ACFTU and immediately affiliated it with the "Red International of Labour Unions", which was subordinate to the Communist International.[3] There is little

1 For example, Chan (1993, 2005, 2006); Harper (1969); Leung (2002); Pringle (2001); Qi (2004); Wu and Liu (2004); Yu (2006); Zhang, X. L. (2007), Zhang, Y. M. (2003); Zheng, H. et al. (1997) etc.

2 At the time, Guangzhou (also known as Canton in some western countries) was controlled by the KMT regional government which was in the midst of preparations for its "Northern Expedition (北伐)". The CCP and the KMT were then still in the "honeymoon" period of the "first co-operation between KMT and CCP (第一次国共合作)" (Zheng et al. (1997), pp. 20–25).

3 Refer back to 2.2.1 of Chapter 2.

disagreement among scholars that the ACFTU was founded directly by the CCP for its own purposes.

Why did the Communist Party want to establish a union organization under its control? Harper believed that the communist party was "a party of elites ... (which) lacks the direct involvement of the masses".[4] The labour union was a mass organization which helped "the party maintain leadership and control over the various sectors of society", playing the role of "transmission belt (纽带)"[5] in the communist political system.[6]

The CCP founded a union organization also for the purpose of gaining legitimacy for its own existence, because, according to Marx in the *Manifesto of the Communist Party*, the Party must be hand in glove with the working class:

> ... The Communists have no interests separate and apart from those of the proletariat as a whole ... The Communists are the most advanced and resolute section of the working-class parties of every country, that section which pushes forward all others ... The immediate aim of the Communist is the same as that of all the other proletarian parties: formation of the proletariat into a class, overthrow of the bourgeois supremacy, conquest of political power by the proletariat ... The Communists fight for the attainment of the immediate aims, for the enforcement of the momentary interests of the working class; but in the movement of the present, they also represent and take care of the future of that movement ...[7]

4 According to the Phoenix TV news report, the Organization Department of the CC-CCP (中共中央组织部) announced that, by the end of 2006, the CCP had more than 72 million members. The CCP, the largest party in the world, has a membership covering workers, peasants, intelligentsia and millionaires (Phoenix TV <www.phoenixtv.com> accessed on 9 July 2007). It seems that the CCP, to some extent, can now rightly claim to be representative and to have a valid "mass base (群众基础)". But it cannot be denied that when the CCP was first established in 1921, it was an elite party lacking mass linkage. Most of its founders, including Chen Du Xiu, Li Da Zhao and the 12 representatives (representing 50 members all over China) attending the CCP's first congress, were basically "cynical" intellectuals (Wu and Liu (2004), pp. 2–27).

5 Lenin originated the concept of "transmission belt", but did not further develop it. It was Stalin who later elaborated its meaning and put it into practice (Qi 2004).

6 Harper (1969), p. 84.

7 Marx and Engels (1848).

Because none of the founding members of the CCP was from the "working class",[8] the question was how the CCP could claim to represent its interests? Entering the political arena as the "vanguard/pioneer of the working class (无产阶级先锋队)",[9] the CCP had to do something to justify this claim.

On the one hand, theoretically, it had to combine its activities with those of the labour movement, while, on the other, the intellectual elite needed a practical agency organization to communicate its revolutionary ideas to the workers. Hence, whether from a theoretical or practical point of view, establishing its own trade union was a necessity for the CCP in its early years. Without it, the very legitimacy of the CCP's existence would have been severely challenged.

After the ACFTU was founded by the CCP, what was the relationship between the two? Harper argued that, since its establishment in 1921, the ACFTU was a typical Leninist union. Its core leadership was dominated by the CCP and control of the union members was top-down.[10] Therefore, from the very beginning, the ACFTU's most important function was "to implement and carry out the party's line/guiding principles/policies (执行和贯彻党的路线方针政策)"[11] and *not* "to represent and struggle for workers' interests".[12]

8 Actually, this phenomenon was typical in the preliminary stage of communist parties around the world.

9 "The Chinese Communist Party is the vanguard/pioneer of the working class (无产阶级先锋队)". This sentence or similar expressions can be found in the first part of all versions of the CCP's constitution since 1921.

10 Harper (1969), p. 86.

11 Before 1949, the ACFTU's tasks revolved around assisting the CCP to seize power, whereas after 1949, they revolved around stabilizing the working class and gearing up production (Zheng et al. (1997), pp. 2398–428).

12 Yu provided some historical proofs for this argument: in 1920s, Liu Shao-qi (who was then in charge of the An-yuan Workers' Club) held that workers should not go on strike at will, for this conduct might lead to the collapse of factories. On the contrary, Li Wei Han (who was then the CCP provincial head in Hu-nan) believed that they must induce the workers to undertake more political struggles, and he tried to imbue the workers with the notion that they were fighting not merely for their

Writing in 2007, Zhang challenged Harper's analysis. He argued that even though the ACFTU aided the CCP's work in the labour movement, there was no subordinate-superior relationship. From 1921 to 1925, when the Chinese Labour Combination Secretariat was an internal department of the CCP, the relationship *was* a direct subordinate-superior one. But after the ACFTU was established in 1925, neither the ACFTU nor any of its grass roots organizations were internal organs of the CCP. It was only according to "usual practice (惯例)" that the CC-CCP had the right to "recommend" that some of its members "run" for election to the ACFTU's major leadership positions. This practice subsequently became a "historical convention (历史惯制)".[13]

By comparing the position of leading ACFTU officials in the CCP during the period 1921–49, we may be able to clarify the relationship between the ACFTU and the CCP at that time. We see that all ACFTU chairs were members of the CCP, except for the first chair, Lin Wei Min.[14] The ranking of ACFTU chairs in the CCP fluctuated as policies changed during the long process of seizing power. Before 1929, when the labour movement was still the focus of the CCP's work, the CCP sent high ranking cadres to

---

immediate economic interests but for eventual national power. For this reason, Liu had a serious debate with Li and others. Liu argued that "you will disrupt the whole An-yuan mining site", while Li and his followers answered, "Why are you so silly, how can we make the workers follow us in revolutionary actions by other means? Our purpose is not to win a bowl of rice for the workers but to agitate them to follow us and eventually take over the state power!" (Yu 2006b).

13 Zhang (2007).

14 Lin Wei Min was a famous labour leader in the early 1920s. He participated in the establishment of the Chinese Seamen's Confederation (中华海员工业联合总会) and was one of the leaders of the famous 1922 Hongkong Seamen's Grand Strike (香港海员大罢工). Lin was recruited as a member of the CCP during his visit to the USSR in 1924, but was not offered an internal post. Generally speaking, Lin can be deemed a transitional figure for the ACFTU when it was first established by the CCP. Lin was seriously ill when he was elected as the first chair of the ACFTU in May, 1925 and spent most of time in hospital after August 1925. He died in 1927. ("Lin Wei Min: a Prominent Figure of China's Labour Movement in the Early Years" (in Chinese), *People's Daily*, "早期中国工人运动著名领袖:林伟民", 人民日报, 28 March 2006).

take up ("run" for) the post of ACFTU chair. Subsequently, after the CCP was nearly destroyed and forced into a military struggle for survival against the KMT, based on support from peasants rather than workers, organizing the labour movement was no longer a central focus. Thereafter, the CCP sent lower-ranking cadres to fill the post of ACFTU chair. The ACFTU's work was virtually suspended from 1934, when the "Long March" began, until 1948 when the CCP consolidated its position in Northeast China in preparation for establishing a national government.[15]

Zhang's argument that the ACFTU was organizationally independent is sustainable, but only in theory. In practice, the ACFTU's work never escaped the shadow of the CCP.[16] Zhang's main point, however, is that when and if political conditions allow, the ACFTU could become autonomous as there is no theoretical or ideological barrier to the ACFTU's independence.[17] Nevertheless the ACFTU was an extension organization established by the CCP for the purpose of seizing power. Though nominally independent, it was and remains dependent on the CCP from an organizational point of view. As the CCP was confronted by a critical war-time environment prior to 1949, the ACFTU's only objective was to help the Party seize power. The relationship between the two was a simple "subordinate-superior" one.

5.1.2 Party-state and ACFTU 1949–79

After establishing the People's Republic of China in October 1949, the CCP began the long and complex process of slowly transforming itself from a revolutionary party with the sole objective of seizing power into

15 Zheng et al. (1997), pp. 2367–80.

16 By analysing the finance, organization, and the history of the development of the ACFTU, Qi concluded that the ACFTU hardly has any "independent space" but is actually a puppet of the party-state system (Qi 2004).

17 For understandable reasons, many Chinese scholars use an obscure writing style when discussing politically sensitive topics. On the surface, Zhang (2007) seemed to be defending the ACFTU, but his underlying meaning can be interpreted in various ways.

a party in power with diversified objectives ranging from establishing a government to promoting production and maintaining social stability.[18] In this prolonged process, the exact relationship between the party-state and the ACFTU, which was supposed to "represent" the working class, is difficult to determine.

Harper argued that after 1949 ACFTU leaders and cadres dealt with the questions of whether the unions had to accept party leadership, and if so, at what level, and whether the unions should view representation of the workers' interests as their central task. Harper believed that these questions eventually led to major conflicts between the union and the CCP after 1949.[19] Zhang, however, implied that conflicts between the CCP and ACFTU were contests for the "power/right of representation (代表权)".[20] Which was better qualified to "represent" the "leading class" in the "socialist" state, or to rule in the name of the "working class"?[21]

18 In this process, there were also complex internal struggles among different factions within the CCP. Mao Ze Dong was particularly unhappy with the relatively conservative policies (the so-called "conciliation policies (调和政策)") of the late 1950s and early 1960s. He believed that the CCP should always retain its "true colour" of being revolutionary (and radical). Therefore, in 1967 he proclaimed the slogan of "continuing revolution under the proletarian dictatorship (在无产阶级专政下继续革命)", and with this slogan as his theoretical basis, escalated the Cultural Revolution. Actually, the CCP, ever since 1949, swayed between the two conflicting characters (a revolutionary party vs. a party in power). At its 16th national congress held in 2002, the CCP made a clear statement that the party is now re-positioned as a party in power (Li 1998; Yu 2002).

19 Harper (1969), p. 89.

20 Zhang (2007).

21 In fact, such a contest for the "power/right of representation (代表权)" was not the first to take place in a "socialist" country. As early as in the 1920s, the so-called "workers' opposition" in the USSR, headed by the chair of the Russian Hardware Labour Union, contended that "the highest form of the working class [combination] is not the Party but the union ... [We] oppose the supreme power of the Party in the political area ..." Later by severe internal struggle, Lenin crushed the "workers' opposition" and pronounced the faction illegal, reaffirming the principle that the union must accept the leadership of the Party (Qi 2004).

If unions viewed "representation of the workers' interests as their central task" and put this into practice, then they were better qualified to "represent" the "working class" and rule the "socialist" state in its name.[22] Such an inference placed the party-state in a difficult ideological position. The party-state had to emphasize the principle that "the unions must unconditionally accept the party leadership"[23] and oppose the idea that representation of the workers' interests was the union's central task.[24] The party-state resorted to internal struggle to defeat the ACFTU.

In the early 1950s, Li Lisan, the executive vice-chair in charge of the daily operation of the ACFTU, contended that there were a number of conflicts of interest in SOEs between the interests of the working class and individual workers, and long-term goals and short-term aims. These conflicts were reflected in many specific daily problems in the workplace. Though Li did not directly propose that the union separate from the Party, he did advocate that the union organize its activities independently with only general ideological leadership by the Party committee. His ideas were strongly criticized at the ACFTU's Party Committee meeting in 1951. His "mistakes" were officially summarized as over-emphasizing the conflict of interest in SOEs, reducing the union to a narrow, economic organization, denying Party leadership over the union, and leading the union down the wrong path of "corporatism".[25]

22 In this case, there would be no question "whether the unions must accept Party leadership". On the contrary, the necessity for the Party's existence would have become problematic.

23 There are actually two problems with the statement that "the unions must unconditionally accept the Party leadership". First, the CCP equated the ACFTU and the "unions", by stealth replacing the concept that "the ACFTU must unconditionally accept the Party leadership" with the concept that "the unions must unconditionally accept the Party leadership". Secondly, as noted previously, even the ACFTU was, at least theoretically, an "independent" organization without a clear-cut subordinate relation to the CCP; now, at last, the CCP had thrown away the last "fig leaf" and clearly positioned the ACFTU as a Party extension.

24 Zhang (2003).

25 Harper (1969); Zhang Y. M. (2003); Zhang X. L. (2007).

Li Lisan's successor, Lai Ruoyu[26] originally adopted the opposite position. But as the political circumstances changed, he began to express different ideas, arguing that protection of employees' material interests and democratic rights should be undertaken by the union.[27] Lai also tried to elucidate the positive relation between the union's activities and higher productivity, contending that the union must have certain legal rights to perform its various functions better. He, too, was eventually condemned openly as a "rightist, opportunist and factionist" at the ACFTU's 3rd Party Committee meeting[28] in 1958.[29]

26 Lai Ruo Yu, unlike Li Lisan, originally was only a local cadre from Shan Xi province. He was rotated to the ACFTU in 1952 and became the chair in 1953. Lai was elected a member of the 8th CC-CCP in 1956 (ranked No. 57) and died in 1958, but was criticized and condemned after his death ("Brief CV of Lai Ruoyu", Party History Research Office of CCP Kunming Committee, available at <http://kmds.km.gov.cn/dsbl/dsrw/lmn/262122599523IIA6H9B6C1KKJD6IIA6H9B6C1KKJD6.shtml> last accessed on 20 January 2009).

27 The published literature of the history of the Party does not explain why Lai Ruo Yu had such a downfall. But judging from his posthumous condemnation, we can see some of the signs of internal struggle within the CCP. In concluding the ACFTU's third party committee meeting, Liu Lan Tao, reserve Secretary of the Central Committee' Secretariat, stated that "the fundamental mistake of Li Lisan and Lai Ruo Yu was to use the union as a battle field to oppose the Party's leadership, to contend for the power with the Party and government, with the intention to domineer over the party and government or separate from the party and government ... The purpose of their anti-party activities was to realize the political ambition of making a "union kingdom" with themselves the national leaders of the working class ..." (Zhang 2007). Ranked only 57 in the CC-CCP, Lai clearly did not have enough strength to "realize the political ambition of making a union kingdom". Was there some one behind him, and if so who? These questions remain unresolved in Chinese political history.

28 As explained in Chapter 3, one major characteristic of China's party-state system is that there are party committees in all the government ministries/departments as well as in "mass organizations" and SOEs. These party committees, though not declared, hold the ultimate decisive power in the corresponding organizations. In the case of Lai Ruo Yu, at the time when this party committee meeting was held, he had just died but was still criticized and condemned, along with some other ACFTU leaders.

29 Harper (1969); Zhang Y. M. (2003); Zhang X. L. (2007).

After these two confrontations, the power of the ACFTU was diminished severely. It no longer advocated sensitive political issues such as maintaining workers' interests and union independence. It had to be "content" with playing the role of "bridge and transmission belt (桥梁和纽带)" between the party-state and the working class.[30]

After 1958, the ACFTU was walking on wire. If it turned a little to the left towards the party-state, it was criticized as "being divorced from the masses (脱离群众)" and condemned as a "bureaucratic scab". If it turned to the right towards the workers, it was denounced as "corporatist", as undermining party leadership or establishing an "independent kingdom (独立王国)".[31] The ACFTU was so lost ideologically that in 1958 it committed to "struggle for the dying-out of unions (为工会消亡而斗争)" and cancelling the unions' organizational structure at or below the county level.[32]

The ACFTU's difficult political situation continued between 1958, when Lai was denounced, and 1966 when the Cultural Revolution began. During the "decade of catastrophe (十年浩劫)",[33] the ACFTU pleased nobody, alienating both the party-state and the workers. The union issue during the Cultural Revolution was quite different from the earlier Li Lisan and Lai Ruoyu incidents. Their problem had been that ACFTU leaders, no

30 Zhang (2007) obscurely suggested that the concept of "bridge and transmission belt (桥梁和纽带)" contains a serious logical problem. If the union is the "bridge and transmission belt" between the party-state and the working mass, then what is the relation between the party-state and the working mass? Are there high mountains or big rivers separating the Party from the mass? Does it mean that the Party is so inherently separated from the mass that it needs an agency (the union) to connect with it?

31 Zhang (2007).

32 Zheng et al. (1997), p. 2428. A further study of the 1950s union issue would have to elaborate on the Chinese political history at the time. For example, Hu argued that the union issue in 1950s had a more complicated underlying linkage with the political triangle conflicts among Mao Ze Dong, Liu Shao Qi and Gao Gang (Hu 2002), while Lin also pointed out that it might have certain connections with the "Anti-rightist Movement" and the "Great Leap-forward Movement" (Lin 2007).

33 A term commonly applied to the Cultural Revolution.

matter what their political motive, posed a political challenge to the party-state from the side of the workers. During the Cultural Revolution, by way of contrast, the ACFTU itself was the political target, attacked by both the party-state and workers, and was forced to cease operations. Workers' organizations, from various political backgrounds, were established and quickly became involved in the vortex of political struggle.[34]

In summary, the party-state and the ACFTU had a very subtle relationship during the period 1949–79. The ACFTU went through different stages, from becoming a "tame puppet" of the party-state while struggling for more autonomous development, to being crushed into submission and finally discarded completely. The questions of whether the union must accept party leadership, and if so, at what level, and whether the union should view representation of workers' interests as its central task constantly confronted ACFTU leaders and cadres. Eventually the ACFTU leaders and cadres dared not contemplate struggle against the party-state in the name of solving problems for the benefit of workers.[35] It remains an open question whether ACFTU leaders struggled against the party-state for the purpose of solving such problems or simply identified problems to

34 We discuss this in more detail in the next chapter.

35 Such a viewpoint was held by Harper (1969). Chan (1993) continued Harper's train of thought and categorized the labour movements during 1976 "April 5th Incident" and 1989 "June 4th (Tian-an-men Square) Incident" as the fourth and fifth conflicts between the union and the party. Pringle (2001) also adopted a similar perspective to explain the labour movement in China since 1949. In my opinion, however, the categorization of the1976 "April 5th Incident" and the 1989 "June 4th (Tian-an-men Square) Incident" as union-party conflict is far-fetched. The 1976 "April 5th Incident" referred to the activities conducted by ordinary Chinese people during a traditional "Qing Ming" Festival to commemorate the late Premier Zhou En-lai and to express their opposition to the Cultural Revolution. The people involved came from all strata of society and workers were only one component. During the 1989 "June 4th (Tian-an-men Square) Incident", the ACFTU's executive vice-president Zhu Ze Hou openly supported the students' movement and issued a public statement, "Five Points on the Present Situation", advocating the advancing of the national congress meeting etc. Some independent labour organizations appeared, the most famous being the Beijing Workers' Autonomy Association, but it is generally accepted that the incident was led by students, with only minor involvement of union and workers.

legitimise their leadership.[36] We cannot, within the limits of this book, explore this issue in greater detail.[37]

5.1.3 Party-state and ACFTU since 1979

After the 9th National Congress of the ACFTU in 1978, the work of the ACFTU was gradually re-established. In the comparatively loose ideological atmosphere of the mid/late 1980s, when political reform was, for the first time, on the working agenda of the party-state, the ACFTU attempted to reform itself. In 1988, it issued a document, "Ideas on Union Reform", openly acknowledging for the first time that it was an "officially operating union (官办工会)"; and proposing to streamline the relationship between the union and party-state, defining the "protection of employees' legal interests and democratic rights" as its top priority. Moreover, it suggested democratic elections at the grass roots level, removing the practice of top-down appointments.[38] However, the June 1989 "Tian-an-men Square Incident" led to the suspension of reform, especially political reform, which had a negative effect on union reform.

36 For example, Li Lisan, as one of the most famous labour movement leaders of the early 1920s, practically presided over the CC-CCP during the ebb of revolution between 1927 and 1929. Later, because of his failure in the CCP's internal "line struggle (路线斗争)", Li was exiled to the USSR for more than a decade. In fact, Li had complex and subtle personal relations with most of the CCP's founding leaders (including Mao, Zhou etc.). It is certainly worth considering whether these factors affected his stance on the union issue during 1950s. Did he use the union with the intention of restoring his own political reputation and power? At least, Mao thought so (Li and Liu 2005).

37 He, F. former secretary of the communist leader Zhang Wentian, pointed out that, as early as the 1940s, the CCP had systematically developed the so-called "Scientific Compilation of Party History (党史编纂学)", allowing the winning sides of the party's internal struggles the right to rewrite the party history according to their interpretation. The truth about some historical events can only be partly recovered and even this entails difficult research and investigation (He 2005, internet edition, chapters 19 and 20).

38 As quoted by Zhang (2003).

During the period of the Tian-an-men Square Incident from late April to early June, 1989, Zhu Zehou, the ACFTU's executive vice-chair, openly supported the students' movement by issuing a public statement, "Five Points on the Present Situation". In the name of the ACFTU, he also donated RMB100,000 to the Red Cross in China for the medical care of the students occupying the Square.[39] We do not know whether Zhu acted alone or on behalf of the ACFTU leadership.[40]

Generally, the ACFTU did not undertake any significant activities during the 1980s. Economic reforms were in their early stages and the interests of workers, especially the majority who were in SOEs, were not yet seriously affected. Enterprises of other ownership types were still in their infancy. Hence, labour-capital conflicts were uncommon. The typical tasks of unions during this period were organizing entertainment and trying to cultivate a sense of harmony in the workplace.

After the re-start of economic reform in 1992, China began a fundamental social transition, with the non-SOE sector quickly developing to become the dominant force in the economy.[41] The ACFTU could no longer comfortably remain in the security of the SOE sector. In 2000, it proposed that "where there are employees, there shall be unions (哪里有职工，哪里就要建立工会)", attempting to reverse the trend of declining union membership.[42] However, Zhang argued that, under the party-state's decision-making logic of "state development (国家成长)" and "capital first (资本优先)", the ACFTU, as a "signboard union (招牌工会)", could not fulfil any undertaking to protect employee interests, as it was a mere tool

39 Ibid.

40 After the incident, Zhu was dismissed from all posts and disappeared from the public view. However, Ni Zhifu, chair of the ACFTU, remained in position until he formally retired in 1998. We may infer that the ACFTU leadership did not share a consensus view about the student movement.

41 See Chapter 3.

42 Speeches by Wei Jianxing and Zhang Junjiu presented on 11 and 12 November 2000 at the Ningbo Conference for New Enterprise Union Construction, available at <http://www.gdftu.org.cn/Articles/9/54/78/200412218553126630.htm> (last accessed on 20 January 2009).

serving the party-state's interest of maintaining social stability.[43] Leung pointed out more directly that the ACFTU was an active agent of surveillance, denunciation and suppression during all incidents of independent union organizing, and its active attempts to establish union branches in private/foreign-owned companies were intended to defend the existing trade union system by denying survival space to potential independent unions. Such actions protected the interests of both the ACFTU and the party-state.[44]

A series of articles written by Chan[45] typifies the complex views of some observers about the relationship between the ACFTU and the party-state in this period. Chan used the theory of "corporatism" to analyse the ACFTU during the new atmosphere of the early 1990s. She concluded that the ACFTU was a corporatist institution, and though it was still under CCP control, it played a more significant role than most analysts believed. She further concluded that the ACFTU will gradually seek independence, and the dynamics of liberalization will eventually reach a critical point when the work of the ACFTU and workers' advocates will be recognized by their constituency. Chan argued that it will then be up to workers to agitate for the right to decide their own destiny and to make use of the ACFTU to further their interests; in other words, to effect change within the existing state corporatist structure.[46]

Nine years later, Chan (2002) was less optimistic, but she still held that, though the ACFTU had not escaped the colour of bureaucracy and monopoly, some of its leaders[47] did their best to uphold labour rights and

43 Zhang (2003).

44 Leung (2002).

45 Anita Chan is Research Fellow in the Contemporary China Centre, Australian National University. Her research focuses on Chinese labour issues. Chan has published widely on Chinese workers' conditions, the Chinese trade union and labour rights issues, and is recognized world-wide as an expert on Chinese labour issues <http://rspas.anu.edu.au/people/personal/chana_ccc.php> (last accessed on 20 January 2009).

46 Chan (1993).

47 For example, the former ACFTU president Wei Jian Xing.

interests[48] within the party-state structure, though their attempts usually ended quietly.[49] After 2003, Chan partly revised her expectations of ACFTU reforms and even began to describe it as "an arm of the party-state".[50] She began to pay more attention to such matters as labour's struggle against capital, "legal right protection (依法维权)", the social accountability movement in enterprises and grass roots union construction.[51]

Leung was less equivocal on this matter, maintaining that the ACFTU, as part of the party-state, exists to legitimize and sustain the CCP [52] and to control workers. Hence the ACFTU places the party-state's requests ahead of the interests of workers.[53] Arguably, in the context of dramatic social transition, relations between the ACFTU and the party-state returned to the type of "mutually-cohering interest relationship" in existence before 1949. The ACFTU and the party-state no longer evaded, as they did in the 1950s, the union's function of protecting workers' rights. On the contrary, they sought together to advance the development of such a function.[54] The reason is that, as discussed especially in Chapter Three, with a poor social security system, labour issues were linked to basic survival. Inappropriate treatment of these issues led to turbulence. Therefore, from the stance of maintaining social stability and their own power, party-state leaders did not want industrial relations to deteriorate. As an extension of the party-state system, the ACFTU bore the responsibility of relieving pressure on the party-state by "... realizing the social function of the union, i.e. at the same time as safeguarding the general interests of the whole nation, trying its

48 To be more precise, these were the rights and interests of (labour-related) corporatists.

49 Chan (2002).

50 Chan and Ross (2003).

51 Chan (2005).

52 Because the CCP, up until 2002 when it changed its constitution, held that it was the vanguard of the working class, representing its essential interests.

53 Leung (2002) commented that "hoping for an organization that is supposed to control the workers to take up the role of struggling for workers' interests is simply as futile an attempt as trying to milk a bull."

54 This is the background of the ACFTU's recent slogan: "organize and protect (workers') legal rights practically (组织起来, 切实维权)".

best to speak out and protect employees' specific interests ..."[55] The party-state changed the positioning of the ACFTU from that of a tool of social control to one of "social stabilizer". Thus, the ACFTU did not cease to be a tool for the party-state.

5.2 Party-state and Employers' Associations

The relationship between the party-state and employers' associations is both simple and complex. On the one hand, it is relatively simple because employers' associations, compared with the ACFTU, have shorter histories with little involvement in the party-state's internal political struggles. On the other hand, it is complex because, unlike employees who have only one legally recognised organization, there are two separate national employers' associations, the CEC-CEDA and ACFIC. Both are less strictly controlled by the party-state than the ACFTU. Moreover, more spontaneous employers' associations have begun to emerge.

In section 3 of Chapter Two, we briefly discussed the history and current status of the CEC-CEDA, ACFIC and other emerging employers' associations, hinting at their relationships with the party-state. In this section, we argue in more detail that each employers' association developed distinctive relationships with the party-state due to the different constituencies and interests amongst them.

5.2.1 Party-state and CEC-CEDA

By looking into the history and status of the China Enterprise Confederation-China Enterprise Directors Association (CEC-CEDA), we see that, by 2008, it had a relatively clear and simple relationship with the party-state.

55 General Provisions in ACFTU (2003).

During the first two decades after 1979 the CEC-CEDA was a direct subsidiary of the State Economy Committee (SEC, 国家经委), once acting also as its training centre. Before 1999, the CEC-CEDA was a "government-run association (官办协会)", and its objectives were

> ... to strengthen the work of the government's [industrial] administration departments, and organize those people who are familiar with the economy to upgrade the management standard of the enterprises (the SOEs) ...[56]

During this period, the CEC-CEDA was akin to an officially-run, semi-academic institution specializing in the topic of enterprise management.[57]

After 1999, deepening economic reform affected the government's industry administration system and was the direct catalyst for the transformation and expansion of the CEC-CEDA. In this process, the CEC-CEDA, including "industry associations" which were loosely connected with it, was given two new functions. One was to act as a diversionary outlet channel for redundant officials during the streamlining of industrial departments.[58] The other was to help the government shift from "departmental management (部门管理)" in a planned economy to "industry management (行业管理)" in a market economy. The CEC-CEDA was one of the institutional options for the government to implement policies and co-ordinate different interest groups.[59] That is to say, like the ACFTU, the CEC-CEDA was supposed to act as an intermediary organization or,

56 Yuan (2004).

57 That is why the CEC-CEDA once also acted as the training centre of the SEC and some of its direct subsidiaries, e.g. the Enterprise Management Press (企业管理出版社), the China Enterprise Newspaper (中国企业报社), and the China Enterprise Training Centre (中国企业管理培训中心) which are all intended to push forward the modernization of China's enterprises (CEC-CEDA's official website: <www.cec-ceda.org.cn> last accessed on 20 January 2009).

58 According to Yu and Huang's study, many officials believed that the industry associations must be well established so that "no matter how the government reforms and streamlines the system, the ex-government staff will still have some ideal places to settle themselves" (Yu and Huang 2007).

59 Yu and Huang (2007); Zheng and Jiang (2003).

in the official language, the "the bridge and transmission belt"[60] between the party-state and enterprises/employers.[61]

After analysing government administration reform, Yu and Huang concluded that the Chinese government's 20-year-long goal was to cultivate the growth of industry associations by dissolving industrial departments so as to loosen the government's control over the economy, which was implemented previously by those departments.[62]

Thirty six nation-wide industry associations headed by the CEC-CEDA cover such diverse industries as machine manufacturing, textiles, electronics, chemicals and coal mining.[63] Most were formed after the relevant government ministries or bureaus were streamlined during the 1990s and subsequently.[64] Most, however, are only loosely connected with the CEC-CEDA and are not direct subsidiaries. In the bureaucratic administrative system, an industry association operated under the supervision of either the relevant government ministry,[65] if the specific ministry remained, or the State-owned Assets Supervision and Administration Commission

60 Article 3 in CEC-CEDA (2003).

61 That is why the CEC-CEDA, together with the ACFTU, is chosen as a member of the NTCLRC (国家协调劳动关系三方会议). We discuss the tripartite scheme in the next section.

62 Yu and Huang (2007).

63 The 36 nation-wide industry associations have very obscure relationships with the CEC-CEDA. There are some hints in the central government's website, but no clear statements, especially regarding the relationships between the CEC-CEDA and the industry associations under the former SETC <http://www.gov.cn/banshi/2005-06/27/content_10191.htm> (last accessed on 20 January 2009).

64 "Searching for the Revoked State Ministries" (in Chinese), *Chinese Youth Newspaper*, "寻访经贸委被撤销的国家局", 中国青年报, 22 February 2001.

65 For example, the China Association of Railway Engineering Construction works under the remaining State Ministry of Railway (铁道部).

(SASAC, 国资委),[66] if the ministry was abolished.[67] After the late 1990s, the CEC-CECDA and the industry associations undertook functions to help the government manage industrial development and encourage self-discipline, co-ordination and mediation within specific industries. Nevertheless, officially-run industry associations faced serious challenges. In particular, the government did not treat them as a mechanism of social self-governance, but regarded them as a different form of departmental management. The majority of the expenses of the industry associations were met by government funding, causing their leaders to think it unnecessary to be responsible to their members. Moreover, industry associations became places where ex-officials were accommodated. The government also conferred some regulatory power on them.[68]

Thus China's industry associations are not independent, civilian intermediary organizations. In 2008, they remain officially under the direct supervision of the party-state. As their location in the system is closer to the party-state than to enterprises and employers, their ability to fulfil the

66 The origins of the ten national industry associations working under the SASAC are as listed below: the China Machinery Industry Federation comes from the former State Ministry of Machinery Industry; the China National Light Industry Council comes from the former State Bureau of Light Industry; the China Iron and Steel Association comes from the former State Ministry of Metallurgical Industry; the China National Textile and Apparel Council comes from the former State Bureau of Textile Industry; the China Building Material Industry Association comes from the former State Bureau of Building Material Industry; the China Petroleum and Chemical Industry Association comes from the former State Ministry of Petroleum and Chemical Industry; the China Non-ferrous Metals Industry Association comes from the former China Non-ferrous Metals Company; and the China Coal Industry Association comes from the former State Ministry of Coal Industry. The China General Chamber of Commerce and the China Federation of Logistics and Purchasing are the only two associations which were not established to accommodate ex-officials. They were directly under the former State Economic and Trade Committee until the SETC itself was (partly) replaced by the SASAC (this information is derived respectively from the official websites of these associations).

67 "The SASAC Is Going to Put Forward Rules to Regulate Industry Associations" (in Chinese), *First Financial Daily*, "国资委将推出 '规范行业协会暂行办法'", 第一财经日报, 8 June 2007.

68 Yu and Huang (2007).

function of "bridge and transmission belt" between the party-state and the enterprises/employers is severely compromised.[69] For this reason, Zheng and Jiang argue that the future of the industry associations depends on how far the government goes in reforming its administrative functions. As economic reform is largely top-down and usually means lessening the power of the government over management, specific departments charged with implementing reform have little incentive to co-operate in handing over power to more autonomous associations.[70] The re-positioning and transformation of industry associations infringe vested interests. For central government policy makers, the extent to which officials and departments are willing to give up power is difficult to discern.[71]

Regarding the evolution of the industry associations since the 1990s, a reasonable observation is that the central policy-makers resorted to the tactic of "boiling the frog in warm water". During the first phase, industrial administrative departments from the era of planned economy were transferred to industry associations in the mixed market economy.[72] During

69 Yu et al. (2002).

70 Zheng and Jiang (2003). From the individual officials' point of view, the reform was virtually a revolution against themselves.

71 An incident of "industry association firing an enterprise manager", which happened in 2006 in Xiang-fan city, Hu-bei province, illustrates the problem. The Xiang-fan Light Industry Council (formerly the Bureau of Light Industry), for economic reasons, attempted to interfere with the transformation of Xiang-fan Aluminum Products Factory (a collectively owned enterprise), but did not succeed. It was so annoyed that it issued a document announcing that the Council had decided to fire the manager of the factory (over which the Council has no legal property rights). Such behaviour was so absurd that the Council was widely denounced and boycotted. Prof. Wu X. M., who is from Wuhan University, argues that the industry associations should be civilian organizations acting between the enterprises and the government; however, the Xiang-fan Light Industry Council still considered itself a part (or extension) of the government and sought to gain economic benefits (or "rents") from its power, instead of serving the interests of the industry and enterprise. Some scholars commented that the official industry associations are weird hybrids of the planned economy and the market economy ("Can Industry Association Fire Factory Manager" (in Chinese), *Xinhua News*, available at <http://news.xinhuanet.com/focus/2006-04/12/content_4376724.htm> last accessed on 20 January 2009).

72 Undoubtedly, the behaviour and performance of officially-run industry associations were not entirely satisfactory during the first phase, though the situation was better

the subsequent second phase, associations were to be transformed further to better suit the requirements of the market economy. If we bear in mind that gradualism was the philosophy behind China's reforms, such a "two-phase" approach is understandable.[73]

As to the use of industry associations to accommodate ex-officials, it is possible to argue that this practice is a form of compensation which "buys" the support of vested interest groups. To the extent that compensation removed an obstacle to reform, it furthered the government's aim of "gradualist" reform. It does not follow, however, that industry associations maintain the status quo when reform moves from one phase to another. As the role and status of industry associations are products of a transitional period during which a market economy is established, pressure from below for further development of industry associations increases. The question for the CEC-CEDA is how to transform itself gradually into an organization which primarily serves the interests of enterprises and employers rather than those of the party-state. Otherwise, it may be dumped by members in the face of competition from other employer associations.

5.2.2 Party-state and ACFIC

Because of its longer history and unique features, the All China Federation of Industry and Commerce (ACFIC) developed a relatively complex relationship with the party-state. From the discussion in Chapter Three, it will be recalled that ACFIC was established formally in 1953 as "a mass

---

than before, when government departments had the legal right to interfere in even the day-to-day operation of enterprises.

73 As pointed out by Fan, the biggest problem with China's reform is that the fait accompli interest groups fostered in the old system could well be the barrier and resistance to the development of the new system. Any attempts to change a system will change the existing layout of interests. A fundamental matter for system transition (reform) is to use part of the bonus gained from efficiency improvement to compensate the losers in the reforms. However, there are some interests that cannot be compensated financially, for example, the sense of belonging to a powerful privileged class (Fan 2008). This helps to explain the obstructive behaviour of some leaders of industrial associations, as in the case described in the last footnote.

organization and a civil chamber of commerce with the characteristics of a 'united front (统一战线)' under the leadership of the CCP, and a participating unit of the National People's Political Consultative Conference (NPPCC)".[74] As a "united front" organization, the ACFIC was quite different from either the ACFTU or the CEC-CEDA. ACFIC was outside the party-state system with relatively more independence and freedom. This did not mean, though, that the party-state let the ACFIC develop without political constraint. From an organizational perspective, the party-state asserted its indirect control over ACFIC through two mechanisms: first, through the United Front Work Department of the CC-CCP (UFWD-CC-CCP, 中共中央统战部); and, secondly, via the "democratic parties (民主党派)"[75] and the NPPCC.[76]

74 Information from <http://www.acfic.org.cn/cenweb/portal/user/anon/page/introducePage.page> (last accessed on 20 January 2009).

75 The so-called "democratic parties" refer to the eight parties which are under the leadership of the CCP. They are the Revolutionary Committee of KMT (RC-KMT), the China Democratic League (CDL), the China National Democratic Construction Association (CNDCA), the China Association for Promoting Democracy (CAPD), the Chinese Peasants' and Workers' Democratic Party (CPWDP), the China Zhi Gong Party (CZGP), the 9–3 (September 3rd) Society, and the Taiwan Democratic Self-governance Alliance (TDSA). These are all small parties which allied themselves with the CCP against the KMT regime before 1949. Cross memberships are commonly found among the CCP and the "democratic parties", and many leaders of these parties were or are themselves members of the CCP at the same time. The CCP used to co-ordinate the membership recruitment issues of these puppet parties, requiring them to focus on different specialties; for example, the CNDCA focuses on economic matters, the CDL on cultural and educational matters, etc. According to the "Civil Servant Law" promulgated in 2005, staff working in the "democratic parties" are treated as civil servants, i.e. part of the party-state system. Actually, from the organizational as well as financial perspective, the "democratic parties" had already been bureaucratized since the 1950s, though without any clear law or formal regulation ("Attentions on the Appointments of Democratic Parties' Members" (in Chinese), *Southern Weekend*, "民主党派任职问题引发关注", 南方周末, 18 January 2007).

76 The National People's Political Consultative Conference (NPPCC, 全国政协) is an organization within the party-state system that provides political accommodation

In the UFWD-CC-CCP's line of control, the party-state was involved in the leadership of ACFIC by appointing one of the vice-directors of the UFWD-CC-CCP as vice-chair of ACFIC. After 1988, this was usually the first vice-chair.[77] In relation to democratic parties and the NPPCC, the party-state manipulated ACFIC elections so that all of its chairs, except for the first (Chen Shutong), were members of the China National Democratic Construction Association (CNDCA, 民建),[78] which is one of the eight "democratic parties" under the leadership of the CCP. ACFIC chairs, from national to local levels, were also offered PPCC vice-chairs at a corresponding level, so that ACFIC was within the NPPCC's management framework, albeit relatively loosely.[79]

Except for macro-level control, the party-state does not interfere too much in the daily operation of ACFIC. Nevertheless, the relationship between the party-state and ACFIC varied over time, as the following brief overview illustrates.

1949–52

After coming to power in 1949, the CCP set about "remoulding the old society" and building a new "socialistic society". This involved reshaping various Chambers of Commerce left over by the KMT period. Conflicts and contradictions were bound to occur, as the new regime was supposed

---

for the "democratic parties" and non-CCP celebrities <http://www.cppcc.gov.cn/zxjj/jianjie_1.html> (last accessed on 20 January 2009).

77 Information is from official websites of the ACFIC <http://www.acfic.org.cn/cenweb/portal/user/anon/page/meetLeaderPage.page> and the UFWD-CC-CCP <http://www.zytzb.org.cn/zytzbwz/introduce/index.htm> (last accessed on 20 January 2009).

78 The CNDCA is "formed by members mainly from the economic circle, having the characteristics of a political alliance (with the CCP), striving to construct socialism with Chinese characteristics, participating in political affairs in the party co-operation and political consultation system under the leadership of the CCP" (official website of the CNDCA <www.cndca.org.cn> last accessed on 20 January 2009).

79 Information is from the official websites of the ACFIC <www.acfic.org.cn> and the NPPCC <www.cppcc.gov.cn> (last accessed on 20 January 2009).

to be building a "socialist country under proletarian dictatorship", while the Chambers of Commerce were typical representatives of the interest of the vanquished capitalist class. China in 1949 was disrupted severely by war and in desperate need of recovery. The new regime had to be cautious when dealing with the Chambers of Commerce as well as "patriotic capitalists", at least for a time, in order to utilize their resources and energy for economic re-construction. Against this background, the CC-CCP issued the "Instructions on Organizing the Federation of Industry and Commerce", trying to arrange a new national industrial and commercial organization to replace the existing Chambers of Commerce. The party-state realized its influence over the new organization mainly by means of personnel arrangement and financial support.[80]

The organizing process of the ACFIC was under the direct leadership of party departments at various levels such as the UFWD. Though key members of the preparatory committee were from business and commerce, the leadership of the original Chambers of Commerce did not stay. The party-state was cautious in selecting personnel and only those with a historical connection to the CCP were chosen.[81]

1952–56

The "Five Antis (五反)"[82] Campaign, which was conducted during February-April 1952, was the dividing line in the evolution of the relationship between the party-state and industrial and commercial interests. This was the first time that the new regime launched a political attack against the capitalist class and individuals. The magnitude and methods of the "Five Antis" Campaign had not been experienced before, though it could not be compared with subsequent nation-wide political campaigns. Such an ideological and political assault shocked even patriotic commercial interests, including the ACFIC's leadership. The deterrent effects of this movement

80 Wei and Yang (2005).

81 Ibid.

82 The "Five Antis (五反)" refer to anti-bribery, anti-nonpayment of taxes, anti-economic fraud, anti-stealing government property, and anti-economic spying.

were significant, forcing individuals who covertly resisted the leadership of the party-state and the ACFIC to begin to co-operate actively, or at least to be seen to be doing so.[83]

After the "Five Antis" Campaign, the UFWD-CC-CCP issued the "Instruction on Re-structuring the Federation of Industry and Commerce", advocating to:

> ... restructure the FIC, firing those who fall into the "Five Antis" range while attracting those who were active in the movement ... the local party committees and governments should control the leadership of the FICs ... SOEs should also take part in the activities of FIC ... the party and the government should realize their operational and political leadership over the FIC by means of the United Front Work Department and the Finance Department ...[84]

In compliance with this direction, the State Council issued a formal regulation, the "General Rules on Organizing the Federation of Industry and Commerce". Xue Muqiao, Director of the Private Enterprise Bureau of the Central Government, made the following statement:

> ... the establishment of FIC was to solve the leadership issue over the organizations in the private sector. The FICs were not merely a replacement of the old organizations but also a means for the state's future remoulding of the private sector; therefore, FICs were not just communication channels between the state and the commercial circle but also served the political needs [of the regime] ...[85]

Subsequently, the ACFIC began to accept more intervention from the party-state. Its work focus shifted gradually from "representing the legal interests of the private sector" to "working under the general mission of the state's transitional period, pushing practitioners and business owners in the private sector to accept patriotic and socialistic education, and promoting the 'socialistic transformation of capitalist industry and commerce' ..."[86]

83 Wei and Yang (2005).
84 UFWD-CC-CCP (1952).
85 As quoted by Wei and Yang (2005).
86 Chen (1953). The "socialistic transformation of the capitalist industry and commerce" refers to the nation-wide nationalization after 1953. Such "transformation" was supposed

1956–79

By the end of the first quarter of 1956, 99% of industrial enterprises and 85% of commercial companies in the private sector became "joint ventures" nominally owned jointly by the state and the private sector, which signalled the basic completion of the "socialistic transformation of capitalist industry and commerce".[87] Until 1979, ACFIC did the political bidding of the party-state. There were barely any independent private business owners or employers and hence ACFIC had no one to represent. After 1958, the ACFIC was state funded and its staff became state cadres.[88] During the Cultural Revolution, as discussed, even the ACFTU, which was supposedly a workers' organization, was attacked. The ACFIC's situation as an organization "representing the capitalists" was worse and its operations were paralyzed until 1979.

1979 to the Present

The ACFIC restarted operations at the Fourth National Congress in 1979.[89] However, because the Chinese economy was still dominated by the state-owned sector, the ACFIC, which was supposed to be suited to the needs of the private sector, lacked a rationale for its existence. Only during the 1990s did the non-SOE sector grow rapidly as economic reforms deepened, forcing the party-state to adjust its policy towards the ACFIC. In 1991, the CC-CCP issued an instruction stating that

to go through two stages: in the first stage, capitalism would be turned into state capitalism; and in the second stage, state capitalism would be turned into socialism.

87 Compilation of documents from Xinhua News Agency <http://news.xinhuanet.com/ziliao/2003-09/03/content_1060054.htm> (last accessed on 20 January 2009).

88 Wei and Yang (2005).

89 Almost 20 years since its last (the third) national congress in 1960. (Information from ACFIC's website. <http://www.acfic.org.cn/cenweb/portal/user/anon/page/deputyConventionPage.page> last accessed on 20 January 2009).

> ... the ACFIC is a mass organization and chamber of commerce with the characteristics of a "united front"; [it] is the government's assistant in managing the non-state-owned economy and a bridge connecting the party/government with the representatives from non-state-owned economy ...[90]

In 1993, with the approval of the CC-CCP and the central government, the ACFIC gained the second title of the China Civil Chamber of Commerce.[91] Subsequently, it shed some of its political colour and provided more business-related services to enterprises and employers and its work moved gradually from implementing party policies to more service-oriented activities, such as providing management training and organizing trade fairs.[92]

It does not follow, however, that the ACFIC became an economic organization serving the needs of enterprises and employers. According to the UFWD-CC-CCP, "ACFIC simultaneously contains the characteristics of united front, economic, and civil organization ... it is a mass organization under the leadership of the CCP, *mainly* for the purpose of forming the 'united front' ..."[93] We also have a hint of this in its personnel arrangements. Huang Mengfu, chair of ACFIC in 2007, was also a member of the CNDCA and the CCP, with a long career in the SOE sector, while the first vice-chair, Hu Deping, was vice-director of the UFWD-CC-CCP. This suggests that the ACFIC's leadership remained under the control of the party-state, and was an indirect extension of the party-state, though its situation was slightly better than that of direct party-state extensions such as the ACFTU and the CEC-CEDA.

90 CC-CCP (1991).

91 "Introduction to the ACFIC", <http://www.acfic.org.cn/cenweb/portal/user/anon/page/introducePage.page> (last accessed on 20 January 2009).

92 <http://www.acfic.org.cn/cenweb/portal/user/anon/page/workdDynamicChannelPage.page> last accessed on 20 January 2009.

93 Information from the official website of the UFWD-CC-CCP <http://www.zytzb.org.cn/zytzbwz/economic/gongshanglian/200804/t20080430_374274.htm> (last accessed on 20 January 2009).

5.2.3 Party-state and Emerging Employers' Associations

In subsection 2.3.3 of Chapter Two, we noted that the party-state's attitude towards spontaneous employer associations and Civil Chambers of Commerce gradually became more accepting as reforms deepened. In December 2005, Guangdong Province, in the front line of reforms, issued the "Regulation on Trade/Industry Associations", providing a much looser environment for the self-association of enterprises within specific trades and industries, while Shenzhen City, "in the front line of the front line", went further and established the "Shenzhen Trade Association Service Department", enforcing a new system of "no official level, no official staffing, no supervisory unit (无级别、无编制、无主管)"[94] for trade associations. These reforms were only trials in a few specific regions. At the national level, the "Regulation on the Registration and Management of Social Organizations" issued by the State Council in 1998 was still in effect in 2008. This regulation enforced a "double examination and double licensing" system. Anyone who sought to establish a social organization, including an employer association, first had to get the approval of the corresponding government industry administration department, then go through the registration process of the civil affairs administration bureau.[95] The examination and licensing processes were so complex and difficult that it was almost futile to attempt them independently without the nod of relevant party-state authorities.[96]

94 As we have discussed previously, many official/semi-official associations still enjoy the benefit and treatment of government departments (i.e. official level and official staffing). For example, the China Machinery Industry Federation comes from the former State Ministry of Machinery Industry; according to its "official level", its chair enjoys all the benefits of a minister.

95 State Council (1998).

96 Gao argues that, in the context of China's current system, a social organization cannot be "legal" unless it meets four "legitimacy standards": firstly, it must be socially legitimate, i.e. it must win the recognition from the society and participants; secondly, it must be legitimate from an administrative perspective, i.e. it must get approval from and be affiliated to certain administration authorities; thirdly, it must be politically legitimate, i.e. it must successfully stand the political examination which requires

Chen and Ma argued, therefore, that winning the support of the party-state system was a "must" for Civil Chambers of Commerce to develop. The Chambers developed vigorously in some areas, such as Wenzhou, simply because the local party-state leadership had a relatively open attitude towards them. Commercial groups, in return, rewarded officials with honorary positions in the organization, providing economic benefits in the form of allowances, or offering a retreat for their retirement from the party-state system.[97]

Spontaneously established Chambers of Commerce successfully opened, sometimes by controversial measures, a new era for intermediary third-party organizations in China.[98] As pointed out by Yu and Lu, before reform and opening-up, China had a very centralized leadership system,

---

that the organization does not breach a political bottom line, or even contributes to the current political order; lastly, it must be legally legitimate, i.e. it must go through the examination and registration process according to the law (Gao 2000).

97 Chen and Ma (2004).

98 It is understandable that, in the context of China, where the party-state holds an overwhelming position, the Civil Chambers of Commerce, to survive and develop, have to make compromises (sometimes even providing corrupt incentives) with officials. The most important thing is that these organizations are spontaneously established by entrepreneurs and employers to protect their own interests, and the existence and development of such organizations depend on whether they can genuinely serve their members. It is this characteristic that distinguishes them from official or semi-official organizations such as the CEC-CEDA and ACFIC. In fact, when the Civil Chambers of Commerce have grown up to a certain level, they no longer need to please government officials. The Wenzhou Fashion Industry Association is an example: in its preliminary stage after establishment in 1994, it invited the heads of most relevant party-state authorities (such as government, PC, PPCC, UFWD, taxation office and police) to be its honorary leaders or consultants. In 2003, after ten years of development, its fourth congress formally decided to stop hiring party-state officials as its honorary leaders or consultants (Chen and Ma 2004). It is worth pointing out that there may seem to be a contradiction to some western readers that a person who is hired cannot be "honorary", but in the Chinese system, a job can be claimed to be "honorary" as long as it is not full time, regardless of how much benefit that job may bring to the incumbent. This is clearly a loophole for corruption. Only recently (since 2007) have some local governments, such as Hangzhou and Xi-an, issued regulations to ban such practices.

confusing boundaries between public and private, state and society, government and people. After 1979, reforms encouraged "smaller government and bigger society", facilitating a process of the state's gradual retreat from social and economic arenas.[99] It is ironic, though, that, in a "socialist country" nominally "led by the working class", the party-state is more willing to experiment with free associations among employers and capitalists than among workers.[100]

5.3 The National Tripartite Conference on Labour Relations Co-ordination

In the last two sections, we discussed the relationships between the party-state and the ACFTU and various employers' associations. The party-state has constantly occupied the leading position in both of these two sets of relationships.

As the ACFTU, the CEC-CEDA and the ACFIC were, more or less, organizational extensions of the party-state, with parallel reporting lines to different bureaucratic bodies,[101] these industrial relations actors had little

99 Yu and Lu (2004).

100 If this situation continues, the power gap between the employers and employees will only become wider. What will the party-state's response be? Will it resort to strengthening individual employees' power by enhancing state intervention, as with the new labour contract law passed in June, 2007? Or will it gradually loosen control over labour unions? Or will it do both? I make no prediction, but the present position seems unstable.

101 As pointed out previously, the ACFTU works under the Employee Works Committee (now called Enterprise Works Committee) of the CC-CCP, being in the line of the party system; the CEC-CEDA works under double-line control of the Ministry of Commerce and the State-owned Assets Supervision and Administration Commission, being in the line of the state system; and the ACFIC works under double-line control of the United Front Work Department of the CC-CCP and the National People's Political Consultative Conference, in the line of the party system.

direct communication with each other. This situation remained until a new scheme, the National Tripartite Conference on Labour Relations Co-ordination (NTCLRC), was inaugurated in 2001, providing a platform for the co-ordination of labour relations above the workplace level.

The NTCLRC's origins can be traced back to August 1990 when the Standing Committee of the NPC approved China's ratification of ILO Convention 144 – the Convention about Tripartite Consultations to Promote the Implementation of International Labour Standards.[102] Theoretically, the Convention comes into force for any member twelve months after the date of ratification has been registered,[103] but China's NTCLRC was not established for almost eleven years after ratification. There was no public explanation for this delay, but two major reasons are possible. First, during the period between the Tian-an-men Square Incident in 1989 and Deng's Southern Tour (南巡) in 1992, economic reform lacked clear direction, marked by a heated ideological debate over whether the reform is "socialist or capitalist".[104] In this context, no one in the party-state or its extensions was willing to take up the role of employers' association, a capitalist organization, in the NTCLRC. Secondly, the economy was dominated by the state-owned sector until the mid 1990s, and labour relations issues were, at least superficially, of secondary importance.[105] The government, though it had ratified the Convention, was under little pressure to establish the tripartite scheme.

102 From its inception in 1919, the ILO has promoted tripartism among member states as a means of giving voice to all parties and preventing labour disputes from becoming intractable. In such a tripartite system, the government consults representatives of employers and employees and involves them in the formulation of socio-economic policies (Shen and Benson (2008), p. 233).

103 Article 8 in ILO (1976).

104 Ma and Ling (1998).

105 This can partly be proved by the statistics of recorded labour disputes, as shown in the next paragraph. Of course, before 1990s, in many SOEs, labour disputes were not always formally recorded. This is one reason why labour disputes seemed to be less serious before the 1990s. According to the bureaucratic principle of "no case no worries", the policy-makers did not need to worry about labour issues (not because they did not exist, but because they were not reported or recorded).

During the latter part of the 1990s, as reform moved forward and the non-SOE sector became more important in the national economy, the issue of labour relations gradually came to the surface as one of the major social problems of the transitional period. According to official data, labour disputes, formally recorded by various labour tribunals across the country, climbed from 9,600 in 1990, when Convention 144 was ratified; to 33,000 in 1995, when the Labour Law was first promulgated; and to 155,000 in 2001, when the Tripartite Conference was eventually founded.[106] During the eleven years between 1990 and 2001, the growth trend in labour disputes was alarmingly explosive, the case numbers more than tripling every five years.[107] Labour issues became a serious social problem confronting China's policy-makers.[108]

In this context, the Tripartite Conference gained the attention of central policy-makers as a possible tool for easing social conflicts and promoting social harmony. According to a memorandum of the Tripartite Conference, in August 2001, the party-state appointed MOLSS to represent the government, the ACFTU to "represent" employees and the CEC-CEDA to "represent" employers. The three formed the National Tripartite Conference on Labour Relations Co-ordination (NTCLRC), with the following responsibilities:

106 NBS and MOLSS (1990–91, 1995–96, 1997–2003) as quoted by Fu and Choy (2004), p. 18.

107 As mentioned in previous discussions, before the 1990s, in many SOEs, labour disputes were not always formally lodged and recorded, making the 1990 base of recorded cases relatively small. Since then, the development of the non-SOE sector, the strengthening of employees' legal consciousness and the Chinese government's greater open-mindedness towards negative statistics all combined to cause recorded labour dispute case numbers to grow quickly. The inherent reliability problems of Chinese statistics make it difficult to estimate the contributions of different factors to the growth of labour disputes.

108 Such concerns can be found in the report of the 17th national congress of the CCP which was held in October 2007. The report mentioned many times the problem of how to let more working people share in the benefits of economic growth, ("Let More Working People Share the Economic Growth" (in Chinese), *People's Daily*, "让更多劳动者分享发展成果", 人民日报, 22 October 2007).

2. Responsibilities and tasks:

I. Research and analyse labour-related economic reform policies and the socio-economic development plan, and propose suggestions for policy-making.
II. Communicate within the circle about problems arising from co-ordination efforts in labour relations in respective areas, research and analyse the situation of national labour relations and development trends, co-ordinate and reach agreement on significant issues concerning the labour relation situation as a whole.
III. Propose opinions and suggestions for the drafting, supervising, and adjusting of labour-related laws, regulations, rules, and policies.
IV. Instruct and co-ordinate the establishment of tripartite schemes at the local level and the negotiation of collective labour contracts in the enterprises; summarize and promote typical and successful experiences.
V. Investigate and analyse collective labour disputes and mass incidents with national influence, propose opinions and suggestions for the solution of such matters.

3. Contents of co-ordination works:

I. Co-ordination on collective (labour contract) bargaining systems;
II. Labour relations in the process of enterprise ownership transformation;
III. Salary distribution;
IV. Minimum wage, work time, rest and vacations, health and safety, special protection for female and non-adult workers, welfare packages, vocational training and other labour standards;
V. Prevention and settlement of labour disputes;
VI. Construction of industrial democracy and union organization;
VII. Other issues concerning the adjustment of labour relations ...[109]

From these responsibilities and tasks we can see that the party-state had high expectations for the NTCLRC, hoping that it would provide an all-around package of solutions for the co-ordination of labour relations, thereby relieving the party-state of problems arising from labour-related matters.

109 Information based on the memoranda of ten meetings of the NTCLRC which were held between 2001 and 2006 <www.molss.gov.cn> (last accessed on 20 January 2009).

Unfortunately, the tripartite system did not live up to expectations. According to the *China Labour Statistical Yearbook*, labour disputes climbed from 155,000 in 2001 to 317,000 in 2006.[110] One may argue that there were complex reasons for the growing trend in labour disputes, while the phenomenon of a high rate of labour disputes is not uncommon during a transitional period.[111] However, the NTCLRC, as a national level mechanism with the direct responsibility to ease labour relations, seems to have had little success.

The memoranda of the ten meetings of the NTCLRC held from 2001 to 2006[112] give little evidence of practical work plans or proposals. Instead, they set out bureaucratic and official formalities. After its establishment in 2001, the NTCLRC did little except set up subordinate organizations at provincial and city levels throughout the country. The tripartite organizations were originally supposed to be a platform for equal communication among the government, employers and employees, but they evolved into yet another organizational "decoration" in the party-state system.[113]

The ineffectiveness of the tripartite scheme is not surprising if we take into account the characteristics of its major participants. According to ILO Convention 144, employer and employee organizations in the tripartite scheme should be "the most representative organizations of employers and workers enjoying the right of freedom of association".[114] As we saw in earlier chapters, both the ACFTU and the CEC-CEDA were, more or less, extensions of the party-state system, with the bureaucratic working style of semi-governmental organizations. As their power was conferred

110 NBS and MOLSS (2007), disc edition, Table 9.1.

111 Yin et al. (2000).

112 Documents are available at <http://www.cec-ceda.org.cn/ldgx/info/more.php?page=oandname=会议与纪要> (last accessed on 20 January 2009).

113 This situation can be summarized by a Chinese proverb: "Tangerines in the southern bank of the Huai River will grow up as oranges in the northern part (淮南为桔，淮北为枳)", meaning that the environment has tremendous influence over the outcome of a policy. Many mechanisms imported from western countries – the tripartite system in this case – have become different things in China, though having the same name.

114 Clause 1 in ILO (1976).

by the party-state rather than deriving from members' authorization and recognition, they had little motivation or pressure to struggle for members' interests. For bureaucrats who took part in the tripartite conferences, it was important to maintain peaceable relations between the people from different departments. No difficult issues were debated, as participants were part of the same bureaucracy. Therefore, conflicts did not emerge in the tripartite conference, as they did in the work place. For this reason, tripartite conferences were usually held in an "over-harmonious environment", without seriously discussing, let alone solving, actual problems.

Other defects of the scheme were of a technical nature. It was a mistake to appoint MOLSS as the sole representative of the government in the NTCLRC. During the transitional period, many labour-related issues such as redundancy caused by SOE transformation, corruption issues in SOEs, and living stipends for laid-off workers, could not be solved by a single government department. MOLSS simply did not have sufficient power to solve these problems. Other issues such as the regulation of the minimum wage, which were originally the responsibility of MOLSS, shifted to the tripartite scheme, lowering the already low efficiency of the government ministry.[115]

These factors combined to make the NTCLRC ineffective. The key problem, however, lay in the absence of freedom of association. It may be argued that if there is neither a free labour union nor free employers' association, there can hardly be effective co-ordination through a "tripartite" scheme. Indeed, in the ILO's tripartite model the three parties are supposed to be independent and strong enough to carry out a meaningful "social dialogue". As pointed out by the ILO, the principles underlying Convention 144 were two other Conventions: Convention 87, the Freedom of Association and Protection of the Right to Organize, and Convention 98, the Right to Organize and Collective Bargaining.[116] Though this indicates that an international consensus emerged over how to establish a successful tripartite scheme, China did not ratify Conventions 87 or 98. The inference

115 Clarke et al. (2002).
116 ILO (1976).

is that China "castrated" Convention 144 by ratifying it without entering into Conventions 87 and 98. It is puzzling that the ILO allowed China to do so, gaining a nominal ratification of Convention 144 with little actual content. Perhaps the ILO considered it better to have China on board to a limited extent than not at all.

Even some official institutes, such as RI-MOLSS, expressed their concern, though cautiously, with careful wording, on the importance of freedom of association, especially for labour organizations:

> ... To ensure just enforcement of the law, there must be a supervising and balancing power to oversee the execution of the government. To achieve this, the fundamental way is to cultivate the workers' own power, i.e. to establish a strong and powerful union, so that it can superintend the behaviour of enterprises and government. Otherwise, it is no use establishing a mediation system led by the government, for it may be an even worse situation of "larger (governmental) power leading to higher extraction of 'rents'". ... The biggest problem for China today is that the union is too weak to protect the workers, and this leads to impairment of the effectiveness of other measures ...[117]

Yin et al., by studying a number of cases in Eastern Europe, pointed out that the tripartite scheme is supposed to be a possible channel for developing new industrial relations in the context of a changing socio-economic environment. When the state gradually withdraws from direct interference in socio-economic affairs, employers and employees, with their representative organizations, can start to take responsibility for their own fate and future. Such a real tripartite scheme played a significant role in the transition process in the former socialist economies in Eastern Europe.[118] However, it is possible to hypothesize that it is exactly for that reason that Chinese policy-makers were highly sensitive to the tripartite scheme. Central policy-makers learnt many lessons from Eastern Europe, and were extremely cautious about any thing that might trigger a domino effect. In this case, a genuine tripartite scheme could be very dangerous to the party-state, as it would open the door for free association and free co-ordination and negotiation.

117 Research Institute of MOLSS (2004a).
118 Yin et al. (2000).

That is the dilemma confronting the party-state. On the one hand, a tripartite scheme represents a clear trend in the emergence of civil society where citizens form their own organizations for co-ordination and negotiation.[119] On the other hand, such an attempt might, sooner or later, lead to a challenge to the power of the party-state, as employees and employers get used to having their own representation.

The conclusion to be drawn is that the party-state preferred to establish a nominal tripartite scheme under its strict control rather than a real one. The party-state shows no intention of allowing the diversification of mass organizations, including employers' and employee associations. Though the policy is relatively looser for employers' associations, the selection of the CEC-CEDA and not the ACFIC or other spontaneous employers' associations as the "representative" of employers indicates that this "tripartite" scheme is a tool to deny space to any potential development of a civil rights movement. For this reason, the NTCLRC has become yet another bureaucratic arrangement. A genuine "tripartite" scheme is unlikely to function effectively before political reform is implemented which brings China into line with ILO Conventions.

Conclusions

In this chapter, we discussed three sets of relationships among China's industrial relations actors at the macro-level, namely between the party-state and the ACFTU, the party-state and employer associations, and the tripartite system. After analysing interactions between the party-state and

119 The information asymmetry between labour and capital implies that conflicts are inherent in the employment relationships; but the interdependency of employers and employees also implies that these conflicts must be solved properly, otherwise no one will win in the long run (Bray et al. 2005). These beliefs set the theoretical foundation for the joint regulation by labour, capital and the state. As Kaufman put it, a joint regulation (by labour, capital and the state) can safeguard the stability of the society and achieve balance between efficiency and justice (Kaufman et al. ed. 2003).

ACFTU during various historical periods, we argued that even though the ACFTU was an extension organization established by the party-state, relations were not always a simple case of "subordinate obeying the superior" but varied during different historical periods. Employers' associations have shorter histories, with little involvement in the party-state's internal political struggles. However, the diversity of employers' associations made the relation between the party-state and various employers' associations no less complicated. Each of the three types of employers' associations has a distinctive relationship, according to its specific characteristics, with the party-state.

The NTCLRC provided a new platform for the co-ordination of labour relations above the workplace level. However, we concluded that though the tripartite system was originally supposed to be a platform for equal communication among the state, employers and employees, it has evolved into yet another organizational "decoration" in China's party-state system.

CHAPTER SIX

Interactions among Grass Roots Unions, Employers and Employees

Introduction

In the last chapter, we explored interactions among the three major industrial relations actors above the workplace level in China, involving the party-state, ACFTU, and employers' associations. We pointed out that they revolved around the party-state, though there were variations in specific relationships in different periods of times.

In this chapter, we shift our attention to interactions among three major industrial relations actors at the workplace level: the grass roots unions, employers and employees. We discuss, firstly, the relationship between grass roots unions and employees, pointing out that, for most of the time, grass roots unions used the employees as tools to serve the will of their superiors – the party-state and the ACFTU. During the Cultural Revolution, employees took the initiative to break the restraints imposed on the grass roots unions. Secondly, we argue that, for historical and political reasons, the ACFTU's grass roots unions interacted with employers during several limited periods: 1921–25, 1949–56 and 1979 onwards. In the first two periods, interactions were more political than after 1979. Though interactions among grass roots unions and employers were more economic after 1979, the bargaining strength of grass roots unions, whether in SOEs or non-SOEs, was restricted by their dependence on the will of the employers. Finally, we analyse relationships between employers and employees in enterprises of different types, showing that the healthy development of relationships depended on the state's ability and willingness to enforce labour related laws and rules promulgated since the 1990s.

6.1 Grass Roots Unions and Employees

In western countries during the twentieth century, both the old political Left and the Right were suspicious of the functions of unions in a capitalist economy, based on the assumption that unions operated too effectively. The Left worried that unions won rights and benefits for workers, reducing their "revolutionary spirit". The Right feared the potential strength of unions and their capacity to dominate labour markets.[1] Neither the classic concerns of the Left nor those of the Right were borne out, however, by the development of China's unions.

As pointed out in Chapter Four, the literature[2] on China's labour unions rarely identifies grass roots unions as a separate industrial relations actor, usually treating the ACFTU and grass roots unions as a whole. The literature that analyses separately the interactions between grass roots unions and employees is even scarcer.[3] As China's economic reform developed, so did industrial relations in the workplace, forcing grass roots unions to evolve, though slowly, to be more economic and service oriented than the upper level ACFTU which, as a part of the "superstructure", concentrated on political issues.[4]

1 Western (1997), pp. 3–13.

2 For example, Chan (1993, 2002, 2003); Leung (2002); Gilbert (2005); Zhang (2003); Qi (2004); Feng (2006).

3 In fact, I have so far found no such literature. Most of the material used for this section comes from other relevant research fields such as history and political science. This lack of research attention is due mainly to two phenomena: on the one hand, research on China's industrial relations has started quite recently, and researchers have tended to focus on macro issues (such as the interaction between the party-state and the ACFTU) rather than on issues at the workplace level; on the other hand, the operation of grass roots unions, especially before 1979, has indeed been closely linked with the ACFTU, and many of their activities have been related to macro-level political issues.

4 However, as the activities of the CCP, the ACFTU and the grass roots unions were highly interwoven (especially in the years before 1949), the discussion in this section will inevitably overlap with that about the party-state and the ACFTU in previous chapters.

6.1.1 Grass Roots Unions and Employees before 1949

As we saw in Chapter Five, the ACFTU, before 1949, was under the absolute control of the CCP and actively facilitated the CCP's objective of seizing power. In this context, how did the ACFTU's grass roots branches carry out their work among employees so as to serve the macro-level objective of seizing power? And what were the relationships between grass roots unions and employees during this period?

Based on the information provided by various sources of literature,[5] we argue that relationships between grass roots unions and employees before 1949 are best divided into three stages. The first, 1921–25, was a stage of agitation, organization and initial action. The second, 1925–27, was one of organized mass mobilisation, while the third, 1927–49, was a period of "hibernation" for the ACFTU as well as for its grass roots unions, as they virtually ceased operation because of the CCP's failure in cities and its strategic shift to "military struggle (武装斗争)" and to "using rural areas to besiege cities (农村包围城市)." There was little to investigate in the interaction between the ACFTU's grass roots unions and employees during 1927–49.

Agitation, Organization and Initial Actions 1921–25

As we saw in Chapter Two, the CCP in August 1921 established the "Chinese Labour Combination Secretariat (中国劳动组合书记部)", the predecessor of the ACFTU, in Shanghai. The most successful branch of the Secretariat was its Hunan provincial section, in which some of the most famous future leaders of the CCP, including Mao Zedong, Liu Shaoqi and Li Lisan, worked. During its peak period, in 1922–23, the Hunan section alone had more than 20 affiliates with a total membership of around 40–50,000 workers.[6]

5 For example, CC-CCP (1945); Jin (2002); Li and Liu (2005); Perry (2008); Wu and Liu (2004); Yang (2002); Yu (2002, 2006a); Zheng et al. (1997).

6 Zheng et al. (1997), p. 2439.

In investigating the question of how the ACFTU's grass roots unions successfully agitated and organised, establishing linkages and relationships with workers, the best case study is Anyuan Railway and Mining Workers' Club (安源路矿工人俱乐部). Anyuan's experiences were unique in the history of the CCP and the Chinese working class for three reasons: first, the Anyuan Strike was one of the most famous early instances of CCP organisation of labour movement activity; second, by 1924, one fifth of all CCP members were in Anyuan; and third, Mao Zedong, Liu Shaoqi and Li Lisan were heavily involved.[7]

According to a number of authors,[8] Mao and Li went to the Anyuan mining site three times before finally settling on the following strategy:

> ... utilize all possible legal methods to obtain legal positions, get close to the working mass ... find, organize and train the progressive elements among them, establish a party branch as the core of united forces ...[9]

In order to put this strategy into practice, the first thing to do was to establish a school for miners' children and a workers' night school, and to use the teaching forum as the media for agitation and propaganda.[10] Imbued with ideological education, workers accepted theories promoted by Li and

7 Ibid. "Chairman Mao Goes to Anyuan (毛主席去安源)" (a painting) and "Burning the Plain (燎原)" (a movie) were the two most influential art works about the Anyuan labour movement. For a long time records of the Anyuan labour movement paid tribute only to Mao Zedong. But according to Li and Liu's research, Mao was involved only in the early stage of Anyuan's labour activities, and most of the detailed work was done by Li Lisan and Liu Shaoqi (Li and Liu (2005), pp. 35–67; see also Perry 2008).

8 Li and Liu (2005); Perry (2008); Yu (2006a).

9 Recollection of Li Lisan as quoted by Li and Liu (2005), p. 37.

10 Yu (2006b) provided some historical detail about what Li and other CCP activists taught in the schools: Li said, "You workers live a very hard life here." The workers responded, "It's hard, but compared with the life in the countryside it's already a lot better here." Li said, "No, your labour is worth 10 dollars, but you are only paid 50 cents; the capitalists and foremen have taken away the other 9.5 dollars." The workers responded, "But I would not be able to earn even 50 cents if I stay in the countryside; the boss deserves the rest of the money." Li said, "Wrong again! There is a great figure

his colleagues. Li then promoted party membership among workers, establishing the CCP's first branch for industrial workers in February 1922.[11] With the CCP branch as the "backbone", workers formed the Anyuan Railway and Mining Workers' Club, which was the embryo of China's grass roots unions.[12]

When the Club was established,[13] Mao and Li believed that the time was ripe for workers to strike for a wage increase and for a formal labour union. The famous "Anyuan Railway and Mining Workers' Grand Strike" was the first in China to be led by a political party and a quasi-union. The employer conceded most of the demands, among which the most significant was recognising the Anyuan Railway and Mining Workers' Club as the representative body of the workers, making it in effect a grass roots union.[14]

Though the CCP used the workers as a power source, workers themselves gained from the strike, economically and in terms of morale.[15] Nevertheless, some workers were satisfied with the outcome, while others were not, agitating for more strike action.[16] Even the leaders themselves had

---

named Marx who told us that the workers are 'exploited' by the capitalists. We can get all the money back by uniting ourselves and struggling against the capitalists."

11 As we indicated in the last chapter, the CCP was founded by intellectual elites. There was no worker involved in CCP's activities until its Anyuan Railway and Mining branch was established.

12 Li and Liu (2005), pp. 42–44.

13 By September 1922, Li had recruited about 10 party members and 30 youth league members in Anyuan, and the Workers' Club had attracted more than 700 members (Li and Liu (2005), p. 47).

14 "Treaty for the Settlement of Anyuan Railway and Mining Workers' Strike" (in Chinese) as quoted by Li and Liu (2005), pp. 60–61.

15 Spiritually, the once downtrodden miners, belittled as beasts of burden before the strike, found a sense of dignity and respect afterwards (Perry (2008), p. 1152), while, from the economic point of view, the workers won a 20% wage increase plus various other compensations such as paid holidays, sick leave and year-end bonus etc. (Li and Liu (2005), p. 61).

16 Liu Shaoqi later recalled how he and Li Lisan had been driven to tears by angry workers who threatened to beat them up when they refused to approve a second strike (Liu 1988 as quoted by Perry (2008), p. 1158).

different opinions, with Li Weihan the more extremist.[17] As pointed out by Western, though many Marxists saw unions as advancing a collective class interest in freedom from the uncertainty of the labour market, Leninists worried that unions delivered only limited short-term gains to workers, while the modest advances in wages and conditions achieved obstructed revolutionary action led by the vanguard party.[18] In the 1920s, the CCP was controlled strictly by the Russian Leninists. Li's radical reaction was not surprising. He believed that the goal was not small-scale reform within capitalism, such as collective bargaining. The Communist party wanted to subvert the system by emancipating the working class from the shackles of the wage system.

In summary, Anyuan was an important early example of how a grass roots union, under the control of the CCP and the ACFTU, worked to agitate and organize employees for industrial action. During 1921–25, the major tasks of the grass roots unions were to "enlighten" the workers in ideological consciousness and tie the CCP's political objectives to the workers' economic demands. The ultimate purpose of these activities was to serve the CCP's political objectives rather than the worker's own interests, but workers' conditions did improve initially.

By studying the experience in Anyuan, similar cases in Wuhan, Shanghai and other cities,[19] and the recollections of Zhang Guotao,[20] a founding member of the CCP and leader of the labour movement during its early years, the CCP developed grass roots unions in the five ways listed below.

First, it established a workers' school.
Second, it identified and developed worker activists and cadres.
Third, it organized a (quasi) union, usually in the name of a workers' club.

17 Refer back to the footnotes of subsection 5.1.1, where we discussed a debate between Liu Shaoqi and Li Weihan regarding strikes as an agitating weapon.
18 Western (1997), pp. 4–5.
19 Zheng et al. (1997), pp. 2478–84.
20 Zhang (1998) Vol. 1., pp. 261–82.

Fourth, it mobilized strikes to demand higher wages and the establishment of a union.
Fifth, it further enlarged the influence of the organization (union and party).

These approaches were effective and successful in helping the ACFTU's grass roots unions gain an anchor point among workers.

Organized Mass Movement 1925–27

After several years of development, the number of grass roots unions under the control of the CCP grew substantially. By May 1925, when the Chinese Labour Combination Secretariat held the Second National Labour Conference in Guangzhou and formally promulgated the establishment of the ACFTU, the ACFTU claimed to represent 165 unions nation-wide with a total membership of 540,000 workers, while the CCP had only 900-odd members at that time.[21]

In the context of the first KMT-CCP's First United Front's "Grand Revolution (大革命)",[22] the ACFTU organized a series of political strikes, the most famous of which were the "May 30 Movement (五卅运动)"[23]

21 Zheng et al. (1997), pp. 306 and 2348.

22 The first co-operation between the KMT and the CCP refers to the two parties' co-operation during 1924–27, which was mediated by the Soviet Union. At the reformed KMT's first national congress, which was held in January 1924 in Guangzhou, Dr Sun Yat Sen announced the KMT's "Three Major Policies (三大政策)", i.e. "Ally with Russia, Accommodate the Communists and Assist the Peasants and Workers (联俄、容共、扶助农工)", symbolizing the start of the co-operation between the KMT and the CCP (Zhang (1998) Vol. 1, pp. 213–323).

23 In February 1925, around 40,000 workers in 22 textile factories owned by Japanese investors began to strike in protest against the Japanese capitalists' beating and laying off of workers without reasons. The CC-CCP had set up a strike committee to organize the movement. On 15 May, the Japanese capitalists shot and killed the worker representative Gu Zheng Hong, who was a communist party member, and injured more than ten other workers. This led to bigger-scale protests. The CCP then established the ACFTU's Shanghai section and organized an anti-Japanese labour

and the "Canton-Hong Kong Grand Strike (省港大罢工)".[24] Both became nation-wide anti-imperialist movements. Because of the link between the CCP and its grass roots unions, labour activities during 1925–27 were highly political. Unlike earlier strikes, which were confined to individual enterprises and demanded mostly economic benefits, subsequent actions were organized on such a scale that they could rightly be deemed to be mass social movements rather than random workplace-level incidents.

When the CCP-led strike action peaked, winning substantial support for the CCP and its unions, it was no longer satisfied with peaceful action. With the divergence between the KMT and the CCP becoming wider and the Northern Expedition War progressing more quickly than expected, the CCP made the decision to seize power in some localities through armed workers' insurrections, of which there were three in Shanghai in 1926–27.

The first two Shanghai insurrections in October 1926 and February 1927 failed because of poor preparation. The CCP established a Special Task Committee[25] to prepare for a third insurrection, forming a several-

---

movement. On 30 May 1925, when the Shanghai workers and students were protesting in Nanjing Road, which was located in the British Concession area, the British police suddenly opened fire into the crowd, causing 13 deaths and dozens of injured. This was the famous "May 30th Incident (五卅惨案)" which led to series of strikes named the "May 30th Movement (五卅运动)" (Xinhua News Agency's compiled materials, <http://news.xinhuanet.com/ziliao/2003-01/20/content_698206.htm> last accessed on 20 January 2009).

24 The "May 30th Movement (五卅运动)" led to the "Canton-Hong Kong Grand Strike (省港大罢工)". After the "May 30th Movement (五卅运动)", some Hong Kong workers went on strikes and marched back to Canton (Guangzhou). On 23 June 1925, when the striking workers and students held a demonstration parade and marched outside, on the other side of a small river surrounding the British and French Concession area, the British and French police opened fire into the crowd, causing about 50 deaths and about 170 injured. The incident triggered the "Canton-Hong Kong Grand Strike (省港大罢工)", in which more than a quarter of a million workers participated, lasting for 16 months (Xinhua News Agency's compiled materials <http://news.xinhuanet.com/politics/2006-06/23/content_4737039.htm> last accessed on 20 January 2009).

25 The special task committee was led by Chen Duxiu, the founder and the then Secretary General of the CCP, and Zhou Enlai, the then military leader of the CCP and later Premier of P. R. China 1949–76.

thousand-strong armed workers' picket to maintain public security. On the 21 March 1927, the CCP took the opportunity, which arose when the KMT's Northern Expedition Army besieged Shanghai but had not yet entered metropolitan areas, to launch the third workers' insurrection. After thirty hours of severe fighting, the CCP seized control of Shanghai at a cost of around 300 workers killed and 1,000 wounded. The CCP established and led the "Shanghai Civilian Council".[26]

The success of this workers' insurrection was the climax of the labour movement in the 1920s, directly triggering the "4–12 (April 12th) Incident",[27] which ended the First United Front. Issues between the KMT and the CCP emerged at the very beginning of their co-operation,[28] and difference became very obvious after the 1926 "3–20 (March 20th) Incident"[29] which resulted in the "Resolution to Reorganize (KMT) Party Affairs".[30] The third workers' insurrection convinced Jiang Jieshi that the CCP was no longer satisfied with peaceful labour action but intended to seize power,

26 "The Three Workers' Insurrections in Shanghai" (in Chinese), *People's Daily*, "上海工人三次武装起义", 人民日报, 29 June 2006.

27 On 12th April 1927, General Bai Chongxi, the commander of Shanghai-Songjiang Military Headquarters, following secret instructions from Jiang Jieshi, induced the local union gangsters (the Green Gang) to provoke fighting with the CCP unions' picket. Bai then disarmed the workers' picket in the name of stopping internal fighting among the workers. On the next day, when the CCP's unions organized a demonstration, Bai opened fire. Many CCP and union members were arrested, detained and even killed (Yang 2002).

28 As early as the first national congress of the KMT, the CCP and Youth League members occupied 10% of the seats, while they counted for only 2% of KMT members. In the Central Executive Committee of KMT, the CCP and Youth League members occupied even more than 25% of seats, with two minister and three deputy-minister positions in the six central departments. This immediately caused severe criticism from all other factions within the KMT, denouncing the CCP as the agent of Soviet Russia with the mission to control the KMT (Zhang (1998) Vol. 1, pp. 213–323).

29 On 20 March 1925, Jiang Jieshi, suspecting a potential anti-Jiang intrigue led by the left-wing of the KMT and the Russian military consultants, declared martial law in Guangzhou and arrested a few military officers who were CCP members (Yang 2002).

30 The direct result of the "3–20 (March 20th) Incident" was the passage of the "Resolution to Reorganize (KMT) Party Affairs", which strictly limited the CCP members' position and power within the KMT (Yang 2002).

at least, locally, by quasi-military force. The CCP's control over Shanghai, the most important industrial and financial centre in China, led Jiang and the right wing of the KMT to break finally with the CCP in 1927.[31]

In summary, during 1925–27, workers joining grass roots unions were industrial actors for the CCP in an organized mass movement. Except for a few fragmentary economic-oriented actions, grass roots union activities were to organize and agitate the working class in support of the CCP's attempt to seize power.

"Hibernation" 1927–49

After the breach with the KMT in 1927, the CCP was forced to shift to "military struggle (武装斗争)" and to "using rural areas to besiege cities (农村包围城市)", ceasing all of the ACFTU and grass roots unions' operations in urban areas. Loyal worker followers of the CCP, if not detained or killed by the KMT, commonly joined in the powerful current of military struggle and became professional revolutionaries and soldiers. After 1927, twenty-two years of military struggle against the KMT, and later the Japanese, virtually re-shaped all CCP members' lives. Intellectuals, workers, peasants – no matter what their origins – all became professional revolutionaries and soldiers by 1949.

6.1.2 Grass Roots Unions and Employees 1949–79

If we compare the relationship between grass roots unions and employees with the relationship between the ACFTU and the party-state discussed in Chapter Six, an interesting phenomenon emerges. When the organisational and political linkages between the ACFTU and the party-state were strong between 1949 and 1958, relationships between grass roots unions and employees were very limited. During the Cultural Revolution, 1966–76, however, when the ACFTU was virtually dumped by the party-state, employee relations with grass roots unions (not the ACFTU branches but spontaneous and semi-spontaneous unions) were most positive. Why did this happen?

31 Jin (2002); Yang (2002).

After 1949, the CCP and the ACFTU consolidated its monopoly of grass roots unions either by accommodating or by prohibiting other unions. Workers were no longer free to associate with each other, and all union cadres were appointed from above rather than elected by members.[32] Union cadres, therefore, had little incentive to serve their members, while workers had little reason to communicate with grass roots union cadres. As we saw in Chapter Six, after two major conflicts between the ACFTU and the party-state during the 1950s, the few union leaders who advocated more independent union operations were criticized and sacked, leading directly to the ACFTU proposal to "struggle for the dying-out of unions (为工会消亡而斗争)", while practically abolishing union organizations at or below the county level.[33] In this context, it is not at all surprising to see that grass roots unions had a limited relationship with employees in the 1950s.

After 1958, unions became a subordinate working department of party organizations at the corresponding level. Grass roots unions accepted unconditionally the leadership of local party committees. In SOE workplaces the core work of grass roots unions was to organize "labour competition (劳动竞赛)", i.e. to work more without being paid more, providing instead "moral rewards" such as red flags or red flowers. Unions abrogated their function of struggling for workers' interests and so workers lost faith in them. Thus, when party control was loosened in the Cultural Revolution, workers threw aside the ACFTU and established spontaneous, alternative grass roots unions.[34]

Workers' "rebellious" organizations during the Cultural Revolution remained very sensitive even decades later. Official accounts mostly followed the tone of the CCP's official "Resolution on Certain Historical Issues since the Establishment of the State (1981)", which condemned rebellious activities. Nevertheless, subsequent research and accounts of personal experiences[35] provide an alternative perspective. The Cultural Revolution

32 Li (2006).

33 Zheng et al. (1997), p. 2428.

34 Li (2006).

35 For example, Fang (2006); Li (2007); Li (1998); Li (2006); Li (2000); Liu (2001, 2006); Shen (2004); Xiao (2006); Yang (1988); Yang (1986); Ye (1993); Zheng (2006).

was due, in part, to the Great Leap Forward's (大跃进) economic disasters which cost millions of lives.[36] It also divided the party-state. After 1962, Liu Shaoqi[37] and Deng Xiaoping exercised day-to-day decision making authority, while Mao "retreated to the second front (退居二线)". Mao decided to regain power by utilizing the only source, other than military force, over which he still had influence, i.e. the "masses".[38] In this contest, student movements (the Red Guards) were encouraged first, followed by labour movements.

Suspecting that workers were discontented with party-state bureaucrats, Mao incited workers to rebel and seize power, thereby conferring a freedom of association banned since 1949.[39] Many scholars[40] believe that this was a mutually reinforcing process. On the one hand, Mao encouraged workers to rebel so as to beat down his political opponents while, on the other, workers utilized macro-level political conflict to pursue their own interests. Hence there are two separate concepts of the Cultural Revolution, one led by Mao, at the macro-level and the other by individuals at the micro-level. Problems were bound to arise from such an unprecedented mass movement as the Cultural Revolution. In fact, relationships among various workers' organizations and factions were so complicated that it is almost impossible to answer basic questions such as which political side a specific workers' organization supported.[41]

For understandable reasons, some of the literature is not formally published, and some people may have intruded their personal emotions into their writing. However, this material does contain precious information about this part of history, at least until further research uncovers better and more reliable sources of information.

36 The exact number of abnormal deaths (from starvation) during 1959–61 has never been released. A widely accepted estimate is 30 million (Yang 2004).

37 As we noted in the previous subsection, Liu was one of the leaders in the Anyuan labour movement.

38 Mao named Liu and Deng as "the Party's Internal Faction on the Road to Capitalism (党内走资派)". Judging from Deng's practice after 1979, especially after 1992, one cannot deny that Mao's claim had some foundation.

39 Yang, X. K. (1986).

40 For example, Liu (2001, 2006); Yang (1988); Yang (1986); Zheng (2006).

41 Li X. Y. argued that up to January 1967, it was still possible to identify whether an organization was on the rebellious side or on the conservative (Liu and Deng's) side,

Liu, studying various "rebellious factions (造反派)", identified nine types of rebellions, of which two concerned workers' organizations:

> … Wang Hongwen style "rebellions" were politically motivated.[42] They attempted to realize power within the party-state system by taking opportunities provided by the Cultural Revolution …
>
> … Struggle-style rebellions were more widespread at the grass roots level and constituted the main theme of rebellions in the Cultural Revolution.[43] Some of these rebellions had the higher objectives of resisting political discrimination and suppression, while others simply gave vent to their dissatisfaction with bureaucrats and cadres. Some of these rebellions ended in much personal abuse …[44]

We now discuss these two types of workers' organizations.

---

mainly by seeing whether the organization had been suppressed by the work unit cadres or the "work team (工作组)". But after 1967, when the army became involved, things became complicated: many rebellious workers' organizations were suppressed, but their titles and "flags" remained in use for the new transformed organizations. After February 1967, all workers' organizations claimed to be "rebellious", and all bad deeds were done in the name of rebellion. This is the reason why "rebellious factions (造反派)" later became so notorious (Li 2000).

42 Wang Hongwen was a CCP member, demobilized soldier and junior "safeguarding cadre (保卫干部)" before the "rebellion". With these three good political qualifications, though he was not part of the party-state privileged class (due to seniority), Wang was far from being a member of the suppressed class. Why did he rebel? The problem lay in the pyramid-like power structure of the party-state. People with good political qualifications, such as Wang, believed that they deserved more, while positions at the top were always limited. Therefore, Wang and others like him also felt "suppressed" and had the intention of "rebelling" for a "fairer distribution" of official positions. For this reason, the Wang Hongwen style "rebellions" were hardly genuine rebellions.

43 Struggling style rebellions were widespread in the grass roots working units. In the 17 years of communist rule before the Cultural Revolution (1949–66), conflicts accumulated between workers and grass roots cadres. As explained by Mao, "… the mass was at odds with (the bureaucrats) but they had no chance to speak out. Now came the Cultural Revolution; the people eventually burst out and made them (the bureaucrats) really awkward …" (Liu 2001).

44 Liu (2001).

Wang Hongwen Style "Rebellious Workers' Organizations"

The most typical Wang Hongwen Style "Rebellious Organization" was of course the one founded by Wang Hongwen himself, the "Shanghai Workers' Revolutionary Rebellion General Headquarters (工总司)". At its peak, it had over 100,000 members (it boasted 800,000), with 30,000 armed pickets.[45] Wang chose the Central Cultural Revolution Team (CCRT, 中央文革) which was controlled directly by Mao and his wife, Jiang Qing. He had a relatively open attitude towards accepting and allying with other "rebellious organizations".[46] Wang came to Mao's notice and rose rapidly through the political hierarchy.[47] In 1968 when most workers' rebellious organizations were disbanded, Wang's organisation survived. In 1972, it was renamed the "Shanghai Workers' Representative Congress (上海市工代会)". No longer a workers' "Rebellious Organization", the Congress became, a new official union in place of the ACFTU until the end of the Cultural Revolution.[48]

Struggle-Style "Rebellious Workers' Organization"

Among struggle-style rebellious organizations, the most famous and influential was the "National Red Labourers' Rebellious General Regiment (全红总)". This was the first labour organization since 1949 to be

45 Shanghai Local History Office <http://www.shtong.gov.cn/node2/node2245/node4471/node56351/node56369/node56371/userobject1ai42970.html> (last accessed on 20 January 2009).

46 This is arguable, however. Shen Fuxiang, leader of a major workers' rebellious organization, the Shanghai Red Workers' Revolutionary Rebellion Headquarters (SRWRRH, 红工司), was dissatisfied with SWRRGH's rejection of the alliance requested by the SRWRRH. Shen did admit, however, that SWRRGH merged numerous workers' rebellious organizations (Shen 2004).

47 Wang was appointed the CCP's vice-chair and was a potential successor to Mao in the early 1970s. He was arrested later in 1976, condemned as a member of the "Gang of Four", and sentenced to life imprisonment. He died in jail in 1986, at the age of fifty-one (Ye 1993).

48 Li (2006).

established spontaneously on the basis of freedom of association, with the aim of struggling for the interests of ordinary, especially temporary, subcontracted labourers. However, as the "General Regiment" existed only for a short time, from November 1966 to March 1967, and most of its leaders were arrested and punished, little material survives about this organization. We therefore rely largely on articles written by two of its founding leaders.[49]

The "General Regiment" was established on 8 November 1966. Fifty workers marched to the headquarter of the ACFTU in Beijing, requesting official recognition of the organization, and simultaneously appealing to the CCP and State Council for revision of the temporary/subcontract labour system, which was implemented in the early 1960s by Liu and Deng. After a month's struggle, the ACFTU registered the "General Regiment". However, the party-state did not respond to the appeal to revise the temporary/subcontracted worker system. Workers surrounded the office building of the State Labour Department and the ACFTU, shouting the slogan "Time to Settle Account with Boss Liu! Thoroughly Eliminate All Exploiting Capitalist Systems!"[50]

At first, the "General Regiment" was a spontaneous grass roots union with specific economic aims, but its targets (Liu and Deng) accorded with political manoeuvres at the highest level. For this reason, the CCRT encouraged an escalation of worker-related political activity. The ACFTU was expelled and its office building occupied on 27 December 1966.[51] The CCRT had achieved its purpose of using the "General Regiment"

49 Fang (2006); Li (2007).

50 Boss Liu refers to Liu Shaoqi, who was then the number two leader in the party-state system (the major target of Mao's power struggle in the Cultural Revolution). Liu and Deng established the temporary/subcontracted worker system in the early 1960s, dividing Chinese workers, though all were working in the state or collectively owned enterprises, into two classes: formal workers and temporary/subcontracted workers, with substantially different welfare packages.

51 From this specific date on, the ACFTU remained paralyzed throughout the duration of the Cultural Revolution.

to defeat the ACFTU,[52] indicating, though, that it should not pursue specific economic demands regarding the temporary/subcontract worker system. If the "General Regiment's" leaders had been as "smart" as Wang Hongwen, it might have become another official "union", or even better. After all, its name contained the word "national" and it physically occupied the ACFTU's headquarters in Beijing. But the "General Regiment" persisted in agitating on behalf of workers, refusing to compromise on the elimination of the temporary/subcontracted worker system. By January 1967, it had broken with all factions within the party-state system[53] and in March the once eye-catching organisation was suppressed after only five months' existence.[54]

We can conclude that workers' rebellions during the Cultural Revolution, together with corresponding workers' organizations, were of two types; "planned", "fake" rebellions, with political targets set by Mao, and "unplanned", "spontaneous" rebellions which emerged when the revolutionary movement was beyond political control. The outcome was that all genuine workers' rebellious organizations were eventually suppressed, some during the 1968–69 "Clearance of Working Class Force (清理阶级队伍)" and others during the early 1970s. The party-state, when suppressing these organizations, claimed that they were penetrated by "bad elements" and refrained from denouncing them as "counter-revolutionary".[55] Mao still tried to maintain the legitimacy of "workers' rebellions" so as to provide some kind of justification for his overthrow of the party-state system which had been in the hands of Liu and Deng.

52 As we saw in the last chapter, Liu Shaoqi had been a major leader in the labour movement in earlier years and himself took up the honorary chairmanship of the ACFTU after 1948. Therefore, the ACFTU was long considered his power base. For this reason, it is understandable that Mao chose the ACFTU as a prime target of attack.

53 At that time, the CCRT was acting as the core of the party system, while Zhou Enlai controlled the state system.

54 Fang (2006); Li (2007).

55 Liu (2001).

In summary, the ACFTU's grass roots unions were mostly idle and inactive between 1949 and 1979. Before the Cultural Revolution, they followed instructions from above, such as encouraging workers to produce more. During the Cultural Revolution, they were displaced by various rebellious workers' organizations.

The Cultural Revolution was the only period after 1949 when Chinese workers were free to associate, though, in the name of political rebellion. Various rebellious workers' organizations were essentially free grass roots unions. However, in the context of extreme political upheaval, no one escaped the internal power struggles of the CCP. Eventually, rebellious workers' organizations were either transformed into new bureaucratic and official unions such as Wang Hongwen's "Rebellious Organisation" in Shanghai or suppressed, such as the "General Regiment" in Beijing. The Cultural Revolution demonstrated that unions and workers were only chessmen in the party-state's political game.

6.1.3 Grass Roots Unions and Employees since 1979

Only by knowing the historical background described above can we appreciate why grass roots unions in China combine "political extension" with "interest protection organizations", even now in the reform era when "economic construction is the central task (以经济建设为中心)". We can well comprehend why a union federation such as the ACFTU must play a dual role.[56] If grass roots unions at the workplace level did the same, conflicts of interests would be bound to happen. However, China's grass roots unions,

56 Of course, this is also true for free labour organizations in western countries, though to a less significant extent. Thus the Australian Labor Party has both formal and informal connections with the Australian unions <www.alp.org.au> (last accessed on 20 January 2009), and the American unions also engage in politics by rewarding friends and punishing enemies among politicians and by lobbying for legislation (Katz and Wheeler (2004), p. 71).

unlike free unions in western economies,[57] were direct subsidiaries of the ACFTU, itself an extension of the party-state. According to Chen and Zhang, many local governments demanded that unions focus more on their political role of co-operating with the government in attracting investment and contributing to the local economy's GDP growth by putting aside their function of protecting labour rights.[58]

As grass roots unions are direct subsidiaries of the ACFTU and indirectly subsidiary to the party-state, they pay more attention to relationships with superiors than to those with members. According to the ACFTU's "Regulation on Enterprise Union's Work (2006)", enterprise unions should, first of all, play the role of the "ACFTU's extensional organization at the grass roots 1orking under the dual leadership of the corresponding party committee and the superior union ..." Only secondarily should the grass roots union "be the representative and protector of employee members and their interests ..."[59] Therefore, the underlying logic of grass roots union operation is that a superior's demand leads to grass roots union action, which fulfils the superiors' request, while, at best, satisfying only some of the members' demands by the way. This arrangement has been in place for a long time, surviving years of economic reforms.

After 1979 and especially since 1992, large numbers of labour disputes surfaced as China's economy changed.[60] In this context, grass roots unions should have played a more active role in protecting employees' interests and rights. In fact, they did little. According to a survey,[61] most interviewees claimed that the unions' concept of "protection of rights (维权)" was usually "dual protection of rights (双维权)", i.e. protection

57 For example, grass roots unions in Australia are voluntary associations, voluntarily affiliated with the Australian Council of Trade Unions, and relying on shared values and interests <www.actu.asn.au> (last accessed on 20 January 2009).

58 Chen and Zhang (2005).

59 Article 2 and 5 in ACFTU (2006).

60 See Chapters 3 and 4 for detail.

61 Han (2005).

of both labourers' *and* employers' rights.[62] In one of Han's interviews, a union chair "proudly" recalled a case in which the union sued an employee to "protect the enterprise's interests". In Han's case study, we notice that a tripartite scheme of unions employers (and their associations) and the state" was transformed into a workplace system of employees, employers and union, in which unions were not representative labour organisations but state-authorized mediation organisations charged with maintaining social stability.[63]

This concept of the union's role reproduced the historical gap between grass roots unions and their worker members. Such unions would not survive in an environment of free association. But the ACFTU's grass roots unions have not only survived but have prospered in terms of affiliation and membership. According to official statistics, by the end of 2006, there were more than 1.3 million grass roots unions, with a membership of almost 170 million, of which 41 million were peasant migrant workers, boasting to be the largest labour union in the world.[64]

Though the "Union Law" defined a union as "a mass organization based on employees' voluntary association",[65] all unions, whether in SOEs or

62 One of the reasons for such a problem lies in the particular meaning of "protection of rights (维权)" in the (communist) official language. As early as in 1921, Lenin proposed that, as there was no longer an "exploiting class" in a socialist society, the union's major task should be to help enhance productivity. However, Lenin admitted that bureaucracy still existed in a socialist society; hence unions maintained the function of protecting labour (from the abuse of bureaucracy). Lenin's thoughts fundamentally shaped the classic "dual function" union theories in all former socialist countries. That is to say, the official notion of "protection of rights (维权)" stems from the out-dated planned economy, where it means protecting labour from the abuse of bureaucracy rather then from the employers' exploitation. For this reason, misunderstandings are bound to happen when the market economy develops, as most people now do not share the concepts and ideological language of earlier times (Feng 2006).

63 In a separate survey, a majority of the interviewees agreed to the statement that a union is a mediation agent rather than an interest representing organization (Feng 2002).

64 NBS and MOLSS (2007), disc edition, Table 11.1/2.

65 Article 2 in National People's Congress (2001).

non-SOEs, were established by the will of the party-state, or its extension, the ACFTU, from top down rather than spontaneously by employees from bottom up. To occupy space in "new emerging enterprises", in 1999 the ACFTU, under guidance of the party-state, adopted the policy of "where there are employees, there shall be unions (哪里有职工，哪里就要建立工会)". Its strategy was "to be led by corresponding party committees, [and to let] party construction drive union construction while [letting] union construction promote party construction, [so that] party and union can be constructed together (各级党委牵头，党建带工建，工建促党建，党工共建)".[66] In this context, a grass roots union construction movement spread nation-wide. Feng, studying several cases, argues that newly established grass roots unions in the non-SOE sectors are basically direct copies of those in SOEs and that their mode of operation does not fit the requirements of the transitional economy's diversified interests.[67] In another survey of employees in over fifty foreign or private enterprises, the majority of interviewees agreed that unions are only forms with little realistic meaning.[68] This belief arose from workers' everyday experience of unions failing to represent their interests. Most did not believe party-state propaganda that the ACFTU strives to establish grass roots unions in the non-SOEs so as to protect employee interests.

Though unions are ineffective in the eyes of employees, they are not necessarily so in the eyes of the party-state and the ACFTU. Han argues that there are two reasons why the party-state and ACFTU established grass roots unions in non-SOEs.[69] First, as a large number of SOEs were either bankrupt or transformed, the ACFTU needed to develop new financial sources to support its 600,000 full-time union cadres at various levels.[70] Secondly, as non-SOEs developed quickly and state controls in these enterprises were comparatively loose, a "control vacuum (控制真空)"

66 <http://acftu.people.com.cn/GB/67574/7041279.html> (last accessed on 20 January 2009).

67 Feng (2006).

68 Liu and Luan (2002).

69 Han (2005).

70 See the discussion in section 2.2.3 of Chapter 2 of China's arrangements for collecting union fees.

among non-SOE workers and the potential subversiveness of spontaneous worker organizations[71] forced the party-state and ACFTU to occupy the space that would otherwise be available for the possible development of free employee associations.[72]

In addition to these "negative" factors, there was perhaps a more positive reason for the ACFTU to establish grass roots unions in non-SOEs. As we saw in the last chapter, the ACFTU played the role of "social stabilizer" for the party-state. Neither the party-state nor the ACFTU wanted social turbulence. The party-state managed to contain labour unrest by showing some tolerance toward workplace-level activities.[73] In this context, the ACFTU needed to establish grass roots unions in non-SOEs so as to prevent labour disputes from becoming social issues.[74] This accords with our earlier argument that unions first fulfil party political requests while in the process only satisfying some worker requests. According to Clarke, the ACFTU was divided internally over the measures taken by grass roots unions to protect employee rights. One faction argued that unions help social stability by involvement in protecting employee rights,

71 To understand such potential subversiveness, one need only look at the cases discussed in the last subsection (regarding the rebellious workers' organization during the Cultural Revolution) or the case of Solidarity in Poland. Solidarity claimed that "we strike to establish an independent union, so that we do not need to use this method (strike) to protect workers' rights". Once there is an independent union that can really represent the workers' interests, any regime that rules in the name of the working class faces a threat to its ruling legitimacy (Zhao 2002).

72 Leung (2002). When interviewed by VOA in 2002, Bao Tong (former member of the CC-CCP and secretary of Zhao Zi Yang) said "... if western countries ask the CCP to give the workers the 'freedom of association' and the CCP refuses, then I would have to say that the CCP is simply too far away from the Chinese working class and Marxism, even far more distant than the western (capitalist) countries ..." <http://www.voanews.com/chinese/archive/2002–10/a-2002–10-03–73-1.cfm> (last accessed on 20 January 2009).

73 Gilbert (2005).

74 In an interview, a grass roots union chair said: "... the superior sends you down to work well and manage the people well so as to maintain social stability ... not [being able to] solve conflicts means not working well, that is the most direct performance appraisal ... if there are appeals and court suits all the time, the cadre (in charge) cannot be considered good ..." (Feng 2006).

while another held that such involvement encourages workers to act more aggressively.[75] Regardless, grass roots unions, the ACFTU and the party-state share the same political objective of retaining power and protecting vested interests.[76] Grass roots union cadres enjoy high standards of salary and welfare packages as members of management teams, having little connection with workers.[77] They take the interests of "the whole", i.e. the whole party-state system, into account. Otherwise every one in the system will lose if the regime collapses.

As we saw in Chapter Four, non-SOE employees realized that official unions could not be counted on and therefore sought co-operation with employers rather than "representation" by unreliable organizations.[78] For this reason, Feng argues that if grass roots unions were genuine about reform, they needed to gradually distance themselves from the party-state system, with the aim of eventual separation.[79] The unions, however, held complex attitudes towards reform. They were not totally blind to their negative image among workers, but like the frog in slowly boiling water, to remain or jump out were not options.[80]

75 Clarke et al. (2004), p. 241.

76 According to the Regulation on Enterprise Union's Work, "union chairs in SOEs shall enjoy the welfare package of deputy positions at the corresponding party-administration level ... (and) union chairs in non-SOEs shall enjoy the welfare package of deputy positions at the corresponding management level ..." (Article 24 in ACFTU 2006d).

77 Feng describes them as people who "look like a party committee member from the left side and a management member from the right side, but not a bit like a member of the working class from any side" (Feng 2002).

78 Han made a comparison of two enterprises and found that the one without a union provided virtually all the activities available in the other (with a union). The study showed that China's grass roots unions are meaningless, because their major activities – for example, entertainments and production competitions – could be arranged (even better, because of a less bureaucratic style) by the Human Resources departments in the enterprises (Han 2005).

79 Feng (2006).

80 Of course, whether or not the party-state would allow them to "jump" out of the system is another question.

Beginning in early 2000, some districts launched direct union elections in an attempt to counter the "representation" problem. By early 2006 in Yuhang District, Hangzhou, Zhejiang Province, 332 or 40% of enterprises with established unions conducted direct elections for their union heads. In these enterprises, no labour disputes developed into broader social issues, with a 95% satisfaction rate among employers and employees, according to a two-year continuous survey.[81]

Direct elections, however, were restricted to selected areas. Guo Wencai, Chief Director of the ACFTU's Organizational Construction Department, commented in 2003 that direct elections at the grass roots level would take place in medium/small non-SOE enterprises, not in SOEs.[82] That is to say, direct elections were restricted to workplaces where the party-state and the ACFTU were unpopular and had less power. It is reasonable to speculate that the party-state and ACFTU saw direct elections as a bargain, trading direct elections for member recognition rather than risking marginalization and rejection by employees. Thus, direct elections are the result of a compromise by the party-state and the ACFTU. As the non-SOE sector becomes more dominant in China's economy, direct elections are likely to come, sooner or later, but it is impossible to tell how soon.

In summary, since economic reforms were launched in 1979, the development of the non-SOE sector led to a more diversified set of social interests. However, the ACFTU's grass roots unions have not adapted thoroughly to the changes. They have developed "frontiers" in non-SOEs by utilizing the party-state's support, but this practice has not won employee recognition and support. Direct elections helped resolve the "representation" problem in part, but it is unclear when direct elections will be conducted across the board.

81 "Direct Election in Grass roots Unions: New Development in the Construction of Democratic Politics" (in Chinese), *Prosecutors' Daily*, "基层工会直选：民主政治建设的新发展"，检察日报，30 March 2006.

82 "Union Reforms in Transitional Period" (in Chinese), *Southern Weekends*, "转型期的工会改革方向", 南方周末, 3 July 2003.

6.2 Grass Roots Unions and Employers

Whereas interactions among grass roots unions and employees were complex, those between grass roots unions and employers were relatively simple. The ACFTU's grass roots unions had little interaction with employers in the period 1956–79, when the party-state was the only employer in China. Unions, as a subordinated extension of the party-state, could then barely have any "interaction" with this "super boss".[83] The only two periods before 1979 in which grass roots unions had direct interaction with employers were 1921–25 and 1949–56.[84] In the following three subsections we focus on the three periods 1921–25, 1949–56 and from 1979 onward.

6.2.1 Grass Roots Unions and Employers 1921–25

In the last section, we saw that during the period 1921–25, the major tasks of grass roots unions were to "enlighten" workers' ideological consciousness and to tie together the CCP's political goals with the workers' economic demands. Grass roots unions generally held an aggressive attitude towards employers while employers had little experience in dealing with the emerging unions. In the context of China's traditional "parenthood" management style, employers tended to adopt a tough and aggressive approach in face of worker agitation. Interactions between grass roots unions and employers were antagonistic during this period, with Anyuan, again, the much studied example.

83 One may argue that, although the union could not "interact" with the national leaders, it might have done so with the workplace managers. But, as we have shown in earlier discussions, at the workplace level, union cadres were treated as members of management and grass roots union cadres rarely had any motivation to act against the managers.

84 As we shall soon see, those union activities were basically political actions in support of the CCP's macro-level policies, though some of them were represented as struggles for the workers' economic benefit.

When the Anyuan Railway and Mining Workers' Club was established in April 1922, its overt objectives were relatively mild. Neither the Hunan local warlord nor the employer paid much attention to it at first. But as its activities became more political,[85] and its aims shifted to "protecting workers' rights and lessening labourers' oppression and pain",[86] the local warlord authority and employer realized that there were other political purposes behind the club's activities. Initially, the employer was reluctant to take tough measures, attempting instead to buy over the club and its members by providing funds and space for club activities. But the restrained attitude of the employer was taken as a sign of weakness or even cowardice by club leaders and its political activities intensified. The employer and local warlord joined in an attempt to shut down the club by administrative power.

Li Lisan, the club's leader, and Mao Zedong, the CCP leader in Hunan, argued that the time was ripe for a strike. On 11 September 1922, they issued three demands: first, that the employer provide official protection for the club; second, that the employer provide half of the club's funding; and third, that the employer pay the workers' salary arrears immediately. All three demands were to be met by the next day or there would be a strike. The famous Anyuan Grand Strike, involving more than 13,000 workers, was provoked in this way.[87] Although the employer used his personal influence to involve the local warlord's army in maintaining stability at the mining site, the army stayed neutral by declaring that there would be no interference unless the workers disrupted social order. Therefore, this strike was

85 For example, in its establishment ceremony parade, the parade troops shouted political slogans such as "Down with the warlords" and "Long live the Communist Party" (Li and Liu (2005), p. 44).

86 Ibid.

87 I have not found any research that discusses in detail how and why a few hundred club members, Youth League members and CCP members could mobilize more than 13,000 workers to participate in the strike. There were probably two major reasons: first, the demands issued by the club contained reasonable elements, so that many non-club-member workers were willing to support the strike as long as the club was there to take the lead; and second, the club's armed pickets had taken measures to prevent other workers from entering the workplace.

relatively peaceful, without a military crack-down such as occurred in some other areas.[88]

Through mediation by local gentry, the employer agreed to sign a deal with the Club after five days, acceding to almost all its demands. In particular, the Club was recognized as the "representative" of the workers. By this means, a strike won the club the power to "represent" more than 13,000 workers in the Anyuan site, regardless of its real membership of only approximately 700 workers.

If we look into the nation-wide labour movement during the period 1921–25, we find that Anyuan's grass roots approach in dealing with the employer was typical. Such an approach can be broken down into the following steps.

First, the grass roots union appears with a relatively mild face, winning the endorsement of the employer and local authorities.

Second, the grass roots union gradually shifts the emphasis of its activities and becomes more political.

Third, when the time is ripe, the grass roots union launches strikes, forcing the employer to compromise and recognize the unions' "representative" position.

Fourth, by utilizing the "representative" position, the grass roots union further develops itself.

Not all strikes, though, followed the Anyuan example in enjoying the neutrality of the army and police. Zheng H. et al's (1997) record of twenty-one major strikes during the period 1921–25 under the leadership of the CCP and its union found that five were repressed completely by military or police forces, eight were held peacefully, and another eight had violent conflicts at first but were later settled peacefully through mediation.

88 For example, the Yue-Han Railway Workers' Grand Strike (粤汉铁路工人大罢工), which was held in the same period under the leadership of the CCP and its union, was suppressed by the army and police, causing hundreds of deaths and injuries (Zheng (1997), pp. 2482).

Between 1925 and 1949, as discussed in the previous section, there was barely any interaction between the grass roots unions and individual employers. For the first two years grass roots unions facilitated the launch of political labour movements, but between 1927–49 operations ceased completely.

6.2.2 Grass Roots Unions and Employers 1949–56

Confronted with the chaotic economic situation in September 1949, the NPPCC passed the "Common Programme (共同纲领)" which acted as a temporary constitution. It set the policy of "(giving) consideration to both public and private interests, benefiting both labour and capital (公私兼顾、劳资两利)" as a key principle for economic construction in the early years of the People's Republic of China.[89] The purpose of this policy was to enhance production and economic recovery. In 1950 the State Council passed the "Temporary Regulation of Private Enterprises (私营企业暂行条例)", putting the party-state's policy of "use, restrict, and remould private capitalism" into a formal regulation.[90]

This was only a temporary policy for the transitional period. Beginning in 1951, the party-state started to act against the private sector. The measures included unifying state purchase and sales, and industry-wide public-private joint-ventures. The aim was to institute "state capitalism (国家资本主义)".[91] The first "Constitution of the People's Republic of China", promulgated in 1954, gave formal recognition to the privileged position of the state-owned economy, calling for the replacement of private enterprise with SOEs.[92] Though grass roots unions took some action against the remaining private employers in the transitional period between 1949 and 1956, by the end of the first quarter of 1956, 99% of industrial enterprises and 85% of commercial enterprises were public-private joint ventures. This signified

89 Article 26 in NPPCC (1949).
90 Zhao and Xie (2002).
91 Yang (2004).
92 National People's Congress (2004), p. 145.

the basic completion of the "socialist transformation of capitalism".[93] Union leaders[94] depended on military units to clamp down on the "old" unions[95] and establish "new" unions within the ACFTU system, while the "new" unions joined with the new administration to confiscate and nationalize so-called "bureaucratic capitalist enterprises (官僚资本企业)".[96] Grass roots unions mobilized employees to oversee employer operations and production, and enhanced the formation of public-private joint ventures. Further, as there were not many grass roots CCP organizations in the early years after "liberation", many local Committees adopted a policy of "establishing unions first and setting up party branches later".[97] For these reasons, grass roots unions played the role of representative of the party-state in the workplaces.[98] Their attitudes towards employers were not those of equal negotiators but of entities in a commanding position.[99]

The national situation was complicated and cannot be described in a simple summary. For example, Liu argued that the success of union development in the early years after "liberation" was due to grass roots unions paying much attention to employees' interests and working hard to solve problems. During those years, unions organized action against the misconduct

93 Compilation of documents from Xinhua News Agency, <http://news.xinhuanet.com/ziliao/2003-09/03/content_1060054.htm> (last accessed on 20 January 2009).

94 For example, Li (2005); Harbin Local History Office (2005); Feng et al. (2002); Su (1985).

95 The "old" unions were those outside the ACFTU system, either established by the employees spontaneously or manipulated by the employers or the KMT government.

96 The so-called "bureaucratic capitalist enterprises" refer to enterprises owned by the KMT government. The management of those enterprises was appointed by the KMT; they were little different from SOEs under the CCP's system (Su S. Z. 1985). The KMT was a weird hybrid of Leninist and Fascist parties, though it originated as a democratic party. Various organizations, including SOEs, existed under both the KMT and the CCP regimes.

97 This policy was also called "enhancing party construction by union construction (以工建带党建)".

98 This was probably the origin of the "representation" issues that we have discussed in 5.1.2 of Chapter 5.

99 Feng et al. (2002).

of some private employers, and did much to improve working conditions and production safety.[100]

In summary, during the period 1949–56, the major tasks of grass roots unions were to implement the party-state's policies and take action against private employers. They helped confiscate "bureaucratic capitalist enterprises", while for ordinary private employers, their policy was "both unite and struggle (又团结又斗争)": i.e., unite with employers during the period of economic recovery, then struggle against them so as to enforce public-private joint ventures.

6.2.3 Grass Roots Unions and Employers since 1979

From 1956 to 1979, no private enterprises operated in China. One may argue that there was a single employer, the party-state, which not only "employed" all workers but virtually controlled all aspects of their lives. Grass roots unions implemented political instructions from the party-state. They launched production competitions, fostered worker acceptance of technical innovation, enhanced production and organized entertainment activities. Grass roots unions in SOEs played multiple roles assisting management and were agents for the party-state within these enterprises.[101]

Feng argues that, in the planned economy, when given certain "official ranking (行政级别)",[102] the interest of the enterprise was not so much to earn a profit as to have access to funds retained by the enterprise after handing money to the state. As a grass roots union's "official ranking" and corresponding welfare package was in accordance with enterprise management's ranking, its interests were linked. Therefore, the function of the Chinese grass roots unions was not to struggle with employers on behalf

100 Liu (2005). But as Liu had been vice-chair of the ACFTU and had worked in the grass roots unions for many years from the 1950s, his words cannot be treated as objective.

101 Zhu (2006).

102 "Official ranking (行政级别)" is a special system in China (especially during the planned economy period), meaning that all working units (whether governmental organizations or SOEs or even schools, hospitals etc.) have their own official ranking which is similar to a bureaucratic hierarchy.

of the employees over the division of profit, as in a free economic system, but to "conspire" with enterprise management to retain more funds from the state. In this sense, the interests of grass roots unions or, at least, their cadres, accorded with, or even depended on, those of management.[103]

The twenty-year-long planned economy from 1956 to 1978 had a profound long-term impact on grass roots unions. Even after almost thirty years of economic reform, the 2006 version of "Regulation on Enterprise Union's Work" stated formally that "union chairs shall enjoy the welfare package of the corresponding deputy-position official in the management".[104] The long held working style of grass roots unions, thus, accustomed union officials to work on the side of the enterprise management. This was so when they were in SOEs, when management was not the real employer, and little changed when they were in non-SOEs, where management was the actual employer or representatives of the employer.[105] Many union cadres found little difficulty in supporting private employers. Whereas before 1979 they supported the party-state, which was the only employer, after 1979 they supported employers of various types. In this sense, we may conclude that Chinese unions have always been subservient to the employers.

The diversity of economic subjects since the late 1970s complicated labour relations more than in the planned economy system. In the context of "strong capital vs. weak labour", with ever-growing labour disputes in the non-SOE sector, employees needed to organize to negotiate collectively with employers to protect their interests. This pressured the ACFTU to establish grass roots unions in the private sector before employees associated spontaneously. To occupy the industrial relations space in non-SOEs, the ACFTU adopted a policy of "establishing [unions] first and regulating later (先建制后规范)",[106] which became a source of trouble in union-employer relationships.

First, to accomplish the "new union establishment" target, many local union cadres allied with employers to establish "signboard unions (招牌工会)". It was not uncommon to see the chairs of many unions in non-SOEs

103 Feng (2006).

104 Article 24 in ACFTU (2006).

105 Feng (2006).

106 "Union Reform Direction in Transitional Period" (in Chinese), *Southern Weekend*, "转型期的工会改革方向", 南方周末, 3 July 2003.

occupied by the owners themselves, their relatives, or members of the management team.[107] A "union" of this kind provided little real protection for employees. From the union cadres' point of view, these "unions" assisted simultaneously in "political performance (政绩) appraisal", developing new financial sources and squeezing the survival space for spontaneous unions, or "hitting three birds with one stone (一石三鸟)".

Secondly, union cadres may not have had the deals with employers discussed above, but because unions were not compulsory in non-SOEs, and were rarely established without employer endorsement, union cadres had to show their "value" to employers in order to win their support. For example, according to Feng, some private employers were willing to establish unions because they promised to help with "mobilizing" workers to work overtime[108] when there were urgent orders. Such a practice faced no legal risk because it was done "voluntarily" by the union.[109] Union cadres were more like salesmen trying to sell their services. But they were selling their services to employers rather than employees.

Thirdly, even where grass roots union cadres worked for the benefit of employees, union activities and the jobs of the union cadres were highly dependent on the tolerance of employers. Union chairs could do little more than mediate between employers and employees.[110]

For these reasons, grass roots unions rarely perform the function of protecting employee interests or acting as employees' representatives to negotiate as equals with employers. After two months' field research in China, two ILO investigators reached the conclusion that grass roots union dependence on employers, rather than dependence on the party-state as perceived by most people, prevents China from developing a modern industrial relations system.[111]

107 Ibid.

108 As we saw in the previous section, "production mobilization" work was not new to the unions at all. The difference is that, in the past, unions mobilized for the party-state, while now they mobilize for the capitalists.

109 Feng (2006).

110 "Direct Election was not a show" (in Chinese), *Southern Metropolitan Paper*, "直选不是做秀, 广东1/3企业基层工会直选产生", 南方都市报, 9 July 2003.

111 Clarke et al. (2004).

In summary, after economic reforms were launched in 1979, grass roots unions underwent a difficult self-transformation. For historical and practical reasons, grass roots unions remain in a relation of dependency with employers and cannot negotiate effectively with them.[112]

6.3 Employers and Employees

Friedman (1977) and Aungles and Parker (1992) argue that management control strategies towards employees lie along a continuum between two extremes. At one extreme the protagonists of Taylorism or scientific management treat employees as "economic men", control them by strict supervision, de-skill and replace humans by machines, reduce the autonomy of staff, and minimize the uncertainty of the management process. At the other extreme is the human-relations or neo-human-relations school, which considers employees as "irrational" or "self-actualising", giving certain conditional delegation powers and autonomy to staff, and emphasizing management by communication, motivation and leadership.[113]

Few companies anywhere completely adopt either strategy. The same firm may apply different strategies at different times towards different employees. As to the question of what management may do under specific circumstances, practice is not as clear-cut as text-book theories.[114] Relation-

112 If China's unions are so desperately hopeless, the natural question arises whether the unions' major functions of bargaining and voice can be replaced by a non-union approach. Freeman and Medoff argued that collective rather than individual actions are necessary and that unions will be more effective than individuals in both the actions of bargaining and of voice (Freeman and Medoff (1984), p. 247).

113 Friedman (1977); Aungles and Parker (1992).

114 Aungles and Parker (1992) argued that, for reasons such as business confidentiality, empirical studies of management are far fewer than those of employees. However, the limited research seems to indicate that managers adopt employee participation for improving productivity rather than from a belief in the autonomy and creativity of the rank-and-file.

ships between employers and employees in China's industrial relations are even more complicated.[115] After 1979 and especially since 1992, enterprise ownership has become highly diversified. Within less than 30 years, enterprises have gone through a rapid process of change. The party-state has gradually reformed governmental functions, especially in the economic area. Much power and authority once in the hands of government has been transferred to the market.[116] But the rapid retreat of government authority and the development of enterprise power have not been orderly.[117] Government regulation, monitoring and enforcement facilities have not usually been in place,[118] and employers have exercised active and decisive power in their interactions with employees, at least at the enterprise level.[119] For this reason, as pointed out in Chapter Four, the relationship between employ-

115 Dowling et al. (1999) discuss the difficulties of comparing industrial relations across national borders. They argue that even for firms operating in different capitalistic countries, such as the US and Germany, there are large differences of style and behaviour.

116 Zheng and Jiang (2003).

117 Huang (2007).

118 China did not have any labour regulations, not to mention any monitoring and enforcement facilities, in place until the mid 1990s. (The Labour Law was promulgated in 1994). Labour protection facilities are still in the process of refinement and cannot provide sufficient protection to labour, as shown in discussion throughout this book.

119 This laissez-faire mentality has led Chinese government departments as well as employers to adopt a Unitarist approach, which tends to look at industrial relations purely from a micro/corporate viewpoint. Taylor, a prominent exponent of the Unitarist approach, believed that there were common interests between labour and capital and that the principal objective of management should be to secure the maximum prosperity for the employer coupled with the maximum prosperity for each employee. Therefore, labour issues could be solved at the corporate level through co-operation between labour and capital (Taylor 1911). However, as we will see in later analysis, Chinese employers seldom follow this philosophy of labour-capital co-operation, but rather utilize their commanding power in the employment relation for their own advantage. At this point, the Radicals' arguments seem more applicable to China: in the context of capitalism, conflicts between labour and capital are systemic and non-conciliatory, as is their power relationship; and the frontier of control at any point of time represents a compromise unsatisfactory to both parties, and attempts to shift this frontier are only to be expected whenever either side feels that circumstances are in its favour (Noon and Blyton 1997).

ers and employees is much affected by the enterprise scale and ownership type, ranging from "sweatshops" to modern enterprises with sophisticated human resource management capacities. Furthermore, as pointed out in Chapter Five, an employee's social group also affects an employer's attitude. Therefore, there are forty different possible relationship types between employers and employees.

This section is a general description of employer-employee relations after 1979, as shown in Table 6.1, concentrating on the employer's "Operation Scale" and "Ownership Type". The following is a general summary of commonly cited situations, but obviously does not describe every enterprise. For example, some medium and small size private enterprises may be good employers, while large MNCs may act irresponsibly towards their employees. There is scope for future research.

	Large Enterprises	Medium and Small Enterprises
State (Collectively) Owned Enterprises	Labour relations in these enterprises are relatively regularized, all with union branches of the ACFTU, but with much corruption in daily operations. Large SOEs in non-significant industries will eventually be transformed. Different interest groups contest with each other in the transitional process, pushing the conflict of labour relations to the forefront. However, the characteristics of this conflict are distinct from those in enterprises of other ownership types.	Labour relations in these enterprises are relatively regularized, most with union branches of the ACFTU, but with much corruption in daily operations. These enterprises will eventually be transformed (most were transformed before 2004). Different interest groups contest with each other in the transitional process, pushing the conflicts of labour relations to the forefront. As the transformations are nearing the end, so are these conflicts.

	Large Enterprises	Medium and Small Enterprises
Privately Owned Enterprises	Many private enterprises remain at the lowest level of management, with regular invasion of labour rights. The majority of these enterprises have no unions, with a few having "bosses' unions". Some large private enterprises are gradually trying human resource management measures to maintain the long-term continuous development of the enterprises.	Many private enterprises remain at the lowest level of management, with regular invasion of labour rights. In some of these enterprises, the exploitation of labour and its miserable situation can be compared with that in the "preliminary accumulation stage of capitalism". The majority of these enterprises have no unions, with a few having "bosses' unions".
Joint Ventures	Many of these enterprises are the products of either the early years of reforms or regulations which constrain the size of foreign investment in certain industries. Their operational model is quite unique, with a combined face of SOE and FIE. All large JVs have ACFTU branches.	Many of these enterprises are the products of the early years of reforms. Most have been transformed to be wholly owned FIEs. Labour relations are relatively regularized, with some having ACFTU branches.
Direct Subsidiaries of MNCs	Practices in these enterprises are generally formalized, with the HR and labour policies compliant with those in the mother companies. Most have no unions, with a few "signboard unions" controlled by the management.	If Direct Subsidiaries of MNCs are of medium or small scale, they are usually only representative offices with a few Chinese employees (usually no frontline labourers). This book does not consider them.

	Large Enterprises	Medium and Small Enterprises
General FIEs	The capital for most of these enterprises comes from Hongkong, Macau and Taiwan Capital, catering to "outsourced" production for international markets. Most have no unions, with a few "signboard unions" controlled by management; but there also exist a few semi-independent unions that have emerged under the "Social Accountability Movement". Labour relations are relatively regularized.	The capital for most of these enterprises comes from Hongkong, Macau and Taiwan, catering to "outsourced" production for international markets. Most have no unions, with a few "signboard unions" controlled by management; but there also exist a few semi-independent unions that have emerged under the "Social Accountability Movement". Labour relations in Medium/Small FIEs have many problems.

Table 6.1 Summary of Industrial Relations in Different Enterprises[120]

From this table, we see that both operation scale and ownership type affect employer behaviour and attitudes towards employees. We also pointed out in Chapter Five that even in the same enterprise ownership segment, labour relations depend on an employee's social group. For example employer policies towards migrant workers differ from those for the urban workers, while employers treat white-collar employees differently from blue-collar employees.

The reason for the employer's dominating position in the employer-employee relationship is largely the lack of government monitoring of the labour market, which allows employers the freedom and flexibility to decide how to deal with employees. The new "Labour Contract Law", promulgated in June 2007, was an attempt by the government to change the situation. Many of its clauses were targeted at widely found abuses of

120 This table is a summary of viewpoints from various works in the literature, including Chen (2003, 2006); Cooke (2004, 2005, 2008a); He and Chen (2006); Huang and Guo (2006); Li (2004); Research Institute of MOLSS (2004b); Taylor et al. (2003); Tong (2003); Wang (2003); Wang (2001); Zhang (2006).

labour rights, particularly in non-SOEs. For example, confronting the problem that many private enterprises did not sign formal labour contracts with employees, the law stated that "if the employer does not sign a written contract with employees within one year of employment, the employer will be deemed to have agreed to an open-ended contract (without specific term limit) ..."[121] In another clause, addressing the commonly found overtime issue in private and foreign-invested enterprises, the law states that "employers must strictly comply with the labour standards, and must not force (openly or in disguised forms) employees to work overtime. If the employers have the need for overtime, OT payment should be made according to the law ..."[122]

The law, if thoroughly implemented, may help promote healthier labour relations in enterprises, no matter what ownership type they belong to, requiring all employers and employees to co-ordinate their relations in a unified legal framework.[123] However, as in the case of many other laws, implementation and enforcement were major concerns. Numerous operational problems arose after the law came into effect in January 2008. For example, some employers over-utilized short-term contracts and sacked employees periodically to maintain flexibility.[124] In face of these problems, the State Council issued a supplementary regulation in September 2008 to provide more specific explanation of the law.[125]

121 Article 14 in National People's Congress (2007).

122 Article 31, ibid.

123 Chen, however, doubted the effectiveness of the law. He argued that the right to organize empowers workers to bargain as a collective with employers, while the right to strike is the last resort for workers when negotiations fail; collective bargaining is thus a derivative right from the two other collective rights. Without the rights to organize and strike, Chinese workers do not have any power to bargain with employers (Chen (2007), p. 73).

124 Interested readers may refer to "Implementation Problems of the New Labour Contract Law", *Jiefang Daily*, 14 March 2008; "Issues triggered by the New Labour Contract Law", *Worker's Daily*, 19 September 2008; "In Response to Hot Issues of the New Labour Contract Law", Official website of central government <http://www.gov.cn/gzdt/2008-04/08/content_939470.htm> (last accessed on 20 January 2009). More journal reports can be found in various media.

125 State Council (2008).

In summary, relationships between employers and employees are very complicated. They depend simultaneously on the scale and ownership type as well as an employee's social strata. The Chinese government attempted to regulate industrial practices by issuing the new "Labour Contract Law". However, the Law's effects await further research.

Conclusions

In this chapter, we discussed three sets of relationships among China's industrial relations actors at the micro level, namely between grass roots unions and employees, grass roots unions and employers, and between employers and employees.

First, except for a short period during the Cultural Revolution, the tradition of grass roots unions in China was to act as tame agents of the party-state. This heritage caused them to function simultaneously as "political extension organizations" and "interest protection organizations", even after 1979. These two different organizational positions are somewhat self-contradictory. I have argued that unions responded to superior party-state ACFTU authorities' requests while satisfying some worker demands along the way.

Second, after studying the history of relations between grass roots unions and employers, we concluded that relationships between grass roots unions and employers varied dramatically in different historical periods: before 1956, form 1956 to 1979, and after 1979.

Third, focusing discussion on employer-employee relationships after 1979, we undertook a general description with particular regard to an employer's "operation scale" and "ownership type". We concluded that industrial relations practices in large enterprises are relatively formalized, while those in medium and small enterprises vary dramatically in accordance with ownership types.

CHAPTER SEVEN

Conclusions and Future Studies

In this concluding chapter, we first summarize all the major findings in the previous chapters, then briefly discuss the implications of the research, and finally point out possible future research topics concerning industrial relations in China.

7.1 Conclusions

7.1.1 A New Industrial Relations Model

Having examined existing literature on general (western) industrial relations theories in the first chapter, I argued that a typical three-party analytical framework does not fit well with the realities of China's industrial relations. Having regard to the classic three-party model and Taylor et al.'s (2003) revised four-party model, I developed a "six party" analytical taxonomy. In this new taxonomy, the six parties are the major actors in contemporary China's industrial relations, namely the party-state, the employers' associations, the ACFTU, the grass roots unions, the employers and the employees. This framework also takes into account the differences between China's macro and micro level environments. Accordingly, it distinguishes the relationships among industrial relations actors above and at the workplace level.

This analytical taxonomy, I believe, is a contribution to the understanding of China's industrial relations. By applying it, researchers can analyse China's industrial relations in a comprehensive manner and draw more sophisticated conclusions about the complicated inter-relationships among different industrial relations actors. The rest of the book presents an overall picture of China's industrial relations based on this taxonomy. Chapters Two to Four of the book focus on the industrial relations actors' own characteristics, leaving to Chapters Five and Six the discussion of relations between them.

To the best of my knowledge, this is the first attempt to deal with the topic in such a comprehensive way, and this book therefore contributes to a more thorough understanding of China's industrial relations, especially for western readers.

7.1.2 The Industrial Relations Actors

Chapters Two, Three and Four of the book discuss in detail the history and current status of the six industrial relations actors in China. The conclusions are summarised below.

The Party-state

The "party-state" system penetrates every aspect of the political, social and economic life of China. As a sub-system of the broader social system, the industrial relations system is no exception. Having regard to the problems of Taylor et al.'s (2003) summary of the party-state structure in China's industrial relations, I suggest a different representation of the relevant party-state structure in industrial relations. I analyse the party-state's roles in industrial relations as legislator and labour market regulator, conciliator, arbitrator and mediator, provider of public goods, employer of labour and labour market developer. The party-state, itself a constant target of reforms in an unprecedented transitional period, has not performed well in these roles, though it has been trying to do so.

The All-China Federation of Trade Unions

Taking into account the ACFTU's history and current status, I conclude that it was and still is an extension of the party-state, with the roles (as set by the party-state) of being "bridge and transmission belt for the connection between the party and the employed masses". The ACFTU enjoys a monopolistic position, legalized by the state, in affairs related to Chinese workers. Being privileged by the party-state, however, does not mean that the ACFTU has no need to perform a role of labour representative or to care about the protection of labour rights. Since the 1990s, the situation has changed very much as the pace of marketization in China has increased, and the ACFTU has become more active in recent years; but it remains a question as to how effective the ACFTU's activities are. Whereas the market economy calls for unions that serve the interests of their members, the ACFTU is constrained by its being an extension of the party-state. The fundamental problem confronting the ACFTU is whether or not to change its role from that of a political (control) organization to that of an economic (service) organization.

The Employers' Associations

There are three major employer associations legally operating in China: the official "Industry Associations" headed by the China Enterprise Confederation-China Enterprise Directors Association (CEC-CEDA); the semi-official "Chambers of Commerce", affiliated with the All China Federation of Industry and Commerce (ACFIC); and the more spontaneously emerging "Civil Chambers of Commerce". These three types of employers' associations are distinct from each other. First, the CEC-CEDA, as a direct descendant and extension of the party-state, has enjoyed a special (though not monopolistic) position as the "representative" of employers in official and semi-official bodies, including the National Tripartite Conference on Labour Relations Co-ordination (NTCLRC) and the ILO. Second, the ACFIC has been positioned by the party-state as a so-called "united front" organization, aiming to unite the employers (capitalists) in industry and commerce. Third, spontaneous employer associations began to emerge in China in the late 1990s and have flourished since 2005. Though the openings for such free associations are still limited and conditional, their emergence is an important change in China's political and industrial relations environment.

The Grass Roots Unions

The positioning, roles and functions of the ACFTU and those of grass roots unions have become quite different from each other in the context of China's transition towards a market economy. Consistent with the new CCP leadership's policy of "constructing an harmonious society (构建和谐社会)", reforms of grass roots unions began to take off after the new leadership came into power in 2003. Measures were taken to reform the grass roots unions so as to match the external changes. Two reforms were the most significant and eye-catching: one affecting the election of the leaders of grass roots unions (the "representation" issue) and the other, the manner in which grass roots unions perform their roles (the "function" issue). I draw two conclusions.

First, the authorities hold a complex attitude towards direct elections in grass roots unions, knowing that they are a two-edged sword. On the one hand, they can help to reduce bureaucracy and enhance the effectiveness and efficiency of the officially-run grass roots unions; on the other, the election of union leaders may trigger domino effects and endanger the political structure, as in Eastern Europe in the 1980s and 1990s.[1]

Second, as the grass roots unions are sandwiched between employees and superior official organs, they are in the difficult position of trying to please both sides – usually without success. It is questionable, therefore, whether they can really play a significant role in protecting workers' legal rights.

1 For this reason, though most of the items in the ACFTU's 1992 document "On Grass Roots Unions' Representative Conference" can be seen as consistent with basic democratic practice, there were also clauses meant to protect the existing system and to avert the bottom-up qualitative change of power that might possibly be triggered by direct elections. The authorities are only willing to grant a relatively greater degree of flexibility and freedom to grass roots unions operating in medium and small and non-state-owned enterprises, which, unlike SOEs, are usually out of the control of the party-state.

The Employers

After 1979, and especially since 1992, the character of Chinese employers has become more diverse. Their businesses range from infamous "sweat shops" to highly modernized enterprises applying human resource concepts. I argue that, besides external factors such as the business and political environments, an enterprise's internal characteristics, in particular its operational scale and ownership type, have even more significant and direct impacts on its industrial relations behaviour. I therefore identify "Operation Scale" and "Ownership Type" as two dimensions for differentiating Chinese enterprises. In accordance with this segmentation, I discuss the attributes of the various types of employers.

The Employees

After clarifying the concept of "employee" and differentiating it from the more political concept of "working class", I argue that a proper stratification of Chinese employees is needed if we are to analyse their situations in contemporary China's industrial relations. By synthesizing (with certain revisions) three existing approaches to stratification,[2] I segment Chinese employees and discuss the three dichotomies: SOE employees vs. non-SOE employees; rural migrant employees vs. urban employees; and white-collar employees vs. blue-collar employees.

7.1.3 Relationships among Actors

In Chapters Five and Six, I discuss in detail nine sets of relationships among China's six industrial relations actors above the workplace level, at the workplace level, and across the different levels. I reach the conclusions detailed below.

2 These were proposed by Ping (2005); Shen (2006); Liu et al. (2005).

First Conclusion: Party-state and ACFTU

After analysing the interactions between the party-state and the ACFTU during various historical periods, I argue that even though the ACFTU was an extension organization established by the party-state, their relations were not always a simple case of "subordinate obeying the superior".

First, during the period 1921–49, when the party was contending for power, the ACFTU was under the direct leadership of the Chinese Communist Party.

Second, in the period 1949–79, the ACFTU went through different stages, from being a tame puppet of the party-state, to struggling (under the manipulation of leaders with political ambitions) for some freedom of development, to being crushed into submission, and finally to being discarded completely.

Third, since 1979, in the context of dramatic social transition, the relationship between the ACFTU and the party-state has returned to a type of "mutually-cohering interest relation" similar to that which existed before 1949, with the party-state changing the positioning of the ACFTU from a social controller to a social stabilizer.

Second Conclusion: Party-state and Employers' Associations

Employers' associations have shorter histories, with little involvement in the party-state's internal political struggles, but the diversity of employer associations has made the relationships between them and the party-state less complicated. Each of the three types of employer associations has a distinctive relationship, according to its specific characteristics, with the party-state.

First, the CEC-CEDA, as a direct extension of the party-state, has gone through various transformations since the 1990s, with new functions set by the party-state, acting as an outlet for redundant officials during the streamlining of governmental (industrial) departments and helping the government shift from "departmental management" in the planned economy to "industry management" in the market economy.

Second, the ACFIC, as a "United Front" organization outside the party-state system, has relatively more independence and freedom; but the party-state maintains its indirect control over the ACFIC through the mechanisms of the UFWD-CC-CCP, the "democratic parties" and the NPPCC.

Third, the party-state's attitude towards spontaneous employer associations has gradually become more accepting as reforms have deepened; but the Civil Chambers of Commerce must still win the support of the party-state system, sometimes by controversial measures, if they are to develop under the current system.

Third Conclusion: Tripartite System

The National Tripartite Conference on Labour Relations Co-ordination provided a new platform for the co-ordination of labour relations above the workplace level. I argue, however, that though the tripartite system was originally supposed to be a platform for equal communication between the state, employers and employees, it has evolved into yet another organizational "knick-knack" in China's party-state system. This is due to the characteristics of its major participants – the Ministry of Human Resources and Social Security (MOHRSS), the ACFTU and the CEC-CEDA – all with bureaucratic working styles as governmental or semi-governmental organizations. The key problem lies in the absence of free associations. The party-state has chosen to ignore this problem because its solution will pose a dilemma – though a tripartite scheme represents an irreversible trend in the emergence of civil society, where citizens form their own organizations for co-ordination and negotiation. It may, sooner or later, lead to a challenge against the totalitarian power of the party-state when people get used to having their own representation.

Fourth Conclusion: Grass Roots Unions and Employees

Except in the short period of the Cultural Revolution, during which spontaneous workers' organizations rebelled against the party-state, grass roots unions in China have a long-held tradition of being tame tools of the party-state. This heritage has caused them to function simultaneously as "political extension organizations" and "interest protection organizations", even after 1979 and in today's environment with economic construction as the central task. These two different organizational roles are somewhat self-contradictory: more often than not, unions are state-authorized mediation organizations, with the purpose of maintaining social stability, rather than representative labour organizations. I argue that the unions respond to superior (party-state as well as ACFTU) authorities' requests while, at best, satisfying only incidentally some of the worker members' demands.

Fifth Conclusion: Grass Roots Unions and Employers

After studying the history of the relations between grass roots unions and employers in various periods, I identify three stages.

Before 1956, the grass roots unions, in dealing with private employers, acted under the guidance of the party-state to implement the party-state's policies such as the "Five Antis" and the "Socialistic Transformation".

From 1956 to 1979, there was a single employer in China, the party-state, which "employed" all of the Chinese working population. Grass roots unions in SOEs played multiple roles in assisting management, as well as being agents for the party-state within enterprises.

After 1979, unions continued the tradition of subservience to the employers (as in the period 1956–79). Whereas before 1979 they supported the party-state (which was the only employer), after 1979 they supported employers of various types. It is the grass roots unions' prolonged dependence on employers since 1956 that prevents China from developing a modern industrial relation system.

Sixth Conclusion: Employers and Employees

Taking into account the diverse types of employers and employees, I identify forty different possible types of relationships between employers and employees in China. Focusing the discussion on the employer-employee relationship after 1979 and attempting a general description of the relationship with particular regard to the employer's "Operation Scale" and

"Ownership Type", I conclude that industrial relations practices in large enterprises are relatively formalized, while those in medium and small enterprises vary dramatically in accordance with ownership types. This is due to the fact that the Chinese government's retreat from economic dominance in the planned economy has led to the other extreme of laissez-faire, leaving the employers with decisive powers in their interactions with employees. However, there have been some signs of change since 2007 when the new Labour Contract Law was promulgated.

7.2 Future Studies

With China's accession to the WTO, its low cost products have out-competed the export industries of most other developing countries, and even the developed countries are now beginning to feel the growing pressure of these products. The low cost of Chinese products was, and largely still is, built on China's over-use of its resources – in particular its human (labour) resources. Therefore, a growing awareness of China's industrial relations issues has spread world-wide.

This book attempts to present to readers a broad description of Chinese industrial relations. By revising the classic three-party model of the western industrial relations theories, I develop a six-party model to take into account realities and practices with "Chinese characteristics". This is the first and, I believe, the major contribution that this book makes to the knowledge of industrial relations, in particular to the study of Chinese industrial relations. Then, following the guidance of the model, we discuss, one by one, the situations of all the six Chinese industrial relations actors as well as the nine sets of inter-relationships between them. This is, as far as I know, the first academic attempt to draw a full picture of Chinese industrial relations in a comprehensive manner.

I believe that the discussions and conclusions of the book will be valuable for those interested in China's social development (in particular, the development of modern industrial relations). I hope that my first attempt to revise a western industrial relations analytical model for adaptation to the realities of China will elicit research interest in the matter from other scholars and stimulate further discussions.

However, as the study of Chinese industrial relations is in its infancy, there are so many frontier areas in need of research that it is impossible for one single book to cover all the major topics. Inevitably, there remain many unsolved issues, calling for further research and analysis. For example, limited by length, we have not touched upon cross-level relationships; but this does not mean that this sub-topic is unimportant.

Cross-level Relationships

I have made some preliminary studies of these cross-level relationships.

The Relationship between Party-state and Employees

When dealing with its theoretical relationship with employees and the working class, the state system basically followed the Party documents; but the state's attitude was relatively clearer than the Party's, recognizing the working class's nominal leadership through all the years. However, the nominal "leadership of the working class", as stated in both the Party's and the state's constitutions, has never been a reality. The actual relationship between the party-state and the employees was at best, as in the pre-reform era 1949–79, based on the party-state bureaucrats' *claim* to be acting "under the leadership of working class" while in return, the party-state rewarded ordinary workers with certain honorary positions and economic benefits. After the reform (especially after 1992), the party-state not only gradually marginalized workers in the country's political life but also set aside its responsibilities for the workers' economic welfare.

The Relationship between Party-state and Employers

Since 1949, there have been several phases in the relationship between the party-state and the employers.

First, during the period 1949–56, the history of the relationship between the party-state, the employers and capitalists was a trilogy of use, restrict and transform. The party-state first used the capitalists for the state's economic recovery, then restricted their development, and finally transformed all private enterprises into SOEs.

Second, during the period 1956–79, the party-state was the only employer in China. There was no interaction between the party-state and the employer, as these two were one.

Third, the relationship between the party-state and the employers since 1979 has gone through three sub-stages: from one of restricted encouragement of private employers (1979–88), to one that returned to ideological caution (1989–92), and finally (since 1992) to one that entailed a new structure of economic-political collaboration between the party-state and the employers (some of the latter being ex-officials of the party-state or ex-SEO cadres).

The Relationship between Employers' Associations and Employers

The right of choice fundamentally differentiates the relationship between employers' associations and employers from that between ACFTU and employees. However, the three types of employers' associations behave differently in the treatment of their employer members.

The CEC-CEDA, as a typical semi-official organization, is most detached from the employers whom it is supposed to "represent".

The ACFIC's central level and grass roots level organizations have very different working styles, with the former being within the control of the party-state while its grass roots branches allow spontaneous Civil Chambers of Commerce to be only "nominally under" the flag of ACFIC and to operate independently.

The newly emerged Civil Chambers of Commerce have provided new choices of association to the employers, in which the leaders are no longer arbitrarily appointed from top down but are chosen at the will of the employer members.

The above are some results of my preliminary study on the cross-level relationships in the Chinese industrial relations arena. We of course need to do more to reach some meaningful conclusions.

Other Research Questions

Besides this, I have identified other research questions, as listed below, that may interest academics in the Chinese industrial relations circle:

1. What is the appropriate approach to tackle China's industrial relations problems? Unitarist, Radical, Pluralist or the three synthesized?
2. Is it possible to define a universal labour standard, taking into account the huge variation in productivity and living standards around the world?
3. Does the ACFTU, as a legally monopolistic organization, have the intention and motivation to trigger self-reform? If so, how effective would the reforms be? If the monopoly position were broken, making room for free association of labour, would there be chain effects such as those leading to the emergence of Solidarity in Poland?
4. Why is it that in a "socialist country" such as China, nominally "led by the working class", the breakthrough of free association reform has come not from the association of employees but from the association of employers (capitalists)? How will the Civil Chambers of Commerce develop in the context of China's mixed system of market economy and authoritarian politics?
5. If there is no reform of the ACFTU and the union system at the macro level, can there be any significant improvement at the micro level in the grass roots unions' operational model, e.g. by having reforms such

as grass roots union elections, or by enhancing the welfare and social roles of the grass roots union.[3]

6. What are the details of the forty possible sets of employer-employee relationships, taking into account the various types of employers and employees? What are the impacts of the employment arrangements on working conditions and the lives of workers and their families?
7. Who, in detail, are the "red top" capitalists with enormous access to political power since 2002? How were they "elected" or selected into the core of the political circle? Can they really represent the interests of ordinary employers and capitalists? What is the extent of collusion between party-state cadres and these capitalists? Will China go along the road to crony capitalism?
8. How big are the income distribution gaps among the employers, the white-collar and the blue-collar employees? What are the correlations between China's general economic growth and the respective income growths of the employers, the white-collar and the blue-collar employees? Who benefits most from China's economic reform?

In addition, more general questions can be asked regarding how Chinese industrial relations affect economic performance and the working lives of different groups of workers, as well as the processes of industrial relations, e.g. labour participation in daily operation/management, labour dispute and settlement mechanisms, or collective bargaining/consultation procedures which lead to collective contracts. There is also an opportunity to incorporate some of the "new" actors, e.g. employment agencies and labour dispute arbitration bodies, into the conceptualization of the industrial relations system in China.

3 There are debates on the welfare and social roles of the grass roots unions. For example, Cooke (2008c) argued that they have a positive impact on employees' working lives and some groups of employees (particularly employees in the public sector) actually desire this function of the trade union. However Feng (2006) dismissed (and even ridiculed) these roles for Chinese unions.

These are undoubtedly large questions in need of cross-disciplinary knowledge and efforts. I intend to tackle one or two of them in my post-doctoral research, but I also look forward to co-operating with interested parties in researching the other untouched topics. Therefore, this book acts as only the beginning of a series of related future studies.

In face of the global financial crisis beginning in late 2008, to avoid beggar-thy-neighbour strategies whereby footloose foreign investors play one low-wage country off against another, and to protect China's labour rights, it is now the right time to seek new strategies for Chinese industrial relations. I hope that this book and my other forthcoming studies will contribute towards a better understanding and a better approach to the solution of Chinese industrial relations issues.

Bibliography

ACFIC (1953), 'Statute of ACFIC' (in Chinese), Public Paper, available at <http://www1.acfic.org.cn/cenweb/portal/user/anon/page/acfic_CMSItemInfoPage.page?appId=00000000000000000122&category=200020&metainfoId=ABC000000000000011339> (last accessed on 20 January 2009); 全国工商联, '中华全国工商业联合会章程', 公告.

ACFIC (2007), 'Statute of ACFIC' (in Chinese), Public Paper, available at <http://www.acfic.org.cn/cenweb/portal/user/anon/page/constitutionPage.page> (last accessed on 20 January 2009); 全国工商联, '中华全国工商业联合会章程', 公告.

ACFIC (2007), 'Statute of ACFIC' (in Chinese), Public Paper, available at <http://www.acfic.org.cn/cenweb/portal/user/anon/page/constitutionPage.page> (last accessed on 20 January 2009); 全国工商联, '中华全国工商业联合会章程', 公告.

ACFTU (1984), 'Temporary Regulation on Grass Roots Union's Work' (in Chinese), Public Paper, available at <http://gh.sicnu.edu.cn/(S(gsjgno45pe2koxfvqtlnxoi5))/showdetail.aspx?id=5&ar_id=133&AspxAutoDetectCookieSupport=1> (last accessed on 20 January 2009); 中华全国总工会, '基层工会工作暂行条例', 公告.

ACFTU (1992a), 'Temporary Regulation on Grass Roots Union's Election' (in Chinese), Public Paper, available at <http://www4.zzu.edu.cn/gh/show.aspx?id=240&cid=10> (last accessed on 20 January 2009); 中华全国总工会, '工会基层组织选举工作暂行条例', 公告.

ACFTU (1992b), 'On Grass Roots Union's Representative Conference' (in Chinese), Public Paper, available at <http://www.qdu.edu.cn/zzjg/ghzhy/UploadFiles/2008102816556557.doc> (last accessed on 20 January 2009); 中华全国总工会, '关于基层工会会员代表大会', 公告.

ACFTU (2003), 'Statute of Labour Unions in P. R. China' (in Chinese), Public Paper, available at <http://www.acftu.net/template/10004/file.jsp?cid=807&aid=42622> (last accessed on 20 January 2009); 中华全国总工会, '中华人民共和国工会章程', 公告.

ACFTU (2004), 'Resolution on Enhancing Grass Roots Union's Work' (in Chinese), Public Paper, available at <http://www.hyedu.com/gh/ShowArticle.asp?ArticleID=1350> (last accessed on 20 January 2009); 中华全国总工会, '关于进一步加强基层工会工作的决定', 公告.

ACFTU (2005a), 'Blue Paper on the Protection of Employees' Legal Rights by China's Union' (in Chinese), Public Paper, available at <http://www.hntj.gov.cn/Vital_Statistics/Policy_Statute/200609270128.doc> (last accessed on 20 January 2009); 中华全国总工会, '中国工会维护职工合法权益蓝皮书', 公告.

ACFTU (2005b), 'Opinions on the Protection of Employees' Legal Rights in the Process of SOE Transformation' (in Chinese), Public Paper, available at <http://www.gzxz.gov.cn/Article/ShowArticle.asp?ArticleID=220> (last accessed on 20 January 2009); 中华全国总工会, '关于在国有企业改制中切实维护职工合法权益的意见', 公告.

ACFTU (2005c), 'Opinions on the Implementation of State Council's "Notice on Further Strengthening the Employment and Re-employment"' (in Chinese), Public Paper, available at <http://www.bjzgh.gov.cn/template/10002/file.jsp?cid=468&aid=6993> (last accessed on 20 January 2009); 中华全国总工会, '关于贯彻落实国务院'关于进一步加强就业再就业工作的通知'的意见', 公告.

ACFTU (2005d), 'Resolution on Adhering to the Socialistic Union Development Route with Chinese Characteristics' (in Chinese), Public Paper, available at <http://51.yq.gov.cn/Article_Show.asp?ArticleID=194> (last accessed on 20 January 2009); 中华全国总工会, '关于坚持走中国特色社会主义工会发展道路的决议', 公告.

ACFTU (2005e), 'Summary of the Joint Meeting between ACFTU and MOLSS' (in Chinese), Public Paper, available at <http://www.hngh.org/content/showContent.jsp?aid=20050402134 4&lu_id=410000000000> (last accessed on 20 January 2009); 中华全国总工会, '全总与劳动和社会保障部联席会议纪要', 公告.

ACFTU (2006a), 'Name List and Resumes of All Current and Previous Chairs' (in Chinese), Official Information, available at <http://www.acftu.net/template/10004/file.jsp?cid=106&aid=41> (last accessed on 20 January 2009); 中华全国总工会, '历任主席名单', 官方网站资讯.

ACFTU (2006b), 'Brief Introduction to All Previous National Congress of ACFTU' (in Chinese), Official Information, available at <http://www.acftu.net/template/10004/file.jsp?cid=107&aid=2536> (last accessed on 20 January 2009); 中华全国总工会, '中国工会历届全国代表大会简介', 官方网站资讯.

ACFTU (2006c), 'ACFTU's Key Responsibilities' (in Chinese), Official Information, available at <http://www.acftu.net/template/10004/file.jsp?cid=804&aid=42616> (last accessed on 20 January 2009); 中华全国总工会, '全总主要职责', 官方网站资讯.

ACFTU (2006d), 'Regulation on the Work of Enterprise' Unions' (in Chinese), Public Paper, available at <http://www.acftu.net/template/10004/file.jsp?cid=701&aid=42680> (last accessed on 20 January 2009); 中华全国总工会, '企业工会工作条例', 公告.

ACFTU (2007), 'Enterprise Union: On the Way to Coordination and Negotiation' (in Chinese), Discussion Paper, available at <http://acftu.people.com.cn/GB/71368/5401223.html> (last accessed on 20 January 2009); 中华全国总工会, '企业工会: 走向协商与谈判', 讨论稿.

AFL-CIO (2006), '301 Petition Letter', Public Paper, available at <http://www.aflcio.org/issues/jobseconomy/globaleconomy/upload/china_petition.pdf> (last accessed on 20 January 2009).

Alesina, A., Ozler, S., Roubini, N. and Swagel, P. (1996), 'Political Instability and Economic Growth', *Journal of Economic Growth*, Vol. 1 No. 2, pp. 189–211.

Alexander, R. and Lewer, J. (2004), *Understanding Australian Industrial Relations*, Southbank, Thomson.

Aungles, S. and Parker, S. (1992), *Work, Organizations and Change*, St Leonards, Allen & Unwin.

Bai N. X. (2003), 'Research on New Models for Mainland China's Union Organization' (in Chinese), Discussion Paper, available at <http://www.usc.cuhk.edu.hk/wk_wzdetails.asp?id=3288> (last accessed on 20 January 2009); 柏宁湘，'对中国大陆工会组织新模式的研究'，讨论稿.

Bamber, G. (2005), 'What Context Does the Asia-Pacific Economic Cooperation Forum Provide for Employment Relations?', Discussion Paper, available at <http://www98.griffith.edu.au/dspace/bitstream/10072/2812/1/30553.pdf> (last accessed on 20 January 2009).

Bamber, G., Lansbury, R. and Wailes, N. (2004), 'Introduction', in Bamber, G. et al. ed. *International and Comparative Employment Relations: Globalization and the Developed Market Economies*, Crows Nest, Allen & Unwin, pp. 1–35.

Banister, J. (2005), 'Manufacturing Earnings and Compensation in China', *Monthly Labour Review*, Aug, 2005, pp. 22–40.

Basu, K., Horn, H., Roman, L. and Shapiro, J. eds (2003), *International Labour Standards: History, Theory, and Policy Options*, Malden, Blackwell.

Bean, R. (1994), *Comparative Industrial Relations*, London, Routledge.

Bell, S. and Head, B. (1994), *State, Economy and Public Policy in Australia*, Melbourne, Oxford University Press.

Bernstein, J. and Shierholz, H. (2008), 'A Decade of Decline', April 16, 2008, EPI Briefing Paper #209, available at <http://www.epi.org/publications/entry/bp209/> (last accessed on 20 January 2009).

Blecher, M. (2002), 'Hegemony and Workers' Politics in China', *China Quarterly*, pp. 283–303.

Blyton, P. and Turnbull, P. ed. (1992), *Reassessing Human Resource Management*, London, SAGE.

Braverman, H. (1974), *Labour and Monopoly Capital: The Degrade of Work in the 20th Century*, New York, Monthly Review Press.

Bray, M., Deery, S., Walsh, J. and Waring, P. (2005), *Industrial Relations: a contemporary approach*, Roseville, McGraw-Hill.

Brooks, J. G. (1920), *Labor's Challenge To The Social Order*, New York, Macmillan.

Budd, J. (2004), *Employment with a Human Face*, Ithaca, NY, Cornell University Press.

Burawoy, M. (1985), *The Politics of Production*, London, Verso.

Cai F. and Yang, T. (2000), 'A Political-economic Study on the Urban-rural Income Gap' (in Chinese), *China Social Science*, Issue 4, 2000, pp. 11–22; 蔡昉/杨涛, '城乡收入差距的政治经济学',《中国社会科学》2000年第4期.

Cai L. (2006), 'Reflection on China, Re-evaluate 4th May (5–4) Movement' (in Chinese), Discussion Paper, available at <http://www.chinavalue.net/Article/Archive/2006/4/19/27364.html> (last accessed on 20 January 2009); 蔡厉, '反思中国 重估五四的价值', 讨论稿.

Cai Y. F. (2005), 'Concerns on Bosses involving in Politics' (in Chinese), *Chinese Economy Weekly*, 24 April, 2005, pp. 45–46; 蔡永飞, '也忧老板执政', 中国经济周刊, 2005年4月24日.

CC-CCP (1921), 'Programme of the Chinese Communist Party' (in Chinese), Public Paper, available at <http://news.xinhuanet.com/ziliao/2002–03/04/content_695953.htm> (last accessed on 20 January 2009); 中共中央, '中国共产党纲领', 公告.

CC-CCP (1945), 'Resolution on Certain Historical Issues' (in Chinese), Public Paper, concise version available at <http://www.zjgdx.gov.cn/Article/dxjy/dsxzd/200511/527.html> (last accessed on 20 January 2009); 中共中央, '关于若干历史问题的决议', 公告.

CC-CCP (1951), 'Explanation on the Leading Role of Working Class and Semi-working Class' (in Chinese), Public Paper, available at <http://big5.xinhuanet.com/gate/big5/news.xinhuanet.com/ziliao/2004–12/16/content_2342137.htm> (last accessed on 20 January 2009); 中共中央, '关于工人阶级与半工人阶级的领导作用问题的解释', 公告.

CC-CCP (1952), 'Classification Standards and Methods for the Treatment of Industrial and Commercial Business Owners during the 'Five Antis' Movement' (in Chinese), Public Paper, available at <http://big5.xinhuanet.com/gate/big5/news.xinhuanet.com/ziliao/2004–12/21/content_2363153.htm> (last accessed on 20 January 2009); 中共中央, '关于在 '五反' 运动中对工商户分类处理的标准和办法', 公告.

CC-CCP (1956), 'Resolution on the Socialistic Transformation of Capitalist Industries and Commerce' (in Chinese), Public Paper, available at <http://news.xinhuanet.com/ziliao/2004–12/30/content_2394487.htm> (last accessed on 20 January 2009); 中共中央, '关于资本主义工商业改造问题的决议', 公告.

CC-CCP (1957), 'Instructions on Dealing with Workers' and Students' Strikes' (in Chinese), Public Paper, available at <http://news.xinhuanet.com/ziliao/2005-01/05/content_2418443.htm> (last accessed on 20 January 2009); 中共中央, '关于处理罢工罢课问题的指示', 公告.

CC-CCP (1981), 'Resolution on Certain Historical Issues since the Establishment of the State' (in Chinese), Public Paper, available at <http://cpc.people.com.cn/GB/64162/64168/64563/65374/4526448.html> (last accessed on 20 January 2009); 中共中央, '关于建国以来党的若干历史问题的决议', 公告.

CC-CCP (1982), 'Report of the 12th CCP's national conference' (in Chinese), Public Papers, available at <http://cpc.people.com.cn/GB/64162/64168/64565/65448/4526430.html> (last accessed on 20 January 2009); 中共中央，'中国共产党第十二次全国代表大会上的报告'，公开文件.

CC-CCP (1987), 'Report of the 13th CCP's national conference' (in Chinese), Public Papers, available at <http://cpc.people.com.cn/GB/64162/64168/64566/65447/4526368.html> (last accessed on 20 January 2009); 中共中央，'中国共产党第十三次全国代表大会上的报告'，公开文件.

CC-CCP (1991), 'In Reply to the UFWD-CC-CCP's Request of "On Solving Issues concerning ACFIC"' (in Chinese), Public Papers, available at <http://www.cmgsl.com.cn/images/zz/5001.htm> (last accessed on 20 January 2009); 中共中央, '中共中央批转中央统战部 '关于工商联若干问题的请示'的通知', 公告.

CC-CCP (2002a), 'Constitution of the Chinese Communist Party' (in Chinese), Public Paper, available at <http://cpc.people.com.cn/GB/64162/64168/64569/65444/4429114.html> (last accessed on 20 January 2009); 中共中央, '中国共产党党章', 公告.

CC-CCP (2002b), 'Report to the 16th National Congress of the CCP' (in Chinese), Public Paper, available at <http://cpc.people.com.cn/GB/64162/64168/64569/65444/4429125.html> (last accessed on 20 January 2009); 中共中央, '中国共产党第十六次全国代表大会报告', 公告.

CC-CCP (2006), 'Resolution on Major Issues Regarding the Building of a Harmonious Socialist Society' (in Chinese), Public Paper, available at <http://news.xinhuanet.com/politics/2006-10/18/content_5218639.htm> (last accessed on 20 January 2009); 中共中央, '关于构建社会主义和谐社会若干重大问题的决定', 公告.

CC-CCP (2007), 'Report to the 17th National Congress of the CCP' (in Chinese), Public Paper, available at <http://cpc.people.com.cn/GB/64162/64168/106155/106156/6430009.html> (last accessed on 20 January 2009); 中共中央, '中国共产党第十七次全国代表大会报告', 公告.

CC-CCP and State Council (2002), 'Notice on the Implementation of Open System in SOEs and COEs' (in Chinese), Public Paper, available at <http://www.yfzs.gov.cn/gb/info/mzzz/xxgk/2003-06/08/1121347646.html> (last accessed on 20 January 2009); 中共中央/国务院，'关于在国有企业、集体企业及其控股企业深入实行厂务公开制度的通知', 公告.

CCTV (2006), '2005 China Annual Employer Investigation' (in Chinese), available at <http://www.cctv.com/program/jdtz/topic/life/C14761/01/index.shtml> (last accessed on 20 January 2009); 央视国际，'2005 中国年度雇主调查' .

CCTV (2007), '2006 China Annual Employer Investigation' (in Chinese), available at <http://news.sohu.com/s2006/cctvndgz2006/> (last accessed on 20 January 2009); 央视国际，'2006 中国年度雇主调查'.

CEC-CEDA (2003), 'Statute of CEC-CEDA' (in Chinese), Public Paper, available at <http://www.cec-ceda.org.cn/china/zc.php> (last accessed on 20 January 2009); 中国企业联合会-中国企业家协会, '中国企业联合会-中国企业家协会章程', 公告.

Chamberlain, N. (1958), *Labour*, New York, NY, McGraw-Hill.

Chan A. (1993), 'Revolution or Corporatism? Workers and Trade Unions in Post-Mao China', *Australian Journal of Chinese Affairs*, No. 29, pp. 31–61.

Chan A. (2002), 'Labour in Waiting: The International Trade Union Movement and China', *New Labour Forum*, Fall/ Winter 2002, pp. 54–59.

Chan A. (2005), 'Recent Trends in Chinese Labour Issues – Signs of Change', *China Perspectives*, Jan–Feb 2005, No. 57.

Chan A. (2006), 'Realities and Possibilities for Chinese Trade Unionism', in Phelan, C. (ed.) *The Future of Organized Labour*, Bern, Peter Lang, pp. 275–304.

Chan A. and Ross, R. (2003), 'Racing to the bottom: International Trade without a social clause', *Third World Quarterly*, vol. 24, pp. 1011–28.

Chan A. and Senser, R. (1997), 'China's Troubled Workers', *Foreign Affairs*, March/April 1997 Issue, pp. 104–17.

Chang K. (2002), 'On the Legislation of Striking Right in China' (in Chinese), Discussion Paper, available at <http://www.dajun.com.cn/bagongquan.htm> (last accessed on 20 January 2009); 常凯， '论中国的罢工权立法'，讨论稿.

Chang K. (2006), 'Adjustment on Human Resource Management and Labour-Capital Relations' (in Chinese), Conference Paper presented at Labour and Personnel Institute of Chinese People's University on 13 January 2006, available at <http://qzone.qq.com/blog/622007983-1229396921> (last accessed on 20 January 2009); 常凯, '人力资源管理与劳动关系调整', 会议论文.

Chen F. (2003a), 'Between the State and the Labour', *China Quarterly*, No. 176, pp. 1006–28.

Chen F. (2003b), 'Industrial Restructuring and Workers' Resistance in China', *Modern China*, Vol.29, No.2, pp. 237–62.

Chen F. (2006), 'Privatization and Its Discontents in Chinese Factories', *China Quarterly*, Vol. 185, pp. 42–60.

Chen F. (2007), 'Individual Rights and Collective Rights: Labor's Predicament in China', *Communist and Post-Communist Studies*, Vol. 40, pp. 59–79.

Chen J. H. (2005), *Memory of State Affairs* (in Chinese), Beijing, CCP Party History Press; 陈锦华, '国事忆述', 中共党史出版社, 北京.

Chen L. S. (2005), 'Protect Labour Rights and Construct a Harmonious Society' (in Chinese), Study Times, 17 November 2005, available at <http://theory.people.com.cn/GB/49154/49156/3864288.html> (last accessed on 20 January 2009); 陈连升, '保护劳工权益与构建和谐社会', 学习时报, 2005年11月17日.

Chen S. T. (1953), 'Opening Speech on the First National Congress of ACFIC' (in Chinese), Public Paper, available at <http://www.ce.cn/xwzx/gnsz/szyw/200705/29/t20070529_11530921.shtml> (last accessed on 20 January 2009); 陈叔通,'在中华全国工商业联合会第一次会员代表大会的开幕词',公告.

Chen S. T. (1956), 'A Report on the Socialistic Transformation of Capitalist Industries and Commerce' (in Chinese), Public Paper, available at <http://www.gov.cn/2008lh/content_899638.htm> (last accessed on 20 January 2009); 陈叔通, '关于资本主义工商业的社会主义改造的报告', 会议发言稿.

Chen S. Y. and Ma B. (2004), 'Chambers of Commerce in Wenzhou: An Institutional Analysis on Self-governance' (in Chinese), *Business World*, Issue 12, 2004, pp. 31–49; 陈剩勇/马斌, '温州民间商会: 自主治理的制度分析', 管理世界, 2004年第12期.

Chen S. Y. and Zhang M. (2004), 'Local Union Reforms and Grass Roots Union Direct Election in China' (in Chinese), *Academics in China*, 2004 vol.6, pp. 37–49; 陈剩勇 / 张明, '中国地方工会改革与基层工会直选', 学术界, 2004年第6期.

Chen X. N. (2005), *The Last Told Memory of Chen Boda* (in Chinese), Hongkong, Sunshine Global Press; 陈晓农, '陈伯达最后口述回忆', 阳光环球出版社, 香港.

Chow I. H. S. and Fu P. P. (2000), 'Change and Development in Pluralistic Settings: An Exploration of HR Practices in Chinese Township and Village Enterprises', *International Journal of Human Resource Management*, 11:4, pp. 822–36.

Clarke, S. (2005), 'Post-socialist Trade Unions: China and Russia', *Industrial Relations Journal*, Volume 36, No. 1, January 2005, pp. 2–18.

Clarke, S. and Lee C. H. (2002), 'The Significance of a Tripartite Consultation in China', *Asia Pacific Business Review*, Volume 9, Issue 2 December 2002, pp. 61–79.

Clarke, S., Lee C. H. and Li Q. (2004), 'Collective Consultation and Industrial Relations in China', *British Journal of Industrial Relations*, vol. 42 issue 2, pp. 235–54.

Clegg, C., Legge, K. and Walsh, S. eds (1999), *The Experience of Managing*, London, Macmillan.

Cooke, F. L. (2004), 'Foreign Firms in China: Modelling HRM in a Toy Manufacturing Corporation', *Human Resource Management Journal*, Vol. 14, No. 3 pp. 31–52.

Cooke, F. L. (2005a), 'Employment Relations in Small Commercial Business in China', *Industrial Relations Journal*, 36:1, pp. 19–37.

Cooke, F. L. (2005b), *HRM, Work and Employment in China*, Abingdon, Routledge.

Cooke, F. L. (2006), 'Acquisitions of Chinese State-owned Enterprises by Multinational Corporations: Driving Forces, Barriers and Implications for HRM', *British Journal of Management*, Vol. 17, S105–21.

Cooke, F. L. (2008a), 'The Changing Dynamics of Employment Relationships in China: An Evaluation of The Rising Level of Labour Dispute', *Journal of Industrial Relations*, Vol. 50, pp. 111–38.

Cooke, F. L. (2008b), 'Employment Relations in China', in Bamber, G. et al. ed. *International and Comparative Employment Relations* (forthcoming), December 2008 version provided by the author.

Cooke, F. L. (2008 c), 'Are Chinese women workers protected? A study of female workers' representational needs, and forms and effects of (un)organizing', International conference, 'Breaking down Chinese Walls; The Changing Faces of Labor and Employment in China', Cornell University, 26–28 September 2008, Ithaca, NY.

Cooke, W. and Noble, D. (1998), 'Industrial Relations Systems and US Foreign Direct Investment Abroad', *British Journal of Industrial Relations*, December Issue, 1998, pp. 581–609.

Cooney, S. (2007), 'China's labour law, compliance and flaws in implementing institutions', *Journal of Industrial Relations*, 49, 5, pp. 673–86.

Cox, T. and Mason, B. (2000), 'Interest Groups and the Development of Tripartism in East Central Europe', *European Journal of Industrial Relations*, Vol. 6 No. 3, 2000, pp. 325–47.

Creighton, B. and Stewart, A. (1994), *Labour Law*, Leichhardt, Federation Press.

Crouch C. (2000), *Coping with Post-democracy*, London, Fabian Society.

Cunningham, L. X. and Rowley, C. (2008), 'The Development of Chinese Small and Medium Enterprises and Human Resource Management: A Review', *Asia Pacific Journal of Human Resources*, Vol. 46(3), pp. 353–79.

Dabscheck, B. (1995), *The Struggle for Australian Industrial Relations*, Melbourne, Oxford University Press.

Dang G. Y. (2007), 'What's Behind the Labour Relation Issues?' (in Chinese), *Southern Weekend*, 24 June 2007; 党国英,'劳资关系问题的背后是什么?',南方周末, 2007–06-24.

Deery, S. (2001), *Industrial Relations: a contemporary analysis*, Roseville, McGraw-Hill.

Desai, M. (2002), *Marx's Revenge*, London, Verso.

Development Research Center, State Council (2005), 'Evaluation of and Suggestion for China's Medical Care System Reform' (in Chinese), Public Paper, available at <http://down.cenet.org.cn/view.asp?id=58268> (last accessed on 20 January 2009); 国务院发展研究中心, '对中国医疗卫生体制改革的评价与建议', 公告.

Dickens, L. and Hall, M. (2003), 'Labour Law and Industrial Relations: A New Settlement?' in Edwards, P. R. (ed.) *Industrial Relations: Theory and Practice in Britain*, Oxford, Blackwell.

Ding D. Z. and Akhtar, S. (2001), 'The Organizational Choice of Human Resource Management Practices: A Study of Chinese Enterprises in Three Cities in the PRC', *International Journal of Human Resource Management*, Vol. 12, No.6, pp. 946–64.

Ding D. Z., Goodall, K. and Warner, M. (2002), 'The Impact of Economic Reform on the Role of Trade Unions in Chinese Enterprises', *International Journal of Human Resource Management*, vol. 13, pp. 431–49.

Dirlik, A. and Meisner, M. ed. (1989), *Marxism and the Chinese Experience*, London, M. E. Sharpe.

Dong B. (2002), 'Labour Law and Reform in China', Paper for International Labour Standards Conference (2002), Stanford Law School.

Dore, R. (2000), *Stock Market Capitalism: Welfare Capitalism*, New York, Oxford University Press.

Dowling, P. and Welch, D. (1999), *International Human Resource Management*, Mason, South-western College Publishing.

Dunlop, J. T. (1958), *Industrial Relations Systems*, New York, NY, Henry Holt.

Fairbank, J. (1983), *The Cambridge History of China 1912–1949 (Part I)*, Cambridge, Cambridge University Press.

Fairbank, J. and Feuerwerker, A. (1986), *The Cambridge History of China 1912–1949 (Part II)*, Cambridge, Cambridge University Press.

Fan G. (2008), 'When to Reach the Other Side of the River' (in Chinese), Southern Weekend, 28th Aug 2008, available at <http://www.nanfangdaily.com.cn/epaper/nfzm/content/20080828/ArticelC16002FM.htm> (last accessed on 20 January 2009); 樊纲, '还要多少年才能抵达河对岸', 南方周末, 2008年08月28日.

Fan J. P., Gao H. Q. and Hu S. W. (2006), 'Income Distribution Reform: A Silent Revolution' (in Chinese), Discussion Paper, available at <http://www.bjqx.org.cn/qxweb/n8973c5.aspx> (last accessed on 20 January 2009); 范剑平, 高辉清, 胡少维, '收入分配体制改革：一场 '静悄悄的'革命', 讨论稿.

Fang L., Chen J. X. and Zhang M. (2004), 'Chinese Entrepreneurs Get Involved in Politics: An Inevitable Phenomenon in the Process of Political Transition' (in Chinese), *Perspectives Eastern Weekly*, Vol. 18 (2004), pp. 32–39; 方亮, 陈键兴, 张玫, '中国企业家从政：政治变局过程中的必然现象', 瞭望东方周刊, 第18期(2004年).

Fang Y. (2006), 'From NRLRGH to the People's Cultural Revolution' (in Chinese), Discussion Paper, available at <http://www.boxun.com/hero/2007/zhongguogongdang/35_1.shtml> (last accessed on 20 January 2009); 方圆, '从 '全红总'谈 '人民文革" , 讨论稿.

Feng G. (2006), 'The Institutional Weakness of Enterprise Unions and the Backgrounds of its Formation' (in Chinese), *Society*, vol.26 (2006), pp. 81–99; 冯钢, '企业工会的制度性弱势及其形成背景', 社会, 卷26.

Feng T. Q. (2003), 'A Fine Adjustment of the Relations among State, Enterprise, Staffs and Union' (in Chinese), Discussion Paper, available at <http://www.usc.cuhk.edu.hk/wk_wzdetails.asp?id=3312> (last accessed on 20 January 2009); 冯同庆，'国家、企业、职工、工会之间关系的良性调整'，讨论稿.

Feng T. Q. (2004), 'The Labour Investigation and Research in China' (in Chinese), *Union Theories and Practices*, Vol. 18 (2004 Issue 5), pp. 6–10; 冯同庆，'中国的劳工调查与研究'，工会理论与实践，2004年第18卷第5期.

Feng X. M., Zhou R. G., Wu X. H. and Nian S. P. (2002), 'Historical Experience on Shanghai's Grass Roots Party Construction in Early Days of Liberation' (in Chinese), *Shanghai Party History and Party Construction*, Issue 2, 2002, pp. 22–29; 冯小敏,邹荣庚,吴祥华,年士萍, '解放初期多种经济成分并存条件下上海基层党建的历史经验及启示', 上海党史与党建, 2002年第2期.

Fishman, T. (2004), 'The Chinese Century', The New York Times, 4 July, 2004, available at <http://query.nytimes.com/gst/fullpage.html?res=9C04E2DC1438F937A35754C0A9629C8B63> (last accessed on 20 January 2009).

Flanders, A. (1965), *Industrial Relations: What Is Wrong With The System?*, London, Faber & Faber.

Frankel, S. and Peetz, D. (1998), 'Globalization and Industrial Relations in East Asia: A Three-country Comparison', *Industrial Relations*, vol. 37, pp. 282–310.

Freeman, B. & Medoff, J. (1984), *What Do Unions Do?*, New York, Basic Books.

Friedman, A. (1977), 'Responsible Autonomy vs. Direct Control over the Labour Process', *Capital and Class*, No. 1, Spring pp. 43–57.

Fu H. L. and Choy D. W. (2004), 'From Mediation to Adjudication: Settling Labour Disputes in China', *China Rights Forum*, No. 3, 2004, pp. 17–22.

Fukuyama, F. (1992), *The End of History and the Last Man*, New York, Penguin Books.

Fukuyama, F. (2004), *State Building*, London, Profile Books.

Gall, G. ed. (2006), *Union Recognition*, Abingdon, Routledge.

Gallagher, M. (2004), 'Time is Money, Efficiency is Life: The Transformation of Labour Relations in China', *Studies in Comparative International Development*, vol. 39, No. 2, pp. 11–44.

Gao B. Z. (2000), 'The Legitimacy Issue of Social Organizations' (in Chinese), *Social Science in China*, Issue 2, 2000, pp. 100–09; 高丙中, '社会团体的合法性问题', 中国社会科学, 2000年第2期.

Gao W. S. (2006), 'Analysis on the Factors Affecting Employment and Income of Peasant Workers' (in Chinese), *Chinese Rural Economy*, 2006 Issue 1, pp. 28–34; 高文书, '进城农民工就业状况及收入影响因素分析', 中国农村经济, 2006年第一期.

Gilbert, S. (2005), 'China's Strike Wave', International Socialism, issue 107, available at <http://www.isj.org.uk/index.php4?id=125&issue=107> (last accessed on 20 January 2009).

Giles, J., Park, A. and Cai, F. (2006), 'How has Economic Restructuring affected China's Urban Workers', *China Quarterly*, pp. 61–95.

Guangdong Provincial Party Committee and Government (2006), 'Decision on Utilizing Trade Associations' (in Chinese), Public Paper, available at <http://www.gdsme.org/ns_detail.php?id=552&nowmenuid=322&cpath=0019:&catid=19> (last accessed on 20 January 2009); 广东省委省政府, '关于发挥行业协会商会作用的决定', 公告.

Guangdong Provincial People's Congress (2005), 'Regulation on Trade Associations' (in Chinese), Public Paper, available at <http://www.chinanpo.gov.cn/web/showBulltetin.do?type=next&id=21995&dictionid=1500&catid=> (last accessed on 20 January 2009); 广东省人大, '广东省行业协会条例', 公告.

Guo A. P. (2006), 'Labour-Capital Relations and the Government's Coordination Effect' (in Chinese), *Journal of Jiangxi Administration College*, vol. 9 (2007 Issue 2), pp. 41–45; 郭爱萍, '劳资关系与政府协调作用的若干思考', 《江西行政学院学报》2007年第9卷第2期.

Guo W. G. (2000), 'Reflection on the Relationships between the Central and Local Authorities' (in Chinese), *Journal of Fujian Party School*, Issue 3, 2000, pp. 23–28; 郭为桂, '中央与地方关系50年略考：体制变迁的视角'， 福建省委党校学报,2000年第3期.

Han H. (2005), 'Attention to the Autonomous Interests of Labour Union System' (in Chinese), Discussion Paper, available at <http://www.usc.cuhk.edu.hk/wk_wzdetails.asp?id=4433> (last accessed on 20 January 2009); 韩恒，'关注工会系统的自主利益'，讨论稿.

Harbin Local History Office (2005), 'Local History of Harbin' (in Chinese), available at <http://dqw.harbin.gov.cn/zy_14.htm> (last accessed on 20 January 2009); 哈尔滨市政府地方志办公室, '哈尔滨地方志'.

Harper, P. (1969), 'The Party and the Unions in Communist China', *China Quarterly*, No. 37 (January–March, 1969), pp. 84–119.

Havel, V. (1985), *Power of the Powerless: citizens against the state in central-eastern Europe*, London, Hutchinson.

Hayek, F. A. (2003), *Individualism and Economic Order* (Chinese Translation), Beijing, San-lian Press; 哈耶克，'个人主义与经济秩序'，三联书店，北京.

He F. (2005), *Notes on Party History* (in Chinese), Hong Kong, Liwen Press, internet edition available at <https://sites.google.com/site/mzdsky/before49/biji> (last accessed on 20 January 2009); 何方, '党史笔记：从遵义会议到延安整风'，利文出版社，香港.

He Q. L. (2003), *The Pitfall of China's Modernization* (in Chinese), Sunnyvale, CA, Broad Press; 何清涟, '中国现代化的陷阱', 博大出版社, 美国.

He Y. H. and Chen X. (2006), 'Sweat Shops: An Epitome of China's Economy' (in Chinese), *Security Times*, 25 July 2006; 何雨华/陈霞，'血汗工厂：中国经济的一个缩影'，证券时报，2006–07-25.

Hebel, J. and Schucher, G. (2006), 'The Emergence of a New 'Socialist' Market Labour Regime in China', GIGA Working Paper No. 39.

Heberer, T. (2005), 'Research on the Chinese Model' (Chinese Translation), *Contemporary World and Socialism*, Issue 5, 2005, pp. 9–11; 托马斯·海贝勒, '关于中国模式若干问题的研究', 当代世界与社会主义, 2005年第5期.

Helliwell, J. (1992), 'Empirical Linkages Between Democracy and Economic Growth', NBER Working Paper No. W4066.

Hirschman, A. (1970), *Exit, Voice, and Loyalty*, Cambridge, Harvard University Press.

Hobbes, T. (1651), 'Leviathan', electronic edition from <www.etestingcenter.com/library/BooksG-I/Leviathan.pdf> (last accessed on 20 January 2009).

Howell, J. (1998), 'Trade Unions in China: The Challenge of Foreign Capital', in O'Leary (ed.) *Adjusting to Capitalism: Chinese Workers and the State*, New York, NY, M. E. Sharpe.

Hu F. C. (2002), 'Re-acknowledgement of Liu Shao-qi' (in Chinese), Discussion Paper, available at <http://www.taosl.net/hufc023.htm> (last accessed on 18 Dec 2008); 胡甫臣, '对刘少奇的再认识', 讨论稿.

Hu X. D. (2001), 'On Separation of Government and Enterprises' (in Chinese), *Journal of China University of Mining & Technology*, Vol. 3 Issue 1, 2001, pp. 70–75; 胡星斗, '论政企不分与政企分开', 中国矿业大学学报, 2001年 3卷 1期.

Huang Y. and Guo W. Q. (2006), 'The Global Network's Labour Rights Protection Activities in China' (in Chinese), *Modern China Research*, vol. 2, 2006, available at <http://www.chinayj.net/StubArticle.asp?issue=060212&total=93> (last accessed on 20 January 2009); 黄岩/ 郭巍青，'跨国网络在中国的劳工维权行动'，当代中国研究，2006年第2期.

Huang Y. P. (2007), 'Chinese Economy: Lose Control or Laissez-faire?' (in Chinese), Discussion Paper, available at <http://www.caijing.com.cn/2007-08-29/100028455.html> (last accessed on 20 January 2009); 黄益平, '中国经济：失去控制还是放任自由？', 讨论稿.

Hyman, R. (1975), *Industrial Relations: A Marxist Introduction*, London, Macmillan.

ILO (1948), 'Freedom of Association and Protection of the Right to Organise Convention (C87)', available at <http://www.ilo.org/ilolex/cgi-lex/convde.pl?C087> (last accessed on 20 January 2009).

ILO (1976), 'Tripartite Consultation (International Labour Standards) Convention (C144)', available at <http://www.ilo.org/ilolex/cgi-lex/convde.pl?C144> (last accessed on 20 January 2009).

ILO (2006), 'The Employment Relationship', available at <www.ilo.org/public/english/standards/relm/ilc/ilc95/pdf/rep-v-1.pdf> (last accessed on 20 January 2009).

Interbrand (2007), 'Made in China: 2007 Brand Study', available at <www.interbrand.com/images/studies/Interbrand_Made_In_China_2007.pdf> (last accessed on 20 January 2009).

Ji H. G. (1999), *Biography of Rong Yiren* (in Chinese), Beijing, Central Literature Press; 计泓赓, '荣毅仁传',中央文献出版社出版，北京.

Jin L. R. (2002), 'New Study on Shang-hai workers' Military Insurrection' (in Chinese), *Shanghai Part History and Party Construction*, 2002 Issue 3, pp. 42–45; 金立人, '上海工人武装起义新考', 上海党史与党建,2002年第3期.

Jing S. P., (2002), 'Open Up A New Prospect for ACFIC' (in Chinese), Conference Report, available at <http://www1.acfic.org.cn/cenweb/portal/user/anon/page/acfic_CMSItemInfoPage.page?appId=00000000000000000122&category=200180&metainfoId=ABC00000000000011401> (last accessed on 20 January 2009); 经叔平, '开创工商联工作新局面', 会议报告.

Katz, H. and Wheeler, H. (2004), 'Employment Relations in the United States of America', in Bamber, G. et al. ed. *International and Comparative Employment Relations: Globalization and the Developed Market Economies*, Crows Nest, Allen & Unwin, pp. 67–90.

Kaufman, B. (1993), *The Origins and Evolution of the Field of Industrial Relations in the United States*, Ithaca, NY, ILR Press.

Kaufman, B., Beaumont, R. and Helfgott, R. eds (2003), *Industrial Relations to Human Resources and beyond*, New York, M. E. Sharpe.

Kaufman, B. and Kleiner, M. ed. (1993), *Employee Representation*, IRRA Series, Madison.

Keller, B. (1991), 'The Role of State as Corporate Actor in Industrial Relations Systems' in Adam, R. (ed.) *Comparative Industrial Relations*, London, Harper Collins Academic.

Kelly, J. (1994), 'Does the Field of Industrial Relations Have a Future?' Conference papers of the British Universities' Industrial Relations Association, Oxford.

Knight, J. and Song, L. (2005), *Towards a Labour Market in China*, Oxford, Oxford University Press.

Lan C. D. and Ren B. P. (2004), 'Reflection on the Social Security Protection for Peasant Workers' (in Chinese), *Social Science Research*, Issue 5, 2004, pp. 106–12; 蓝春娣/ 任保平, '关于农民工社会保障问题的思考', 社会科学研究, 2004年第5期.

Lansbury, R. and Wailes, N. (2004), 'Employment Relations in Australia', in Bamber, G. et al. ed. *International and Comparative Employment Relations: Globalization and the Developed Market Economies*, Crows Nest, Allen & Unwin, pp. 119–45.

Lee C. K. (1998), 'The Labour Politics of Market Socialism. Collective Inaction and Class Experiences Among State Workers in Guangzhou', *Modern China*, Vol. 24 No.1 (January 1998), pp. 3–33.

Lee C. K. (2002), 'From the Specter of Mao to the Spirit of the Law: Labour Insurgency in China', *Theory and Society*, vol. 31, pp. 189–228.

Leonard, E. (2005), 'Governance and Concerted Regulation of Employment in Europe', *European Journal of Industrial Relations*, Vol. 11 No. 3, 2005, pp. 307–26.

Leung T. (2002), 'ACFTU and Union Organizing', China Labour Bulletin, available at <http://www.hartford-hwp.com/archives/55/292.html> (last accessed on 20 January 2009).

Li B. T. (2007), 'The Whole Story of NRLRGH' (in Chinese), Discussion Paper, available at <http://www.boxun.com/hero/2007/zhongguogongdang/7_1.shtml> (last accessed on 20 January 2009); 李伯特, ''全红总'始末', 讨论稿.

Li J. Q. and Wang S. Z. (2005), 'Chambers of Commerce and Local Governments' (in Chinese), *Journal of Zhejiang Provincial Party School*, Issue 5, 2005, pp. 5–13; 李建琴/王诗宗, '民间商会与地方政府：权力博弈、互动机制与现实局限', 中共浙江省委党校学报, 2005年第5期.

Li P. L., Zhang Y., Zhao Y. D. and Liang D. (2005), *Social Conflicts and Class Consciousness in China Today* (in Chinese), Beijing, Social Sciences Academic Press; 李培林, 张翼, 赵延东, 梁栋，'社会冲突与阶级意识'，社会科学文献出版社，北京.

Li Q. (2004), *Urban Migrant Workers and Social Stratification in China* (in Chinese), Beijing, Social Science Academic Press; 李强, '农民工与中国社会分层', 社会科学文献出版社, 北京.

Li R. (1998), *Memoir of Lushan Meeting* (in Chinese), Zhengzhou, Henan People's Press; 李锐，'庐山会议实录'，河南人民出版社.

Li S. S. and Liu Z. K. (2005), *The Mystery of Li Lisan* (in Chinese), Beijing, People's Press; 李思慎/ 刘之昆，'李立三之迷'，人民出版社，北京.

Li W. H. (1953), 'On the Utilization, Restriction, and Transformation of Capitalist Industries and Commerce' (in Chinese), Conference Speech, available at <http://www.zytzb.org.cn/zytzbwz/theory/lchy/200804/t20080430_373741.htm> (last accessed on 20 January 2009); 李维汉, '关于利用、限制和改造资本主义工商业问题的意见', 会议发言稿.

Li X. (2006), 'The Working Class Leads All?' (in Chinese), Modern China Research, Issue 2, 2006, available at <http://www.chinayj.net/StubArticle.asp?issue=060205&total=93> (last accessed on 20 January 2009); 李 逊, '工人阶级领导一切？', 当代中国研究, 2006第二期.

Li X. Y. (2000), 'Examining the Cultural Revolution by the Common Points of Rebellious Faction and 1959's Rightist Faction' (in Chinese), Discussion Paper, available at <http://www.chenzhou.gov.cn/Article/Class75/Class78/200312/Article_20031212084929.html> (last accessed on 20 January 2009); 李宪源, '从造反派与五七年右派的共通点审视文革', 讨论稿.

Li Y. M. (2006), 'Enhancing Employment and Social Harmony' (in Chinese), *Study Times*, vol. 363, available at <http://www.studytimes.com.cn/WebPage/xxsb/html/5003.html> (last accessed on 20 January 2009); 李玉梅, '积极扩大就业, 促进社会和谐', 学习时报, 363期.

Li Z. Y. (2005), 'Memory of Labour Movements in Early Days of Liberation' (in Chinese), Conference Speech, available at <http://www.bbzx.gov.cn/detail/news.asp?id=400> (last accessed on 20 January 2009); 李振友, '回忆解放初期的工人运动', 会议发言稿.

Lin J. (2005), 'China's Labour Law System' (in Chinese), Conference Paper, available at <http://news.xinhuanet.com/politics/2008-01/31/content_7532925.htm> (last accessed on 20 January 2009); 林嘉, '我国的劳动法律制度', 学术会议论文.

Lin J. H. (1997), 'A Brief History of the Red International of Labour Unions', Discussion Paper, available at <http://myy.cass.cn/file/1997040114219.html> (last accessed on 20 January 2009); 林建华, '红色工会国际的历史述略', 讨论稿.

Lin Y. H. (2007), 'Debates on the Union's Operational Policies in 1950s' (in Chinese), *Study Times*, Vol. 380/381, available at <http://www.studytimes.com.cn/WebPage/xxsb/html/3250.html> (last accessed on 20 January 2009); 林蕴晖, '1950年代关于工会工作方针的争论', 《学习时报》, 380/381期.

Lipson, L. (1993), *The Great Issues of Politics*, Englewood Cliffs, Prentice Hall.

Liu A. Y. (2003), 'Options for Workers' Action During SOE Reform Process' (in Chinese), *Sociological Research*, 2003 Issue 6, pp. 1–13; 刘爱玉，'国有企业制度变革过程中工人的行动选择'，社会学研究,2003年第6期.

Liu C. Z. (2003), 'Chinese Entrepreneurs' Political Expectations' (in Chinese), *Corporate Culture*, 2003 Issue 2, pp. 50–53; 柳传志, '中国企业家的政治预期', 企业文化,2003年第2期.

Liu G. K. (2001), 'Analysis on the Rebellious Movement and Rebellious Faction in the Cultural Revolution' (in Chinese), Discussion Paper, available at <http://www.cnd.org/CR/ZK03/cr165.hz8.html#4> (last accessed on 20 January 2009); 刘国凯, '文化大革命造反运动及造反派之评析', 讨论稿.

Liu G. K. (2006), 'On the People's Cultural Revolution' (in Chinese), Beijing Spring, January Issue, 2006, available at <http://beijingspring.com/bj2/2006/280/20051231114953.htm> (last accessed on 20 January 2009); 刘国凯, '论人民文革', 北京之春, 2006年1月.

Liu J. (2004), 'On the Erosion of State-owned Assets' (in Chinese), *Party's Working Style and Anti-corruption*, Issue 4, 2004; 刘洁, '论国有资产流失的成因与对策', 党风与廉政, 2004年4期.

Liu J. Z. (2006), 'A Study of Labour Relations in SOEs under New Situation' (in Chinese), *Academic Exploration*, 2007 Issue 2, pp. 41–50; 刘建洲, '新时期国有企业劳动关系研究：一个劳动者视角的分析', 学术探索, 2007年第2期.

Liu K. B., Yan C. Z. and Wang M. (2005), *Modern Workers: The Evolvement & Tendency towards Market Economy* (in Chinese), Changsha, Hunan People's Press; 柳可白, 阎春芝, 王玫, '当代工人: 市场化的演变与趋势', 湖南人民出版社, 长沙.

Liu K. M. and Luan Z. (2002), 'Organization's Predicament or Strength' (in Chinese), Discussion Paper, available at <http://www.usc.cuhk.edu.hk/wk_wzdetails.asp?id=3291> (last accessed on 20 January 2009); 刘开明/ 栾志，'组织的困境或力量'，讨论稿.

Liu S. (2005), 'The Current Situation of China's Working Class' (in Chinese), Discussion Paper, available at http://www.wyzxsx.com/Article/Class17/200507/2509.html (last accessed on 20 January 2009); 刘实,"当前中国工人阶级状况'，讨论稿.

Liu S. Q. (1955), 'On the Socialistic Transformation of Capitalist Industries and Commerce' (in Chinese), Conference Speech, available at <http://news.xinhuanet.com/ziliao/2004-12/27/content_2386189.htm> (last accessed on 20 January 2009); 刘少奇, '关于资本主义工商业的社会主义改造问题', 会议发言稿.

Liu W. (2006), 'Income Distribution Fairness and Justification for the Reform' (in Chinese), Xinhua Digest, 2006 Issue 16, available at <http://qkzz.net/magazine/1001–6651/2006/16/424141.htm> (last accessed on 20 January 2009); 刘伟, '收入分配的公平命题与改革的合理性', 新华文摘, 2006年第16期.

Liu X. B. (2004), 'How Did Mao Rob Private Assets' (in Chinese), Discussion Paper, available at <http://www.boxun.com/hero/liuxb/190_1.shtml> (last accessed on 20 January 2009); 刘晓波, '毛泽东如何抢劫私人财产', 讨论稿.

Liu Y. Y. and Zhang L. (2005), 'In Search of the Lost "Right to Strike"' (in Chinese), Discussion Paper, available at <http://www.usc.cuhk.edu.hk/wk_wzdetails.asp?id=4010> (last accessed on 20 January 2009); 刘运亚/ 张力，'寻找失落的罢工权'，讨论稿.

Locke, J. (1681), 'Two Treatise of Government', electronic edition from <www.etestingcenter.com/library/BooksJ-L/Two Treatise of Government.pdf> (last accessed on 20 January 2009).

Luo C. P. (2005), 'New Bottom Line for China's Classification System' (in Chinese), *New Beijing Daily*, 20 September 2005; 罗昌平, '我国保密制度重置底线', 新京报, 2005–09-20.

Luo X. H. (2001), 'In Search of the Redundant Bureaus' (in Chinese), *China Youth*, 22 February 2001; 罗旭辉, '寻访经贸委被撤销的国家局', 中国青年报, 2001–02-22.

Ma L. C. (2008), *Thirty Years' Contests* (in Chinese), Nanjing, Jiangsu People's Press; 马立诚, '交锋三十年', 江苏人民出版社, 南京.

Ma L. C. and Ling Z. J. (1998), *Contests: Three Major Liberation of Thought in China* (in Chinese), Beijing, China Today Press; 马立诚/凌志军, '交锋: 当代中国三次思想解放实录', 今日中国出版社, 北京.

Ma M. (2003), 'On the New Type of Relationships among Government, Chambers of Commerce and Private Enterprises' (in Chinese), *China Business*, 2003 Issue 12, pp. 58–64; 马敏, '论新时期政府、商会和民营企业的新型关系', 中国工商, 2003年第12期.

MacFarquhar, R. and Fairbank, J. (1987), *The Cambridge History of China 1949–1965*, Cambridge, Cambridge University Press.

MacFarquhar, R. and Fairbank, J. (1991), *The Cambridge History of China 1966–1982*, Cambridge, Cambridge University Press.

Maitland, A. (2002), 'Reebok in China: Worker Elections in Two Supplier Factories', *Financial Times*, 12 December 2002.

Mao W. T. (2005), 'On the Procedural Treatment of Labour Dispute Settlement' (in Chinese), Discussion Paper, available at <http://www.lawbook.com.cn/lw/lw_view.asp?no=5565> (last accessed on 20 January 2009); 毛卫厅, '对劳动争议处理仲裁前置程序的思考', 讨论稿.

Mao Z. D. (1949), 'On the People's Democratic Dictatorship' (in Chinese), Vol. IV, Selected Works of Mao Ze Dong, available at <http://www.mzdlib.com/mzdwk/zyzz/display.asp?Reco_ID=155> (last accessed on 20 January 2009); 毛泽东, '论人民民主专政', '毛泽东选集'第四卷.

Marginson, P. and Sisson, K. (1994), 'The Structure of Transnational Capital in Europe' in Hyman, R. and Ferner, A. (ed.) *New Frontiers in European Industrial Relations*, Oxford, Blackwell.

Marx, K. and Engels, F. (1848), 'Manifesto of the Communist Party', English edition of 1888, edited by Friedrich Engels, available at <http://www.marxists.org/archive/marx/works/1848/communist-manifesto/index.htm> (last accessed on 20 January 2009).

Maskus, K. (1997), 'Should Core Labour Standards be Imposed Through International Trade Policy', Paper for the World Bank, International Trade Division, available at <http://www.worldbank.org/html/dec/Publications/Workpapers/WPS1800series/wps1817/wps1817.pdf> (last accessed on 20 January 2009).

Mayo, E. (1945), *The Social Problems Of An Industrial Civilization*, Harvard School of Business Administration Press, Boston.

Mazur, J. (2000), 'Labour's New Internationalism', Journal of Foreign Affairs, January/February 2000, available at <http://www.foreignaffairs.org/20000101faessay7/jay-mazur/labor-s-new-internationalism.html> (last accessed on 20 January 2009).

McClelland, J. S. (1996), *A History of Western Political Thought* (Chinese Translation), Haikou, Hainan Publishing House (2002); '西方政治思想史'，海南出版社（2002中文版），海口.

McCormack, R. (2006), 'Good Luck Competing Against Chinese Labour Costs', Manufacturing & Technology News, Volume 13, May, 2006, available at <http://www.manufacturingnews.com/news/06/0502/art1.html> (last accessed on 20 January 2009).

Medium-small Enterprise Research Centre, Social Science Academy of China (2005), 'The Development Of China's Private Economy' (in Chinese), Internal Discussion Paper; 中国社科院中小企业研究中心, 我国民营经济的发展历程, 内部讨论件.

Meng Q. R. (2001), 'Enlightenment of Lenin's "New Economic Policy"' (in Chinese), Social Science edition, *Journal of Shangdong University of Science and Technology*, 2001 Issue 1, pp. 1–5; 孟庆仁, '从哲学上看列宁新经济政策的启示', 山东科技大学学报, 社科版200101 .

MOC (2007), 'World Top 500's Investments in China' (in Chinese), Public Paper, available at <http://www.bjcbd.gov.cn/enterprise/food/food7498.htm> (last accessed on 20 January 2009); 商务部, '世界500强等跨国公司对华投资情况', 公告.

MOH (2004), 'Investigation Report of the 3rd National Health Service' (in Chinese), Public Paper; 卫生部, '第三次国家卫生服务调查报告', 公告.

MOHRSS and NBS (2008), 'Statistics Communiqué for Labour and Social Security Development' (in Chinese), Public Paper, available at <http://www.stats.gov.cn/tjgb/qttjgb/qgqttjgb/t20080521_402481634.htm> (last accessed on 20 January 2009); 人力资源和社会保障部/国家统计局, '2007年劳动和社会保障事业发展统计公报', 公告.

MOLSS (2006), 'Labour Supply and Demand Analysis for Quarter Two of 2006' (in Chinese), Public Paper, available at <http://w1.mohrss.gov.cn/gb/zwxx/2006-09/14/content_133368.htm> (last accessed on 20 January 2009); 劳动和社会保障部, '2006年第二季度部分城市劳动力市场职业供求状况分析', 公告.

MOLSS (2007), 'Labour Supply and Demand Analysis on the Current Labour Market' (in Chinese), Public Paper, available at <http://www.gov.cn/gzdt/2007-06/13/content_647157.htm> (last accessed on 20 January 2009); 劳动和社会保障部, '当前劳动力市场供求状况分析报告', 公告.

MOLSS and NBS (2005), 'Statistics Communiqué on Labour and Social Security Development' (in Chinese), Public Paper, available at <http://www.bzld.gov.cn/show.php?contentid=426> (last accessed on 20 January 2009); 劳动和社会保障部/国家统计局, '2005年度劳动和社会保障事业发展统计公报', 公告.

National People's Congress (1994), 'Labour Law of P. R. China' (in Chinese), Public Paper, available at <http://www.cau.edu.cn/xgh/FAGUI/guojia/ldf.html> (last accessed on 20 January 2009); 全国人大, '中华人民共和国劳动法', 公告.

National People's Congress (2001), 'Union Law of P. R. China' (in Chinese), Public Paper, available at <http://www.acftu.net/template/10004/file.jsp?cid=805&aid=42620> (last accessed on 20 January 2009); 全国人大, '中华人民共和国工会法', 公告.

National People's Congress (2004), *Comparison of All Versions of P. R. China's Constitutions and Amendments* (in Chinese), China Legal Study Press, Beijing; 全国人大, '中华人民共和国宪法历次修正对照表', 中国法制出版社, 北京.

National People's Congress (2006), 'Labour Contract Law (draft)' (in Chinese), Public Paper, available at <http://www.lawbook.com.cn/fzdt/newshtml/20/20060320231100.htm> (last accessed on 20 January 2009); 全国人大, '中华人民共和国劳动合同法(草案)', 公告.

National People's Congress (2007a), 'Labour Contract Law' (in Chinese), Public Paper, available at <http://www.ldht.org/Html/lifa/lfjc/038834.html> (last accessed on 20 January 2009); 全国人大, '中华人民共和国劳动合同法', 公告

National People's Congress (2007b), 'Employment Promotion Law (in Chinese), Public Paper, available at <http://www.molss.gov.cn/gb/zxwj/2007-08/31/content_194642.htm> (last accessed on 20 January 2009); 全国人大, '中华人民共和国就业促进法', 公告.

National People's Congress (2007c), 'Labour Dispute Mediation and Arbitration Law' (in Chinese), Public Paper, available at <http://www.molss.gov.cn/gb/ywzn/2008-01/10/content_219148.htm> (last accessed on 20 January 2009); 全国人大, '中华人民共和国劳动争议调解仲裁法', 公告.

NBS (2005), 'Data Communiqué for the First National Economic Census' (in Chinese), Public Paper, available at <http://www.stats.gov.cn/ZGjjpc/cgfb/> (last accessed on 20 January 2009); 国家统计局, '第一次全国经济普查主要数据公报', 公告.

NBS (2006), 'Survey Report on Peasant Workers' Living Conditions in Cities' (in Chinese), Public Paper, available at <http://www.stats.gov.cn/was40/reldetail.jsp?docid=402358407> (last accessed on 20 January 2009); 国家统计局, '城市农民工生活质量状况调查报告', 公告.

NBS (2007), 'China Statistics Year Book 2007 – On-line Data' (in Chinese), available at <http://www.stats.gov.cn/tjsj/ndsj/> (last accessed on 20 January 2009); 国家统计局, '中国统计年鉴 2007– 年度数据在线查询'.

NBS (2008), 'China Statistics Year Book 2007 – On-line Data' (in Chinese), available at <http://www.stats.gov.cn/tjsj/ndsj/> (last accessed on 20 January 2009); 国家统计局, '中国统计年鉴 2008– 年度数据在线查询'.

NBS and MOLSS (2007), *China Labour Statistical Yearbook* (in Chinese, disc edition), China Statistics Press, Beijing; 劳动和社会保障部/国家统计局, '中国劳动统计年鉴 2007', 中国统计出版社, 北京.

NBS and MOLSS (2008), *China Labour Statistical Yearbook* (in Chinese, disc edition), China Statistics Press, Beijing; 劳动和社会保障部/国家统计局, '中国劳动统计年鉴 2008', 中国统计出版社, 北京.

NBS and SAIC (1998), 'Regulation on Dividing Enterprises' Registration Type' (in Chinese), Public Paper, available at <http://www.jmsedu.net/info/jiaoyu/05/Product2/Law/20_Work_trade_administration/20_Work_trade_administration2214.htm> (last accessed on 20 January 2009); 国家统计局/国家工商行政管理局, '关于划分企业登记注册类型的规定', 公告.

Ning N. and Wang X. L. (2006), 'Market Fundamentalism Steps Down from the Sacred Forum' (in Chinese), Business Weekly, 7th April, 2006, available at <http://www.swzk.cn/Html/Global/064714081924348.html> (last accessed on 20 January 2009); 宁南/ 王晓玲, '市场原教旨主义走下神坛', 商务周刊, 2006-4-7.

Noon, M. and Blyton, P. (1997), *The Realities of Work*, London, Macmillan.

NPPCC (1949), 'Common Programme' (in Chinese), Public Paper, available at <http://news.xinhuanet.com/ziliao/2004-12/07/content_2304465.htm> (last accessed on 20 January 2009); 全国政协, '共同纲领', 公告.

Offe, C. (1996 a), *Varieties of Transition*, Oxford, Polity Press.

Offe, C. (1996 b), *Modernity and the State*, Cambridge, MIT Press.

O'Leary, G. ed. (1998), *Adjusting to Capitalism: Chinese Workers and the State*, New York, East Gate.

Pan P. (2002), 'China Labour Unions Offer Little Protection', *Washington Post*, 16 October 2002.

Party History Research Office, CC-CCP (2001), *Brief History of the Chinese Communist Party* (in Chinese), Beijing, CCP Party History Press; 中共中央党史研究室, '中国共产党简史', 中共党史出版社, 北京.

Perry, E. (2008), 'Reclaiming the Chinese Revolution', *The Journal of Asian Studies*, Vol. 67, No. 4 pp. 1147–64.

Ping X. Q. (2005), 'Labour Relations in Private Enterprises' (in Chinese), Discussion Paper, available at <http://www.usc.cuhk.edu.hk/wk_wzdetails.asp?id=5029> (last accessed on 18 Dec 2008); 平新乔，'民营企业劳资关系'，讨论稿.

Polaski, S. (2003), 'Trade and Labour Standard: A Strategy for Developing Countries', Paper for Trade, Equity, and Development Project, Carnegie Endowment for International Peace, available at <http://www.carnegieendowment.org/publications/index.cfm?fa=view&id=1148> (last accessed on 20 January 2009).

Pringle, T. (2001), 'A Summary of the Chinese Labour Movement since 1949', China Labour Bulletin, August 2001, available at <http://www.hartford-hwp.com/archives/55/290.html> (last accessed on 20 January 2009).

Qi D. T. (2004), 'The Independency and Development Trend of China's Union' (in Chinese), Perspective, 31 July 2004, available at <www.oycf.org/oycfold/httpdocs/Perspectives2/Chinese/Chinese_15_07302004/4a_Qi_Dongtao_Final.pdf> (last accessed on 20 January 2009); 祁冬涛, '论中国工会的独立性及发展方向', 视角, 2004-07-31.

Qiao J. (2003), 'China's Labour Relations and Union Strategies under a New Wave of Re-structuring' (in Chinese), Conference Paper, available at <http://www.usc.cuhk.edu.hk/wk_wzdetails.asp?id=3343> (last accessed on 20 January 2009); 乔健，'新一轮结构调整下的中国劳动关系及工会的因应对策'，学术会议论文.

Research Institute of MOC (2004), 'Reform Directions and Suggestions for Trade Associations' (in Chinese), Internal Discussion Paper, available at <http://www.chinanpo.gov.cn/web/showBulltetin.do?type=next&id=17652&dictionid=1835&catid= > (last accessed on 20 January 2009); 商务部研究院, '同业商协会改革方向及建议', 内部讨论稿.

Research Institute of MOLSS (2004a), 'The Current Situation of Labour Relations and the Selection of its Adjustment Model in China' (in Chinese), Key References of Economics, vol. 15, 2004, available at <http://www.usc.cuhk.edu.hk/wk_wzdetails.asp?id=3806> (last accessed on 20 January 2009); 中国劳动与社会保障部劳动科学研究所，'中国劳动关系现状与调节模式选择'，经济要参，2004年第15期.

Research Institute of MOLSS (2004b), 'China's Labour Relations in Transitional Period' (in Chinese), Internal Discussion Paper, available at <http://www2.nwsuaf.edu.cn/gonghui/flash/word/lt7.doc> (last accessed on 20 January 2009); 中国劳动与社会保障部劳动科学研究所，'转型时期中国劳动关系研究'，内部讨论稿.

Rosen, S. (2000), 'International Labour Organizations', Paper for CU Labour Seminar, 18 September 2000.

Rousseau, J. (1762), 'The Social Contract', Translated by G. D. H. Cole, public domain, Rendered into HTML and text by Jon Roland of the Constitution Society, available at <http://www.constitution.org/jjr/socon.htm> (last accessed on 20 January 2009).

Santoro, M. (2003), 'Defending Labour Rights: On the Barricades and In the Boardroom', The Brown *Journal of World Affairs*, Winter/ Spring 2003 – Volume IX, Issue 2, pp. 303–19.

Sarantakos, S. (1993), *Social Research*, Melbourne, MacMillan.

Shanxi Provincial ACFTU (2006), 'Tentative Rules on Direct Democratic Election of Grass Roots Union Chair in Shanxi Province' (in Chinese), Public Paper, available at <http://qgh.tyjcp.gov.cn/DetailServlet?siteID=6&infoID=110> (last accessed on 20 January 2009); 山西省总工会, '山西省基层工会民主直接选举工会主席试行办法', 公告.

Sheehan, J. (1998), *Chinese Workers: A New History*, London, Routledge.

Shen F. X. (2004), 'My Years during the Cultural Revolution' (in Chinese), Discussion Paper, available at <http://www.boxun.com/hero/shenfx/> (last accessed on 20 January 2009); 沈福祥, '我的文革岁月', 讨论稿.

Shen J. and Benson, J. (2008), 'Tripartite Consultation in China: A First Step towards Collective Bargaining?' (in Chinese), *International Labour Review*, Vol. 147 (2008), No. 2–3, pp. 231–48.

Shen Y. (2006), 'Social Transition and the Reformation of Working Class' (in Chinese), *Sociological Research*, vol. 2, 2006, pp. 13–37; 沈原，'社会转型与工人阶级的再形成'，社会学研究，2006年第2期.

Shen Z. H. ed. (2007), *Brief History of the Relationship between China and USSR* (in Chinese), Beijing, Xinhua Press; 沈志华主编,'中苏关系史纲 (1917－1991)', 新华出版社,北京.

Shi X. Y. (2005), 'Social Transformation and Labour Conflicts in the Corporate Level' (in Chinese), Discussion Paper, available at <www.sociology.cass.cn/shxw/cyshx/P020060413303129210800.pdf> (last accessed on 20 January 2009); 石秀印，'中国企业层面的社会结构演变与劳资冲突'，学术会议论文.

Shi X. Y. (2006), 'The Social Flow of Workers and its Underneath Logics' (in Chinese), Discussion Paper, available at <www.sociology.cass.cn/shxw/cyshx/P020060205328791712983.pdf> (last accessed on 20 January 2009); 石秀印，'工人的社会流动及其内在逻辑'，学术会议论文.

Singh, G. (2001), 'Culture as a Guide to Manage the Labour-Relations Function in a Global Economy', Publication No. 109, Fall 2001 Ciber Working Paper Series, Center for International Business Education & Research, San Diego State University.

Skidelsky, R. (2005), 'The Chinese Shadow', The New York Review of Books, Volume 52, 2005, available at <http://www.nybooks.com/articles/18437> (last accessed on 20 January 2009).

Smith, A. (1776), *An inquiry into the nature and causes of the wealth of nations*, Electronic book 1998, Adelaide, The University of Adelaide Library.

Somers, G. ed. (1969), *Essays in Industrial Relations Theory*, Ames, IA, Iowa State University Press.

State Council (1988), 'Temporary Regulation on Private Enterprises' (in Chinese), Public Paper, available at <http://www.law-lib.com/law/law_view.asp?id=5113> (last accessed on 20 January 2009); 国务院, '私营企业暂行条例', 公告.

State Council (1993), 'Regulation on the Settlement of Enterprise Labour Dispute' (in Chinese), Public Paper, available at <http://www.gov.cn/ziliao/flfg/2005-08/06/content_20937.htm> (last accessed on 20 January 2009); 国务院, '企业劳动争议处理条例', 公告.

State Council (1995), 'Regulation on the Employees' Working Hours' (in Chinese), Public Paper, available at <http://www.law-lib.com/law/law_view.asp?id=15573> (last accessed on 20 January 2009); 国务院, '关于职工工作时间的规定', 公告.

State Council (1998), 'Regulation on the Registration and Management of Social Organizations' (in Chinese), Public Paper, available at <http://www.law-lib.com/law/law_view.asp?id=399> (last accessed on 20 January 2009); 国务院, '社会团体登记管理条例', 公告.

State Council (2002), 'Current Situation of Labour and Social Security in China' (in Chinese), Public Paper, available at <http://www.gov.cn/zwgk/2005-05/26/content_1369.htm> (last accessed on 20 January 2009); 国务院, '中国的劳动和社会保障状况', 公告.

State Council (2003), 'Regulation of State-owned Enterprise Reforms' (in Chinese), Public Paper, available at <http://www.sasac.gov.cn/gzjg/xcgz/200408100189.htm> (last accessed on 20 January 2009); 国务院, '关于规范国有企业改制工作的意见', 公告.

State Council (2004), 'Regulation on Labour Security and Inspection' (in Chinese), Public Paper, available at <http://www.gov.cn/banshi/2005-08/05/content_20619.htm> (last accessed on 20 January 2009); 国务院, '劳动保障监察条例', 公告.

State Council (2006), 'On Solving the Issue of Peasant Workers' (in Chinese), Public Paper, available at <http://www.gov.cn/jrzg/2006-03/27/content_237644.htm> (last accessed on 20 January 2009); 国务院, '关于解决农民工问题的若干意见', 公告.

State Council (2007), 'Regulation on Employee Annual Leaves' (in Chinese), Public Paper, available at <http://www1.www.gov.cn/zwgk/2007-12/16/content_835228.htm> (last accessed on 20 January 2009); 国务院, '职工带薪年休假条例', 公告.

State Council (2008), 'Regulation on the Implementation of Labour Contract Law' (in Chinese), Public Paper, available at <http://www.gov.cn/flfg/2008-09/19/content_1099500.htm> (last accessed on 20 January 2009); 国务院, '劳动合同法实施条例', 公告.

Su S. Z. (1985), 'Democratic Reforms in SOEs in Early Days of Liberation' (in Chinese), *Journal of Hubei Finance Institute*, Issue 6, 1985, pp. 81–85; 苏少之, '解放初期国营企业的民主改革', 湖北财经学院学报, 1985年第6期.

Sun L. P. (2004), *Imbalance: the Logic of a Fractured Society* (in Chinese), Beijing, Social Science Academic Press; 孙立平, '失衡: 断裂社会的运作逻辑', 社会科学文献出版社, 北京.

Sun Y. F. (2003 a), 'Union Reform's Direction in Transitional Period' (in Chinese), *Southern Weekend*, 3 July 2003; 孙亚菲, '转型期的工会改革方向', 南方周末, 2003-07-03.

Sun Z. and Liu Y. L. (2004), 'Reflection on Migrant Worker Shortage: Reframing a New Labour Relation' (in Chinese), *China Newsweek*, 2004 Issue 29, pp. 18–27; 孙展, 刘英丽, '中国首遇民工荒反思：重塑劳资关系新格局', 新闻周刊, 2004年29期.

Supreme Court (2001 and 2006), 'Explanation on Certain Legal Issues in the Trial of Labour Dispute I & II' (in Chinese), Public Paper, available at <http://www.law-lib.com/law/law_view.asp?id=15286> (last accessed on 20 January 2009); 最高人民法院, '关于审理劳动争议案件适用法律若干问题的解释(一/二)', 公告.

Tang K. L. (2006), 'Chinese Style of "Wealthy People Politics"' (in Chinese), *Talents*, 2006 Issue 5, pp. 42–48; 唐凯林, '中国式的富人政治' , 英才, 2006–05.

Tao Q. (2007), 'Harmonious Governance of the Society' (in Chinese), *Journal of Humanities*, 2007 Issue 3, pp. 157–64; 陶庆,'社会和谐治理：'正当妥协'的宪政地方性知识', 人文杂志, 2007年第3期.

Tao X. J. ed. (2003), *Discussions on 'Rule of Law' and 'Rule of Man'* (in Chinese), Beijing, Social Science Literature Press; 陶希晋，'法治与人治问题讨论集'，社会科学文献出版社, 北京

Taylor, B., Chang, K., Li, Q. (2003), *Industrial Relations in China*, Cheltenham, Edward Elgar.

Taylor, F. (1911), *Scientific Management*, reprinted in 1972, Westport, Greenwood Press.

Tong X. (2003), 'Efficiency Contract in the Union Practice' (in Chinese), Discussion Paper, available at <http://www.usc.cuhk.edu.hk/wk_wzdetails.asp?id=3322> (last accessed on 20 January 2009); 佟新，'工会实践中的效率合约'，讨论稿.

Tong X. (2005), *Labour Relations and Industrial Democracy under Globalization' in 'Chinese Experience: Enterprise Governance and Employee Democratic Involvement in Transitional Society* (in Chinese), Beijing, Social Science Literature Press; 佟新，'全球化下的劳资关系与产业民主'载'中国经验: 转型社会的企业治理与职工民主参与', 社会科学文献出版社, 北京.

UFWD-CC-CCP (1952), 'Instruction on Re-structuring the Federation of Industry and Commerce' (in Chinese), Public Papers, available at <http://news.xinhuanet.com/ziliao/2002-03/04/content_2358804.htm> (last accessed on 20 January 2009); 中共中央统战部,'关于改组工商业联合会的指示', 公告.

Ulman, L. and Gerlach, K. (2003), 'An Essay on Collective Bargaining and Unemployment in Germany', Institute of Industrial Relations Working Paper Series iirwps-092-03, University of California.

Walder, A. (1993), 'Workers, Managers and the State', *China Quarterly*, No. 127, Special Issue: The Individual and State in China (Sep., 1991), pp. 467–92.

Wang G. X. (2006), 'Has the Working Class Led and Can it Lead?' (in Chinese), Discussion Paper, available at <http://www.boxun.com/hero/2006/wangguangxian/7_1.shtml> (last accessed on 20 January 2009); 王光宪,'工人阶级领导过吗？工人阶级能领导吗？？', 讨论稿.

Wang J. H. (2005), 'Union Reforms and the New Developments in China's Grass Roots Democracy' (in Chinese), *Social Science Journal of South China Normal University*, 2005 Issue 5, pp. 35–59; 王金红，'工会改革与中国基层民主的新发展'，华南师范大学学报社科版, 2005 年第5期.

Wang L. C. (2003), 'Union in the Context of Market Economy' (in Chinese), Discussion Paper, available at <http://www.usc.cuhk.edu.hk/wk_wzdetails.asp?id=3342> (last accessed on 20 January 2009); 王立成，'市场经济下的工会：企业工会力量的成长'，学术会议论文.

Wang M. C. (2001), 'Several Serious Problems in the Labour Relations in Private Enterprises' (in Chinese), *Ningbo Economics Journal*, February 2001; 王明才, '当前私营企业劳动关系中存在的几个突出问题', 宁波经济丛刊,2001年2月.

Wang Q. X. (2004), *Labour Law in China* (in Chinese), Beijing, Law Press; 王全兴, '劳动法', 法律出版社, 北京.

Wang W. G. (2006), 'Decoding Wealthy People' (in Chinese), *Fortune Owners*, 2006 Issue 5; 王武钢, '解读富人' ，财经人物, 200605.

Warner, M. ed. (2000), *Changing Workplace Relations in the Chinese Economy*, New York, St Martin's Press.

Webb, S. and B. (1920a), *The History of Trade Unionism*, reprinted in 2003, New York, Palgrave Macmillan.

Webb, S. and B. (1920b), *Industrial Democracy*, reprinted in 2003, New York, NY, Palgrave Macmillan.

Wei C. (2006), 'Let Everyone Have a Sense of Satisfaction' (in Chinese), Global Sources, available at <http://career.ceconline.com/article/viewArt_100011_8000005703_1_N.htm> (last accessed on 20 January 2009); Celine Wei，'让每个人获得满足感'，世界经理人.

Wei W. X. and Yang T. S. (2005), 'State Intervention and the "Socialistic Transformation" of Chambers of Commerce (1949–1956)' (in Chinese), *Journal of Central China Teachers' University* (Humanities and Social Sciences), 2005 Issue 5, pp. 62–69; 魏文享/杨天树, '国家介入与商会的'社会主义改造'(1949–1956)', 华中师范大学学报(人文社会科学版), 2005年第5期.

Western, B. (1997), *Between Class and Market*, Princeton University Press, Princeton.

World Bank (1997), 'World Development Report 1997', available at <http://www-wds.worldbank.org/external/default/WDSContentServer/IW3P/IB/1997/06/01/000009265_3980217141148/Rendered/PDF/multiopage.pdf> (last accessed on 20 January 2009).

Wright, E. O. (2000), 'Working-Class Power, Capitalist-Class Interests, and Class Compromise', *American Journal of Sociology*, Volume 105 No. 4, pp. 957–1002.

Wu Q. J. (2006), 'On the Formation of Western Working Class: A Reflection of China's Transitional Period' (in Chinese), *Sociological Research*, 2006 Issue 2, pp. 182–203; 吴清军, '西方工人阶级形成理论述评——立足中国转型时期的思考', 社会学研究, 2006年第二期.

Wu X. F. and Han L. (2006), 'A Study on the Urban-rural Difference since Reform' (in Chinese), *Xinjiang Rural Economy*, Nov 2006, pp. 4–9; 吴学凡/韩林, '改革开放以来中国城乡差别问题研究', 新疆农垦经济, 2006.11.

Wu Y. and Liu H. (2004), *Focusing on Rostrum: the Way to Power (1921–1949)* (in Chinese), Changsha, Hunan People's Press; 吴钰, 刘华清, '聚焦主席台: 问鼎天下 1921–1949', 湖南人民出版社, 长沙.

Xiao G. Q. (2006), 'Villain and Red Guards: Two Types of Rebellious Faction in the Factories' (in Chinese), Discussion Paper available at <http://blog.tianya.cn/blogger/post_show.asp?BlogID=293723&PostID=4468438&idWriter=0&Key=0> (last accessed on 20 January 2009); 萧功秦,'痞子与红卫兵：工厂造反派的两种类型',讨论稿.

Xinhua News Agency (2009), 'The Government Restructurings since the Establishment of P. R. China', Compilation of Xinhua News Agency Material, available at <http://news.xinhuanet.com/ziliao/2003-03/06/content_761776.htm> last accessed on 20 January 2009; '新中国成立以来的历次政府机构改革',新华社资料汇编.

Xu X. H. (2003), 'Analysis on the Subject of Chinese Union' (in Chinese), Discussion Paper, available at <http://www.usc.cuhk.edu.hk/wk_wzdetails.asp?id=3340> (last accessed on 20 January 2009); 徐小洪，'中国工会的主体性分析'，讨论稿.

Xu X. J. (2006), 'Reforming China's Unions According to Deng Xiao Ping's Requirements for Unions in the New Era' (in Chinese), Discussion Paper, available at <http://www.chinaelections.org/NewsInfo.asp?NewsID=95684> (last accessed on 20 January 2009); 许晓军,'按照邓小平对新时期工会的基本要求将中国工会建设成工人自己的组织',未刊讨论稿.

Xu Y. P. and Shi X. Y. (2006), 'The Formation of Working Class' (in Chinese), *Journal of Xuehai*, 2006 Issue 2, pp. 27–40; 许叶萍/石秀印，'工人阶级形成：体制内与体制外的转换'，学海，2006年2期.

Yang K. S. (2002), 'Jiang Jie-shi's path from Incident 3–20 to 4–12' (in Chinese), *Journal of Historical Science*, 2002 Issue 6 pp. 70–79 & Issue 7 pp. 63–73; 杨奎松,'蒋介石从'三二〇'到'四一二'的心路历程',史学月刊,2002年第6一7期.

Yang X. G. (1988), *The Captive Spirits* (in Chinese), Hongkong, Oxford University Press; 杨曦光(杨小凯)，'牛鬼蛇神录'，牛津大学出版社，香港.

Yang X. K. (1986), 'Breakthrough of the Socialist System During the Cultural Revolution' (in Chinese), *Intellectuals*, Issue 4, 1986; 杨小凯,'中国文化大革命对社会主义制度的突破',知识分子,1986第4期.

Yang X. K. (2004), 'Economic History of the People's Republic of China (1950–1978)' (in Chinese), Discussion Paper, available at <http://www.boxun.com/hero/yangxk/64_1.shtml> (last accessed on 20 January 2009); 杨小凯,'中华人民共和国经济史(1950–1978)',讨论稿.

Yao W. Y. (1968), 'The Working Class Must Lead in All Matters' (in Chinese), Red Flag, 1968 Issue 2, available at <http://www.hkcommunist.org/forum2008/forumx/archiver/?tid-52.html> (last accessed on 20 January 2009); 姚文元,'工人阶级必须领导一切'，红旗,1968年第2期.

Ye Y. L. (1993), *Biography of Wang Hongwen* (in Chinese), Changchun, Literature and Art Press; 叶永烈,'王洪文传',时代文艺出版社,长春.

Yi X. R. (2003), 'Wealthy People Involved in Politics is a Return to the Old System' (in Chinese), Discussion Paper; 易宪容, '富人从政是向旧体制复归', 讨论稿.

Yin J. M. (1998), *Insiders' Story: Truth Left Over By the Historical Figures* (in Chinese), Beijing, Chinese Youth Press; 尹家民，'知情者说——历史关键人物留给后世的真相', 中国青年出版社, 北京.

Yin J. Z., Stelzer, L. and Yang, W. (2001), 'Tripartism in Eastern Europe: A Model for China's Trade Union Reform?', *American Asian Review*, Vol. XIX (1), pp. 501–31.

Yu H. (2002), *Industrial Associations and their Development in China* (in Chinese), Beijing, Economic Management Press; 余晖, '行业协会及其在中国的发展：理论与案例'，经济管理出版社, 北京.

Yu J. R. (2002), 'Terminating the Revolutions' (in Chinese), Conference Paper presented on 19 December, 2002 at Beijing University, available at <http://www.usc.cuhk.edu.hk/wk_wzdetails.asp?id=2624> (last accessed on 20 January 2009); 于建嵘, '终结革命', 学术会议论文.

Yu J. R. (2006a), 'Situation of the Chinese Working Class' (in Chinese), Hong Kong, Mirror Press, partly available at <http://www.tecn.cn/data/detail.php?id=18336> (last accessed on 20 January 2009); 于建嵘, '中国工人阶级状况：安源实录', 明镜出版社， 香港.

Yu J. R. (2006b), 'Working Class and Socio-political Development in China' (in Chinese), Conference speech presented on 15 July 2006 at Beijing Sanwei Bookstore, available at <http://www.cul-studies.com/jiangtan/jianggao/200607/4229.html> (last accessed on 20 January 2009); 于建嵘, '中国工人阶级状况与社会政治发展', 会议演讲稿.

Yu J. T. (2004), 'Anti-corruption Calls for Reform on the Party's Internal Power Structure' (in Chinese), *Party Construction*, 2004 Issue 4, pp. 38; 于津涛, '反腐败呼唤改革党内权力架构', 党建文汇, 2004年第4期.

Yu J. X. (2006), 'Industrial Association: In Search of Positive Interaction with Enterprises and Government' (in Chinese), *Comparative Economic & Social Systems*, 2006 Issue 2, pp. 118–23; 郁建兴, '行业协会: 寻求与企业、政府之间的良性互动', 经济社会体制比较, 2006年第2期.

Yu J. X. and Huang, H. H. (2007), 'Research on Chambers of Commerce and Local Governance' (in Chinese), *Journal of Ningbo Party School*, 2005 Issue 6, pp. 25–33; 郁建兴/黄红华, '民间商会与地方治理研究：问题与方法', 宁波市委党校学报, 2005年第6期.

Yu J. X and Lu, M. Z. (2004), 'The Rise of Chambers of Commerce in Wenzhou and the Research on "Wenzhou Model"' (in Chinese), *Academic Monthly*, 2004 Issue 5, pp. 30–36; 郁建兴/吕明再, '温州商会的兴起与温州模式研究的范式转型', 学术月刊, 2004年第5期.

Yu J. X. and Wu, Y. (2003), 'The Rise of China's Civil Organization and the Transformation of State-Society Relationship' (in Chinese), *The Journal of Humanities*,

2003 Issue 4, pp. 142–49; 郁建兴/吴宇,'中国民间组织的兴起与国家—社会关系理论的转型', 人文杂志, 2003年第4期.

Yuan B. H. (2004), 'The Establishment and Development of CEC' (in Chinese), CCTV interview, available at <http://www.cec-ceda.org.cn/cec25/speaker_yuanbh01.htm> (last accessed on 20 January 2009); 袁宝华, '中企联的创立与发展', 央视访谈.

Yue F. Y. (2000), *Head of Central Statistics Bureau: Xu En Ceng* (in Chinese), Beijing, United Press; 岳付玉, '中统巨枭——徐恩曾', 团结出版社, 北京.

Zhang B. B. (2006), 'A Win-win Perspective on Enterprise Development' (in Chinese), CCTV interview, available at <http://www.cctv.com/program/jdtz/topic/life/C14761/20060322/101595.shtml> (last accessed on 20 January 2009); 张本波，'个人企业社会共赢的企业发展观', 央视访谈.

Zhang C. S. (2005), 'Discussion on the Reform and Improvement of the People's Congress System' (in Chinese), Conference Memorandum; 张春生, '关于人民代表大会制度改革与完善的讨论'，会议纪要.

Zhang G. T. (1998), *My Recollections* (in Chinese), Beijing, Dong Fang Press; 张国焘, '我的回忆', 东方出版社, 北京.

Zhang H. Y. (2003), 'CCP Members with Private Business Owner's Background' (in Chinese), Study Times, 2003 Issue 11, available at <http://www.xslx.com/htm/szrp/shts/2003-11-12-15353.htm> (last accessed on 19 December 2008); 张厚义，'私营企业主阶层中的共产党员', 学习时报, 2003–11.

Zhang H. Y. (2007), 'China's Private Business Owner Class' (in Chinese), Internal Discussion Papers, available at <www.sociology.cass.cn/shxw/shgz/shgz42/P020080218335108758352.pdf> (last accessed on 20 January 2009); 张厚义, '中国私营企业主阶层', 内部讨论稿.

Zhang J. X. (2006), 'Current Status of Discrimination Treatment Confronted by Peasant Workers' (in Chinese), *Journal of Hubei University of Economics*, 2006 Issue 2, pp. 101–03; 张建新, '农民工遭遇差别对待的现状评析与对策', 湖北经济学院学报, 2006年第2期.

Zhang X. L. (2007), 'Re-recognition of Unions' Characteristics' (in Chinese), Internal Discussion Papers, available at <http://www.law-lib.com/Lw/lw_view.asp?no=6086> (last accessed on 20 January 2009); 张喜亮, '工会性质再认识', 内部讨论稿.

Zhang Y. H. (2003), *Bygones are not Like Smoke* (in Chinese), Beijing, People's Literature Press; 章诒和, '往 事 并 不 如 烟', 人民文学出版社, 北京.

Zhang Y. M. (2003), 'Straightening Out the Conflicts: Relations Between Labour Union and Party-State in China' (in Chinese), *21st Century*, September 2003, available at <http://www.cuhk.edu.hk/ics/21c/supplem/essay/0308024g.htm> (last accessed on 20 January 2009); 张允美，'理顺与冲突：中国工会与党-国家的关系'，二十一世纪, 2003年9月号.

Zhao D. H. (2002), *Chinese Interpretation of Western Philosophy* (in Chinese), Harbin, Hei-long-jiang People's Press; 赵敦华, '西方哲学的中国式解读', 黑龙江人民出版社.

Zhao Q. Q. (2006), 'Tide of Reforms from the Bottom' (in Chinese), Discussion Papers, available at <http://www.unicornblog.cn/user1/zlzqq/9131.html> (last accessed on 20 January 2009); 赵启强, '来自底层的改革浪潮', 讨论稿.

Zhao Z. F. and Xie Z. G. (2002), 'The Development of Civil Laws in China' (in Chinese), *Journal of Legal Studies*, 2002, Issue 5, pp. 3–6; 赵中孚/ 解志国, '论我国民法的发展历程', 法学杂志, 2002年第5期.

Zheng H. eds (1997), *General History of Chinese Communist Party* (in Chinese), Beijing, Central Literature Press; 郑惠 等, '中国共产党通志', 中央文献出版社, 北京.

Zheng J. H. and Jiang J. (2003), 'The Predicament and Solutions for the Development of Chambers of Commerce' (in Chinese), Conference Paper; 郑江淮/江静, '民间商会发展困境和对策', 学术会议论文.

Zhou E. L. (1955), 'On the Socialistic Transformation of Capitalist Industries and Commerce' (in Chinese), Conference Speech, available at <http://news.xinhuanet.com/ziliao/2004-12/28/content_2388221.htm> (last accessed on 20 January 2009); 周恩来, '关于资本主义工商业社会主义改造的几个问题', 会议发言稿.

Zhou S. P. (2003), 'Reflection on the Management of State-owned Assets' (in Chinese), *Economic Research*, Issue 11, 2003; 周绍朋, '关于国有资产管理问题的思考', 经济研究资料, 2003年第11期.

Zhu C. J., Cooper, B., Cieri, H. and Dowling, P. (2005), 'A problematic transition to a strategic role: human resource management in industrial enterprises in China', *International Journal of Human Resource Management*, 16:4, pp. 513–31.

Zhu C. J. and Dowling, P. (2002), 'Staffing Practices in Transition: Some Empirical Evidence from China', *International Journal of Human Resource Management*, 13:4, pp. 569–97.

Zhu L. (2006), 'What Kind of Representatives Do the Employees Need?' (in Chinese), *China Business Operation Paper*, 17 July 2006; 朱力, '员工需要什么样的代言者?', 中国经营报, 2006年7月17日.

Zhu Y. and Warner, M. (2000), 'Changing Approaches to Employment Relations in the People's Republic of China', in Bamber, G. et al. ed. *Employment Relations in the Asia-Pacific: Changing Approaches*, Singapore, South Wind.

Trade Unions Past, Present and Future

EDITED BY CRAIG PHELAN

This series publishes monographs and edited collections on the history, present condition and possible future role of organised labour around the world. Multi-disciplinary in approach, geographically and chronologically diverse, this series is dedicated to the study of trade unionism and the undeniably significant role it has played in modern society. Topics include the historical development of organised labour in a variety of national and regional settings; the political, economic and legal contexts in which trade unionism functions; trade union internationalism past and present; comparative and cross-border studies; trade unions' role in promoting economic equality and social justice; and trade union revitalisation and future prospects. The aims of the series are to promote an appreciation of the diversity of trade union experience worldwide and to provide an international forum for lively debate on all aspects of the subject.

Volume 1 Craig Phelan (ed.): Trade Unionism since 1945: Towards a Global History. Volume 1: Western Europe, Eastern Europe, Africa and the Middle East.
467 pages. 2009. ISBN 978-3-03911-410-8

Volume 2 Craig Phelan (ed.): Trade Unionism since 1945: Towards a Global History. Volume 2: The Americas, Asia and Australia.
364 pages. 2009. ISBN 978-3-03911-950-9

Volume 3 Pablo Ghigliani: The Politics of Privatisation and Trade Union Mobilisation: The Electricity Industry in the UK and Argentina.
293 pages. 2010. ISBN 978-3-03911-961-5

Volume 4 Heather Connolly: Renewal in the French Trade Union Movement: A Grassroots Perspective.
260 pages. 2010. ISBN 978-3-0343-0101-5

Volume 5 Magaly Rodríguez García: Liberal Workers of the World, Unite? The ICFTU and the Defence of Labour Liberalism in Europe and Latin America (1949–1969).
354 pages. 2010. ISBN 978-3-0343-0112-1

Volume 6 Jeffrey Sluyter-Beltrão: Rise and Decline of Brazil's New Unionism: The Politics of the Central Única dos Trabalhadores.
481 pages. 2010. ISBN 978-3-0343-0114-5

Volume 7-8 Forthcoming.

Volume 9 Tracy Carson: Tomorrow It Could Be You: Strikes and Boycotts in South Africa, 1978–1982.
325 pages. 2011. ISBN 978-3-0343-0119-0

Volume 10 Laura Ariovich: Organizing the Organized: Trade Union Renewal, Organizational Change and Worker Activism in Metropolitan America.
310 pages. 2010. ISBN 978-3-0343-0132-9

Volume 11 Indira Palacios-Valladares: Industrial Relations after Pinochet: Firm Level Unionism and Collective Bargaining Outcomes in Chile.
268 pages. 2011. ISBN 978-3-0343-0136-7

Volume 12 Zhining Ma: The ACFTU and Chinese Industrial Relations.
260 pages. 2011. ISBN 978-3-0343-0205-0

www.ingramcontent.com/pod-product-compliance
Ingram Content Group UK Ltd.
Pitfield, Milton Keynes, MK11 3LW, UK
UKHW021851100926
8556IPUK00020B/1176

9 783034 302050